NOTHING
IS MISSING

NOTHING IS MISSING

A MEMOIR OF LIVING BOLDLY

NICOLE WALTERS

SIMON ELEMENT

New York   London   Toronto   Sydney   New Delhi

Library of Congress Cataloging-in-Publication Data
Names: Walters, Nicole, 1985– author.
Title: Nothing is missing : a transformational memoir / Nicole Walters.
Description: New York : Simon Element, 2023. | Includes bibliographical references and index.
Identifiers: LCCN 2023020662 (print) | LCCN 2023020663 (ebook) | ISBN 9781668000953 (hardcover) | ISBN 9781668000960 (paperback) | ISBN 9781668000977 (ebook)
Subjects: LCSH: Walters, Nicole, 1985– | African American businesspeople— Biography. | Women millionaires—United States—Biography.
Classification: LCC HC102.5.W3474 A3 2023 (print) | LCC HC102.5.W3474 (ebook) | DDC 338.092—dc23/eng/20230605
LC record available at https://lccn.loc.gov/2023020662
LC ebook record available at https://lccn.loc.gov/2023020663

ISBN 978-1-6680-0095-3
ISBN 978-1-6680-0097-7 (ebook)

Names and identifying characteristics of some individuals have been changed.

For Daya, Krissy & Ally

CONTENTS

NOTHING

IS MISSING

PROLOGUE

EVERYTHING IS RIGHT. EVERYTHING IS WRONG.
NOTHING IS MISSING.

The paralysis caught me off guard. I felt a tingling above my right cheek-bone, and a heaviness on that side of my face. I'd woken up to the bright Los Angeles sunshine but when I'd smiled at myself in the mirror, like I do every morning, I noticed that my eye wasn't turning up at the corner, and that there was a wrinkle at my jawline. Was I aging suddenly? Was it an allergic reaction? I took an antihistamine just in case. I was in the habit of pushing off my health. I didn't expect at thirty-six that I'd be sitting in a doctor's office asking why half my face was paralyzed and wondering if I'd be able to support my girls.

If you don't already know me, I can pop a big back-of-the-teeth smile; it helps me connect with people right away. But it has also been armor and a mask for me; something I can use to make me look way happier than I feel. But the paralysis stole my smile. When I look back at photos from that spring, I see what I was feeling. I couldn't hide it.

That is so different from what so many of us do, which is just grin and bear it, and make sure everything looks a certain way. Let's stop pretending like everything's okay. My smile is back, and with it I can tell some truth and I can hide a lot, but I don't want to hide anymore. If we're meeting in this book for the first time, I want us to live in truth. If you're returning, I want us to continue in truth.

I'm Nicole Walters. I've built a business, Inherit Learning Company, a digital education firm that has afforded me many different things. It has afforded me a home. It's taken care of my kids. It's given me vacations and luxury and, more than anything, it's given me impact, visibility, and stability. And these are all things I lacked growing up. These are all things I thought that if I had them that I'd made it.

But what I found was that the business, the TV show that grew out of it, and all the chaos of my family life was distracting me from the deep inside work I needed to do. I was struck with anxiety. I was worried about the future. I was recovering from trauma—from years and years of a crazy childhood and trauma that I was living day-to-day in my own home. My health scares, my burnout—they were symptoms of a bigger problem.

At first, I leaned into what I already knew—you might have done this in your own life. When things start going a little haywire, when you start seeing chaos on the horizon, you double down on what you know. I did more business. I booked more events. I gained more clients. I created content. I launched a TV show on a major network in the middle of a pandemic. And I served over fifteen thousand people in my consulting company. Business is something I understand, so I kept trying to do business, and much like you, because we're all like this a little bit inside, I managed to keep it all together. I was changing lives. I was serving well as a consultant, a mother, a wife, but all the while I was struggling to take care of myself.

I was so worried about serving—because it's precious to me to be able to show up for people and not just the people in my family, my kids, but you too—that I served at the expense of myself. I love helping people find their purpose. And I love giving people the practical tools to make change happen. But I couldn't keep doing that good work if I didn't nurture myself first. I couldn't continue to ignore that my health and well-being mattered—and, frankly, it's hard to put yourself second when your facial paralysis stares at you as a stark reminder of your choices first thing every morning.

———————

I'm writing this book because I've been through a lot. I know you've been through a lot too, and we're all going to keep going through things because that's life—hard things will arise and you will have to deal with them. I've done a lot of things wrong but I've also learned a lot. So, when I see people suffering through things, I want to speak up. The majority of us just don't know that there are answers out there and we think we have to figure it out on our own. I spent most of my life figuring things out on my own; I did a lot of things the hard way, and I want to give you all the information I can, because the more information you have the more options you have.

If you're anything like me, friend, when stuff like this happens, you can get really hung up on how you could have done everything better. I followed the steps. I did the plans. I bought the courses. I got the mentors. I went to therapy. I showed up in every way. I did every single thing I was supposed to and everything was wrong.

But, after therapy, after leaning into God[*] (if that gave you pause, go on and read the footnote), after the endless support of my family

———————

[*]   If you've read this far, you've already noticed that sometimes I'm going to mention God. So I want to tell you that I'm a bootleg Christian. I'm the off-brand-Walmart-version-of-Lucky-Charms kind of Christian. Can I tell my story effectively and not mention God? No, I can't. That would be denying something that is, I believe, true, and the only reason I would be denying it is out of fear of pushing people away, because I don't want people to think I'm trying to push religion on them. But I also don't want it to be too "Sneaky Jesus." This is simply the language I speak, just like some people speak Japanese or Swahili. But don't worry—if that isn't the language you speak, you'll still understand these stories and what they've come to mean to me. If you speak woman-trying-to-do-it-all or motherhood or daughterhood or sprawling-unpredictable-messy-life, you'll understand, because I speak them fluently.

and friends, and after a whole lot of time recovering, I realized that the truth is that in this season nothing is missing. Everything's very wrong. Everything is also very right. But nothing is missing.

Nothing's missing because I've created the tools to support myself. Nothing is missing because long before I reached this point, I started learning hard lessons. Nothing is missing because I invested in the friendships and the family and the people to support me through these transitions. Sometimes the hardest part, friend, and I'm sure you can relate to this, isn't finding the tools—it's remembering to use them.

We have to use the tools we've worked so hard to acquire. We have to use them because we are deserving. I'm deserving. You are deserving.

———————

I've lived the past fourteen years of my adult entrepreneurial life feeling very alone in my pain. Feeling like I couldn't quite share the completeness of what I was going through because it was mine and mine alone to carry. But as I've begun to live boldly and out loud, as I've begun to share my story, I've learned that if you walk in transparency, if you're willing to lean on the people around you, grief and gratitude and healing and happiness can coexist. I hope that putting my experiences out here makes it easier to believe that you can survive it all.

Once you read this book, we will be on a path together. On this journey we're going to encounter the stuff of life. There are so many things I've never shared because they were too hard or too raw. But, when I decided to write this book, I knew I had to be honest, to tell you the real story. Because the truth is I wasn't born with wealth, confidence, or vision. I was born into poverty and pretty early on I realized that no one was coming to save me. When I learned that I was able to save myself, everything was different. And I want it to be different for you too.

I want you to know that you're not taking this journey alone. I've been there. And all along the way I'll be by your side. But I must tell you: You've got to be willing to get uncomfortable. And if you're not willing to get just a little bit uncomfortable so you can live a more comfortable, better life, well, close this book right now. Seriously. That's called having personal boundaries. At this point, if you've already bought the book, I'll give you the freedom to step away. However, I'll also remind you that you made an investment. You made a commitment. There was a moment, even if brief, that made you open this book and start reading. Trust that moment.

A lot of people spend a lot of time waiting—for that perfect mentor, life coach, tool, or resource to skyrocket them to wealth, happiness, and peace. All the while, they suffer as they stumble from one shiny object to the next until the day they realize that no one is coming to save them and that they already have everything they need. That's when all hell breaks loose and they enter a new season.

Sometimes people want to hold on to things that no longer serve them. But you have to let go so that your hands are free to grab whatever it is you're supposed to be chasing. I say this as the person who likes to take all her Target bags up the stairs at once. I want to hold a lot. If there was a queen of baggage, call me Samsonite. But I am learning that sometimes taking two or three trips is the better option. Why break your back in the process? Your new life is going to cost you your old one. When we leave our parents' home or head off to college or get married or become parents, we always leave some of who we were behind and start over as a newer self. As we move through life, we also learn that it's not always our choice to start over. And if there's one lesson I want to share with you, it is that we better get really good at building from scratch, because at any point in time, life is going to ask us to do just that.

I hope my story serves you; I hope it reminds you of the tools you already have and that you don't need to pretend to be perfect and strong and never eat carbs. All we need to do is be honest, and willing to show up for the hard work, and learn as we live. And hopefully, each time we start over, things will be better than they were before.

Sometimes you have these incredible seasons during which you are disproportionately happier, where the hard is easier to hold (because, let's be honest, there's always hard). But sometimes we come into a season during which it is disproportionately harder. Until recently, I didn't realize how frequently we feel as if we can't have happiness during those hard periods, as if we aren't allowed to experience joy in the face of suffering, grieving, or struggling. But the truth is this: All you need is a mustard seed of joy and a willingness to enjoy it.

This book is all about living with joy. Chasing joy and truth. And friend, I'm grateful we get to do it together.

PART ONE

CHAPTER ONE

THE AMERICAN DREAM IS ABOUT OPTIONS

I was born Nana Abena Kobi Forson. *Nana* means "chief" or "queen." Abena is the day of the week I was born on—Tuesday. Kobi was my paternal grandfather's name. Forson is the family name my father chose when he left his village in Ghana.

When I was little, I looked up at my mom as we were crossing the street and asked her why she'd chosen my name. She told me that my father had picked it. Something in the way she said it made me ask, "What did you want to name me?" A glimmer of a smile rippled across her face. "I wanted to name you Nicole."

My mom met my dad when she was eighteen, and in the shadow of his narcissism she never developed her belief in herself. She is smart, hardworking, and faithful, with glowing skin and a warm smile. She was meticulous about her appearance. As a kid, I knew my mom was gorgeous. Her hair was always done—braids, pressed out, or with some kind of curl. My favorite look was her Toni Braxton '90s–style pixie cut. She tweezed her eyebrows, painted her nails red, and never left the house without eyeliner, mascara, red lipstick, and a handbag. Purses were her indulgence. She had one in every color and every fabric from patent leather to faux crocodile skin. In our tiny one-bedroom apartment there was a whole chair dedicated to the avalanche of handbags. And Mom always chose one that looked good with her outfit.

On weekend afternoons when the Ghanaian community of Washington, DC, would meet at the soccer field, she'd look cute in her mom jeans, her sweatshirt, her Keds, and a handbag. We'd pull up to the field in my father's cab. It was black and tan with a red diamond on the front doors. I scrambled out of the car and stood in a sea of cabs—yellow, checkered, and other Diamond Cab Company cars.

Ghanaian highlife blasted out of a boom box, the rhythm powerful enough that all the life on the field held to its beat. My dad joined the guys to play soccer.

I scanned the bleachers to see if any of my cousins were there yet—everyone was related one way or another. (Which meant that any auntie could whoop any kid's tail if she caught them misbehaving.) We, the kids, ran around making our own fun, turning the tree into base and running across the grassy fields half watched by the older kids who stood around talking to one another. When we got tired, we begged our mothers for a little money to buy a Ziploc bag of bofrot—a perfect sphere of sweet fried dough.

The wives sat and talked. They gossiped about who was having babies and who wasn't, whether buying real estate in Northern Virginia made sense. They pooled money: Who needs help with school fees? Who needs help to take care of a tombstone, or to send a body back to Ghana? What can you give? They collected and passed out flyers for all the memorials and outdoorings—a baby shower after the baby comes. It is a ceremony and celebration welcoming the baby into the community. They're often held at big halls, with a DJ and dancing and trays of delicious Ghanaian food. Everyone would talk about who was going back to Ghana. Could you check in on this family member? Can you take a letter to this person? Can you take a little extra money for my family? Can you take a small gift to my father? The soccer field was also where new arrivals were embraced. Housing was procured, jobs found, community offered. The women also held business strategy sessions. In Ghana, women run everything—the markets, the restaurants, the barbershops. Even villages are run by queen mothers, not chiefs.

Most immigrants are entrepreneurial by nature or necessity, and my mother's friends were no exception. We always had a lot of friends and family who were trying their hand at business—opening a bread shop, developing a skincare line, selling fabric, or opening a restaurant. Many of the men were cabdrivers and their wives were starting some sort of business alongside working, or going to school, or caring for the kids.

At the field, there was always a woman selling kenkey, a starchy ball made with fermented corn flour and wrapped in a cornhusk. We would buy enough for the week and my mother would serve it with fresh steamed fish and red pepper sauce. Sometimes someone brought back cloth or other things from Ghana to sell. Aunt Efua, one of Mom's closest friends, sold a Ghanaian bread out of the trunk of her car. She'd pull up to the field in an old hatchback stacked full of bread and at the end of the evening she'd drive off, her car empty. Mom would always buy a loaf or two, and Auntie would always slip us an extra. The loaves came in clear plastic bags with green twist ties. The bread was sweet and soft and I'd sink my teeth into it as I watched the grown-ups play soccer and sit and catch up.

I grew up in this environment where everybody had a side hustle. My mom, though, always had a "good" job—meaning she worked nine-to-five and got a salary and benefits. She had taken typing classes, which gave her an edge. Instead of working for minimum wage at a fast-food restaurant, she worked as a secretary and receptionist at the front desk of a fancy condo. My mom had never finished school and felt like she wasn't that smart. So, even though she was the one who made the regular money and benefits, she always deferred to my dad.

But at the end of the day, as in most households, if there was a gap, she was the one who filled it.

My mom was more CEO than entrepreneur. She didn't necessarily want to start a business, but she always wanted to run one. She would see all her friends building businesses from the ground up and she would help with packaging and design. She was always consulting, but what she really wanted was to invest and help them grow. Her friends would tell her, "Bring a little money, Maggie. You can put it in." But she always ran it by my dad and he always said no.

The one place I saw her fly was Ghana. Not only did she know how to navigate that world but she also didn't have my dad there telling her she couldn't. My parents couldn't afford for all three of us to go, so he would usually stay in DC and work. We'd always go back after their tax refund came in. They'd use some money to fix the cab, they'd send some money home, and they'd buy two airline tickets.

I remember watching my mom step off the plane in her homeland with an edge, an air of confidence I never saw when we were in DC. While we were there, Mom was always hustling. She listened and paid attention. When she heard about a new gold mine, she bought a couple of bars; when she heard that some land overlooking the beach was being released for purchase, she scraped together the cash to buy it.

I remember seeing my mom's entrepreneurial spirit in a whole new way one day at Takoradi Market Circle. This was the market we'd visit each day to get fresh groceries. The yellow and red building that formed its outer ring was adorned with stalls and surrounded by hawkers— some of whom were connected to a stall, some of whom were free-lancers, people with something to sell. There were people with baskets on their heads, kids selling batteries or candies, old women with bread piled sky-high. Inside the ring was a riot of abundance. Rows upon rows of stalls you could get lost in. There were sellers with planks of wood atop bright stools—beheaded fish stacked into pyramids, mountains of yams, carts of fresh coconuts—and vendors set up with every manner of household items, from plastic buckets to tablecloths.

My mom and I wound through the maze until she stopped at an

old shipping container. Outside it a woman was selling a cup of rice to an elderly woman. She scooped a cup out of a big sack that sat beside a rainbow of fruits and vegetables at the front of the stall. Behind her were toiletries and paper goods, lotions, soaps—it was the Walmart of Takoradi Market. The place was just big enough for the shopkeeper to stand inside and bring people whatever they wanted.

When she saw my mother, the shopkeeper dug into her waistband, where she kept her money tied in a folded-up piece of cloth. She handed my mother a stack of bills. I'd been taught to stay out of grown folks' business, but my curiosity won out. As we walked away, my mom slipped the money into her pocket without saying anything. "Who's that lady?" I asked.

"Oh, that's my stall. She rents it from me."

I looked at my mom in amazement. She was an operator! She must have seen the pride bubbling up in me because she leaned close and said, "Don't tell your father."

I looked at the booth again and this time I noticed that it had something none of the other stalls had—a few items from America. Staring at the shelves, I remembered all our trips to Ross and Marshalls, where my mom would pick up perfume or special lotions. Here, she was selling them at a premium.

When I took a job in the corporate world and had to understand markets and margins, I realized that all those years earlier I had been learning about business from my mom. She understood market differentiators, how to make a product stand out. She understood margins. She knew you had to check on your business, not just let it run. She understood things she was never taught. I learned these things watching her in an African market.

My parents struggled to get to America, but the minute they arrived they began talking about when they would go home. Unlike most immigrants, they didn't build a long-term plan for America. They never wanted to buy a house; they wanted to go home to Ghana. But they also wanted me to succeed here. My father used to point to all the giant buildings in Washington that housed businesses and empires and he'd tell me, "Your name can either be on the outside of a building or you can clean one." He saw the world in black and white and felt there was no room for the in between.

My dad was a combination of incredibly bright and wildly simple. He had an understanding of where he wanted to get to, but would mostly tread water with occasional moments of growth. He had a vision of success, but did not use all his tools to achieve it. He was a team of one, working by himself for himself, believing that he was the only person who could do anything. Then there was my mom, telling me not to tell my father about her business dealings. Can you imagine being in a household where everyone is working as an island? No wonder we never got anything done. So, when it came time for me to build a life for myself, I didn't know exactly what it could look like. I didn't even grow up thinking I would have a house. I had to learn how to envision a life of stability and enough for myself.

I was traumatized by my father. I was also loved by him. My dad worked hard. He got himself to the United States and has worked every job known to humankind—he was a postal worker, he drove an ice cream truck, he worked at a drugstore, and, finally, he spent twelve to fifteen hours a day driving a cab around Washington. He liked it for a lot of the same reasons people are drawn to entrepreneurship—no one controls your income. You can work as many hours as you need to. You can choose where you're going to go and what fares you're going to pick up. He treated his cab like it was his office.

A lot of the other drivers wore jeans and a T-shirt; unless you were driving a luxury car, there was no need for a suit jacket. But my dad always wore khakis and a button-down shirt, a leather belt and loafers, and a gold necklace and watch. He wore an obscene amount of cologne that blended with the medley of smells in the cab, the cheap Calvin Klein knockoff mingling with the scent of rice and whatever stew my mom had made the night before and whatever stink the city offered—the stench of the Potomac or the fishy smell wafting off the wharf. In the front seat beside his lunch was his manifest, where he wrote down each of his fares in beautiful cursive, and several copies of the *Washington Post*, which he bought every morning and passed me the comics to read on the way to school.

I grew up in a household where everything was a little bit right. For instance, my father always had a slightly off interpretation of idioms and colloquialisms. Instead of saying never look a gift horse in the mouth, he said, "Never look a gift house in the mouth." When I asked him to explain the saying he expounded, "Because if someone wants to give you a house, you have to take it. You don't sit there and ask them 'Why do you have the house?' You just take the house." His logic works, but it is not correct.

My dad was an avid NPR listener. One day we heard a segment with a finance guru who said, "If you treat your money well, your money will treat you well."

That evening at home I found my dad standing over the ironing board, which sat open in the foyer where it doubled as a table for keys and mail and a place for us to line up our shoes when we came through the door. There was a pile of crumpled money to his left. Dad took a bill, laid it flat, vigorously shook the green can of Niagara brand starch, then sprayed and ironed that dollar bill until it looked like new money, except for the rivulets of dirt that had been caked into the creases. The iron huffed and steam rose around his mustache and clean-shaven cheeks. He carefully placed it in a tidy pile on his right. As he worked, little puffs of steam chugged out of the iron. When he noticed me staring, he said, "Nana, if you treat your money well, your money will treat you well."

I was young but I was pretty sure this wasn't what the person on the radio had meant. Even then I sensed that money was a tool.

———————

My parents were terrible with money. Their pattern was to get a lump sum of money, take care of a bunch of overdue bills, buy groceries, hold on to $200, and then just drip that out for as long as possible. They just didn't know better. They didn't understand resources. I looked at the madness and chaos of our life and thought, *This can't be it.* It didn't make sense.

Meanwhile, I had an imaginary butler named Jenkins who would bring me drinks and things. Some kids play house or cops and robbers, but I played rich.

I sat perched on the blue couch that doubled as my bedroom. It was a big, unsightly double seater with blue tufted upholstery that was also a pullout bed. My parents had claimed it after another tenant left it behind. Our apartment was a mess of old things—everywhere there were stacks of bank boxes filled with papers, or piles of things to be sent back home. There were old figure skates (a necessity in Ghana?), old clothes, and soccer cleats that had been on sale. Our Goodwill was Ghana. And besides the chaos of saved things, our home was dirtier than you could see at first. If I touched a windowsill or baseboard my finger came away dark with dust. When you sat still after nightfall, the cockroaches would come out.

But when I played rich, all that disappeared. I'd cross my legs and pretend to sip tea and then I'd hustle over to my pretend elevator, which I rode in to get to my important meetings. Jenkins would call me cars and fix mistakes when he'd messed something up. And I, I was rich.

As a kid I was always trying to figure out the American system, figure out the American dream. You know the dream I mean—having the house, the car, the kids, the white picket fence, and, especially for immigrants, having more than your parents.

It wasn't until I was almost thirty that I realized that the American dream wasn't just the house, the car, the kids, the white picket fence. The American dream is about options. While we all have choices, it is the number of choices we get that matters. When you look at something like slavery, the only choices people had were to work or die.

So, I grew up seeing someone navigating two societies—one where you play by the rules and there's a premade structure for getting ahead, and one where there is no structure, no rules, and the only way to get ahead is if you drive and design a game plan for yourself. Nana. Nicole. African. American. You can be in this world but not of this world, and Africans in America are like that too. Think of the array of Thanksgiving dinners across the country—mine has jollof rice, maybe yours has pierogies or pasta, but we all have turkey. We're in America but we're not of America. On the other hand, it doesn't get more American than being a first-generation child born to immigrant parents in Washington, DC.

As children, many of us are taught to reduce success to money or merit—that if we work hard good things will come. But that's just not true. Some of us have enormous obstacles to summit, some of us are born with privilege, and most of us are raised with a very narrow definition of success. Perhaps you were taught to define your success through marriage and family, through fiscal wealth, through your career. Or maybe you were the lucky one who was taught that you can define your own success and happiness, and that it is enough to be constantly growing your options. I was always told I needed to get a good education, to always excel, to never make mistakes, and I was told that if I did those things, I could be a doctor or a lawyer and have more wealth than the generations that came before me. This was the definition of success handed to me by my immigrant father.

My mom taught me that you could make your own rules. But I also noticed that she only ever did it when my dad wasn't there. She was always limited in her moves based on her self-imposed boundaries. She never wanted to tell anyone about her ideas because she was always worried someone would make fun of her, or that it might go wrong and she'd be embarrassed. That mindset really diminished her impact. She was the first person in whom I could see the consequences of not believing in yourself.

My mother's highest purpose in life was serving others, even if it meant she would often end up being a doormat. My mother didn't have boundaries, and she spent so much time in service to others that she never pursued anything for herself. That's what she was taught to do. She was taught to do it because that *is* what women do—they are selfless. A great woman is taught to set herself on fire to keep others warm. At the end of the workday, she would talk about all the things she deserved, and yet she spent most of her time not pursuing any of them. One of her dreams was to live in an apartment with a balcony, but we always lived on the first floor. The building had twenty-two floors, and most of the apartments had balconies, but even though apartments with balconies became available often enough, my parents never moved.

Joy itself was a privilege my parents felt we couldn't afford. Both of my parents believed that anything that gives you joy had to be treated in a miserly way. The tragedy of poverty is that it creates a scarcity mindset that shows up everywhere. Neither my father nor my mother talked about happiness. The American dream I was raised with, and maybe you've felt this too, was about arriving at a destination, as if success were preprogrammed in the GPS and would be announced when you arrived there.

But I have learned that the true American dream has a different endgame. Money gives you freedom. Freedom gives you choices. And choices are what we are all truly chasing. Financial freedom radically expands your choices—if and whom you will marry, what you will do for work, where you will live. The more wealth you acquire, the more options you have.

When you have options, you have the luxury of designing your own life rather than making choices out of necessity. Rather than living in the run-down apartment because it's the only one you can afford, when you have options you can choose between homes in neighborhoods with good schools or beautiful parks, or small things that make your everyday life better, more enjoyable, more satisfying. Once you realize that the American dream is about options, you can figure out how to give yourself more choices. What does that mean? What resources do you need? What tools do you need? What's your path?

I have recently learned that if you're not willing to lean into the little microcosm of happy that God has given you, you're saying that you don't think you deserve it. You're saying that you don't want to receive that tiny, tiny bit of joy that could make your hard season just a little bit easier. Believe it or not, that tiny bit of happy is the thing that will fuel you to get through that season of hard. Every day you have the option to choose happiness. That is one of your options every single day. And exercising that choice can change everything about a hard season. It's just that we think seasons only change with something major—a big sack of money landing on the front porch, or a dreamy new partner stepping into your life. But the truth is it doesn't have to look like that. It can look like a tiny mustard seed of joy.

CHAPTER TWO

FIERCE CLARITY

Part of the reason that clarity is so important to me as an adult is that I spent a lot of my childhood confused. I grew up in a house where clarity was a foreign concept, and things would happen out of nowhere. My dad's rage would flare up suddenly. But even when he wasn't angry, he was unpredictable and so was our life. Would we have money? Would we have food? Would things change suddenly? My super-secretive dad always had some sort of plot and that was kind of what I thought it looked like to live life. It wasn't effective, and his plots weren't good examples of how to live in America or raise children. I have a few specific memories from my childhood that reinforce this.

———

Dad slammed the cab's tan door and started walking fast. He was a quick mover and I was always scrambling to keep up. My short legs moved like an eggbeater trying to match his pace. My backpack bounced against my shoulders. He grabbed my wrist tightly. I wanted him to loosen his grip but was terrified he would let go. He pulled me toward the Hill, the little grassy stretch outside our apartment complex where the contents of someone's life were strewn about. People were passing through all the things that would mean something to a person and plucking up choice bits—a cast-iron skillet, plates, dressers, a boom box, lamps; one lady had her arms wrapped around a framed mirror.

There was a pit of worry in my stomach. I looked at my dad and there was a focused look on his face as we raced inside to get my mom and JJ, another cabdriver who lived in the building.

As soon as my parents saw the cream laminate pedestal table, my father dropped my wrist. My mom scooped up two wooden chairs with woven cane backs, one under each arm.

"What are you doing?" I asked. "This is someone's stuff."

"Oh, they don't want it anymore because they got evicted," my father explained sternly.

I didn't know what *evicted* meant, but I did know that this was all wrong. Who wouldn't want all their stuff? Why weren't we protecting it until they came back? It seemed like everyone was collectively, publicly stealing. Is this what happens if you don't pay your bills? I already knew the fridge could be empty or rent could be late. My parents were always talking about not having money. I was terrified that one day I was going to come home and all our things would be outside being picked over by our neighbors.

The grown-ups started heading back into the building and I realized no one was holding my hand. Afraid I'd be left behind, I scurried ahead, hovering close to Dad's leg as he and JJ shuffled the table inside.

———————

I was sitting beside Dad in the cab as he picked up fares when he announced that he had to stop and beg our landlord for rent time. He always said "beg," never "ask."

"Hey, Forson. Rent's due," the landlord said.

Inside the tiny office, precarious stacks of papers towering above me, I did my best to look small and demure while my father begged for more time. Dad spun some story about my being sick. I'd been absolutely fine, but I knew better than to say anything. I just stared at the floor and adopted the submissive, sad look I'd learned from Dad. Then, as soon as Mr. Bernstein told Dad to bring rent in by the fifteenth, we thanked him profusely and sweetly.

Around the eighth of the month we'd roll in with a wad of cash, because my dad didn't have a checking account, and settle up.

Bowing at the feet of white people for favors was something I grew up with. It was exhausting. All opportunity came bestowed by a white person, and being at the mercy of someone else's whimsy meant we lacked certainty. We were never evicted but the uncertainty remained. It remains to this day.

———————

One time Dad and I came home late in the afternoon. It must have been winter because the sun was already low in the sky. Dad flipped the light switch just inside the front door and nothing happened. Without saying anything, he threw his keys on the ironing board and stepped inside. I trailed behind him, flipping the switch myself—there was the satisfying click but no light. I doubled back. The lights in the hallway were on. We were having our own blackout.

The apartment was really quiet. I turned the little black knobs on the lamps, the light switches in the closet and the bathroom. I even tried the fridge, determined to figure out what was wrong with the electricity. Dad was standing in the kitchen by the stack of flyers we'd gotten at the last soccer game and speaking into the phone's receiver. "I'll be there. Tomorrow. I have my kid at home."

"None of them are working," I whispered to myself.

"Shhhh." He waved his hand to quiet me.

I waited in the living room. Everything in there was seventies cool, from when my father was single. There was a two-seater bar made of wood and a gold velvet couch covered in plastic. There was the blue couch where I slept. When we first got it, I pulled out the bed and made it every night, then refolded it every morning. But heaving the metal frame out was hard, and I'd always wake up with the bars digging into my back. My dad laid some planks of wood over the bars, but they were hard. Eventually, I gave up and started making my bed on the couch, since those cushions were thicker than the mattress. I started to do less and less for myself until I just curled up each night with a pillow and white quilted blanket with brown teddy bears, each wearing a different-colored bow tie. At night, I'd pull it tight around me praying I wouldn't feel the cockroaches skittering over me.

As the sun went down, I waited on the blue couch for my father to finish negotiating and heat up some food.

We didn't get evicted and the lights came back on. But the next month we had to visit Mr. Bernstein again.

Would you be surprised if I told you that I have always been a talker? I was always riding around with my dad in his cab talking to the passengers. When I was three, one of his passengers commented on how loquacious and inquisitive I was and asked my dad where I was going to go to school. To hear my dad retell it, it was an event. "No, no, no, you can't send her to a regular school. People in DC, you don't do that if you have a kid like this one. You don't send her to regular public school. Nobody does this. There are better schools that you need to send her to." No matter how the exchange went down, the result was that my dad was introduced to an admissions person at a fancy private school and everything, including my tuition, was figured out.

I inhaled my education. At school I felt good. At school I felt happy and safe. At school all my needs were met and there was always someone there who was nice to me. I knew I was doing well—even when I struggled, I never felt like struggling was a bad thing; it was just an indication that I needed to learn something and keep working at it. School was a magical place filled with information, kindness, and teachers who were always encouraging me to do more. It was also filled with clarity. In school, unlike at home, it was always very clear what to do to get what result. When we learned about child labor, I started a letter-writing campaign and wrote to politicians all over the world. But when I asked for postage for a letter to Cambodia, my dad complained, "Stop using all my stamps." That's how it went with him.

One time Dad and I walked down the hallway to my classroom for a parent-teacher conference. Everything was quiet except for the shuffling feet of a few other families coming and going from their conferences. It felt special to be in school after hours, the building empty of people but still full of life.

I was chatting away and beaming. "Oh, this is where I have music and we're doing recorder right now," I said and flung my arm proudly toward the music room.

I took language arts in a cozy subterranean room filled with books and posters. My dad sat beside me in front of the teacher's desk, his body scrunched into a kid-sized desk. In front of him was a name tag shaped like a pencil and a piece of extra-wide-ruled paper with the dotted lines running across the page to help corral our letters into proper formation. As my teacher spoke, my dad took notes—his impeccable cursive at odds with the wide lines.

My teacher gave us a warm smile, showed my dad samples of my work, and complimented my curiosity, my independence, the way I excelled at reading and discussion, and the fact that whenever I didn't understand something I asked for support.

"She's a delight. She's such a great kid."

I felt warm in the glow of her attention.

"But what can she work on?" Dad asked, and when my teacher didn't say anything he pushed. "You can tell me the truth."

He held his pen poised over the paper, ready to chronicle my failures. My face went hot, and I avoided my teacher's eyes.

"Well, Nana is very social, and we definitely want to make sure we're balancing that out in the classroom." My dad took notes so that he could be pointed in his critique later. "But she always gets all her work done." She doubled back to say how well I was doing, though my dad wasn't listening. He started getting loud. "We're always telling her she talks too much."

There was a knock at the door, and I noticed the look of relief on my teacher's face when another family came in.

Before we'd even reached the double doors that led outside, the words shot out of him: "Don't be an embarrassment." My stomach twisted. "Nana, you have to do what you're supposed to do. If you're too difficult, they will kick you out. They don't have to have you."

The cold air hit my face and I pulled my coat tight.

My father took quick strides down the hill to where he'd parked the taxi. I scurried to keep up, but even a few feet behind him I could feel the rage rippling off him. "I pay too much money for this," he said, even though I was there on a major scholarship and he paid only $1,000 a year of a $30,000 tuition.

Confused, I slid into the car quietly, making myself as small as possible in the passenger seat. Dread pooled in my stomach as I thought about the long drive home. Dad could go off for hours, only stopping out of sheer exhaustion. Sometimes we had family meetings, which were time for him to sit and rail while Mom and I just waited for the onslaught to end.

In the car he gave me the silent treatment. The crackle of the radio made my stomach flip. Would he take a fare? Would I have to sit in the car beside his seething? Maybe if he got a fare to Dulles he'd be in a better mood.

He didn't pick up the radio. He didn't pick up a fare. He drove in stony silence until we were home. I was scared. I could feel the heat pulsing off him, but it was his quiet that frightened me most.

Without a word, we walked into the building. The elevator shook and clanked as it carried us up. Every day I feared it would plummet to the ground and I would die. That afternoon, I wished it.

I trailed behind him down the hall. Mom took one look at my tear-stained face and said, "Go clean yourself up."

In the bathroom, I saw my ashy face in the mirror. From there I could hear Dad going on and on about how I was messing up at school and bringing shame upon them. I hovered outside the kitchen, hungry but waiting for his tirade to end. Then he blew past me and disappeared into the bedroom. The door always stuck and he had to push it hard twice, slamming it to get privacy.

Mom handed me a bowl of white rice with red stew. "Oh, stop it. It's just your father. You and him are just the same. You both talk too much. You know what you're supposed to do? Just do it so you don't have to hear his mouth."

I sat at the kitchen table, the bowl of rice warm in my hands. I watched a cockroach scurry along the wall.

The problem was I didn't know what I was supposed to do. I didn't know what I had done wrong. I didn't understand at all.

My father struggled with my exuberance and was always trying to tamp down my excess. His lessons were confusing. *Speak up. All the kids know the answer. Why don't you know the answer?* But then, *You talk too much, put your hand down. That's enough.* At school meetings I'd always raise my hand with a question and my dad would literally grab my hand and pull it down. But I always wanted all the information and knew we didn't have it. To my father, saying that you don't understand was not an acceptable answer; it was a disgrace. He never let me forget how much I had to prove.

"You're Black. You're poor. You're a woman. You already have three strikes against you." He wasn't saying that these were diminishing things, he was telling me that these were real factors in how the world would see me and that my success depended on my perfection. He was telling me I should be grateful that I'm in this space and ashamed for being less than perfect. He wanted me to understand there were consequences for getting it wrong that applied to me in a different way.

One afternoon I needed to wash my gym uniform. The uniform was Irish-green shorts and a gray shirt with our school's name printed on it. In my best writing I wrote my name, Nana Forson, in the white banner that ran along the bottom of the shirt. We had gym a few times a week and would be penalized if we didn't have our uniforms. The other kids had three or four, but I had only one, and if it was dirty and it wasn't the day we went to the Laundromat, I'd either have to wear it dirty or ask my mom to clean it.

My mom wasn't home and my uniform was crusty with mud and had to be washed before class the next day. I decided to take matters into my own hands. I took two buckets to the tub, just like my mother did. I remembered that she put bleach on the clothes to get them very clean.

I filled the first bucket with hot water, detergent, and bleach. It was a pallid yellow and made my nose burn and my eyes water. I turned my head and dropped the uniform in. "It should soak," I said to myself and went to watch TV. When I came back I scrubbed the fabric the way I'd seen my mother do. Then I rinsed it out in the second bucket. When I pulled out the shorts I noticed a bright yellow-and-white spot stretched across the fabric. I knew it wasn't right and hoped it would go away when they dried. I carefully slipped them onto an old wire hanger from the dry cleaners where my dad took his clothes. The metal sagged beneath their weight when I hung them on the shower curtain rod and watched, confused, as the green dripped into our dingy white tub. I was doing my homework on the couch when my dad came home.

"Nana!" His anger rang through the bathroom walls straight into my heart.

"Yes, Daddy." I racked my brain as I hurried toward him. What had I messed up? He rounded the corner, whipping a wet piece of cloth across my body.

Confusion swooped over me.

He whaled on me and yelled "Look what you've done!" over and over as the wet cloth snapped against my skin again and again. Bleach spewed across the walls, its acrid scent burning the air. Then there was the bite of metal.

The shorts fell to the ground and he hit me with the hook of the hanger. Welts were rising on my skin. I screamed, begging him to stop.

My skin burned. I huddled in the hall, my arms wrapped around my head.

There was knocking on the unlocked door and a man's voice called out as he let himself in. "It's too much." It was our Gambian neighbor, a chef at a nearby restaurant. "It's too much," he said again, like he didn't disapprove of the beating but that there were limits that had to be obeyed.

Dad waved the shorts in the air like evidence. "Look what she did!"

The color dripped from my shorts as he held them in his hand—the Irish green had gone a vivid yellow with white spots like acid-washed jeans.

Our neighbor quieted my father and led me down the hall to his apartment, where he fixed me a bowl of rice and stew. Then he went to calm my dad down.

His kitchen was quiet. The stew was warm and rich, and a little chunkier than my mom's, the onions sliced rather than diced. I was hungry, but I couldn't eat. I was struggling to breathe, my throat clotted with emotion, and the simple act of swallowing felt too hard to do. My head was buzzing and my body was burning. The bleach had set fire to the flock of cuts across my forearms.

Later that evening, my mom collected me from our neighbor's apartment. My heart was beating in my throat, my mouth dry.

As I cleaned out the buckets in the bathroom, the acrid smell turned my stomach, and I noticed the blood on my arms for the first time. My father had never beaten me this badly. No matter what I had done, I knew that he was wrong. The fact that he had made me bleed was wrong. When he broke my skin, he had broken some unspoken rule.

I didn't understand what had happened until I found my mother in the kitchen and she explained that bleach was only for white clothing. Finally, I understood that I'd ruined my gym uniform and my parents would be forced to spend $14 on a second uniform for me. But, in the storm of my father's rage, in the torrent of my fear, all there had been was confusion.

———————

When I was seven and my little sister was born, I parented her with a shield and a wall.

Maame's outdooring happened at our apartment. My parents couldn't afford a hall, a DJ, or catering. But my mother was dressed to the nines and our community showed up. Twenty or thirty aunties and uncles piled into our apartment. I'd never seen the house so busy. At an outdooring, the oldest person in the community holds the newest life and blesses the baby. Uncle Tony was the eldest in our community; he blessed my sister, and he'd blessed me when I was born. I was so proud to hold Maame, that day and always. Being a big sister was a blessing.

As soon as Maame was born, my priority was to make sure she didn't experience what I was experiencing. I wanted her to have clarity. To have unconditional love. To have boundless joy. To be celebrated. To be supported. And to believe in her own feelings. I tried to make sure the rage never met her. I was her protector and the person who tried to solve her problems. I taught her games and how to tie her shoes, I helped her with her schoolwork, and I remembered her birthday. By the time I was eleven, I was a primary caregiver, and in the summer she was my charge.

Maame looked like a little version of me, and for the first three years of her life I didn't even call her by her name. I called her "Sister," because I was so damn proud to be a sister. She'd follow me around the apartment, and we were in constant conversation. She would ask questions; I would explain things—what things were and how they worked. I explained how to be safe—what to do and what not to do. I even explained how the day was going to go so she always had clear expectations and no surprises.

Around the holidays my mom would often be mad and exhausted. Two days before Thanksgiving one year, she announced, "I'm not cooking. I'm tired, and no one does anything for me. Why should I put in all this effort?"

I just accepted that she felt that way, but I wasn't going to let it stop Maame and me from celebrating. This was a problem I could solve.

"I want to have Thanksgiving," Maame said, a smile spreading across her face.

I gathered up what money I could, no more than fifteen dollars, bundled Maame into warm clothes, and together we walked the twenty-five minutes to Safeway. I wasn't big enough to lift her into the shopping cart, so we pushed it together. It felt heavy as I steered it down the aisles. I kept Maame close as I checked all the prices, calculating what we could afford.

Maame pointed excitedly at fruit snacks with Arthur, a popular kids' cartoon character, on them and I had to explain that we had only so much money. "Maame, I can't really buy everything you might want, but I am going to pick up stuff to try to do Thanksgiving." We got a pouch of powdered Idaho potatoes, some canned corn, a can of cranberry sauce, a bottle of Schweppes Raspberry Ginger Ale—because it was pink—so we had something special, and some chicken that was on sale, though it was still the most expensive thing. Maame saw a box of cereal with rainbows on it and asked if we could get it. I explained again that we didn't have enough money, but I promised her a donut at the end of the trip. They were decadent glazed orbs, dripping with icing and sprinkles, and they cost only fifty cents. We shared one on the way home.

We hauled our stash home and I began to cook. Our kitchen was marked with symbols of our family's dysfunction. We had a broken pot lid that had been damaged one night when my parents were fighting. We'd had the same dull, never-sharpened knife at least since I was born twelve years before, and my mom would just press harder and harder to chop things with it, so even tomatoes presented fierce resistance. Everything was done the hard way.

Once I got started, my mom walked into the kitchen, peering into the pot with the broken lid where I'd started boiling water to make the potatoes. "You're doing that wrong."

"That isn't seasoned properly," she said as she peered over my shoulder, checking the spices I sprinkled on the chicken, until finally she couldn't contain herself and huffed, "Let me just do it." She then began buzzing around the kitchen, adding all these other dishes to the meal, and before I knew it she was cooking a Thanksgiving dinner of her own devising.

There wasn't a big family sit-down, but my sister and I feasted, toasting with Schweppes. That night after she'd put on her PJs and climbed into bed, we lay side by side giggling in the dark. I imitated our parents telling us to do our homework and she exploded in laughter until my dad walked in and told us to be quiet.

My sister is my one person. So, when fall came around again and Dad told me I was going to boarding school, my only thoughts were: *I can't not be around my sister* (double negative on purpose). *She can't be here by herself. We go together.* Then Dad told me Maame was going too. She was too little, but I pretended to be happy about it, because she was five and a half and I didn't want her to be scared.

The school was meant for gifted inner-city youth, for kids who didn't have the resources but would benefit from having the tools. Maame and I lived in the same house with our dorm parents, a married couple who lived in and supervised the home, raising a small group of students as if they were their own. The electricity was always on, there was always food on the table, no one ever worried about money. And I realized that all the problems I'd grown up with had solutions.

Living with my parents was a study in instability. The consistency and stability of life at school threw into relief the chaos I'd grown up with. Little by little I came to understand that I had to build my own stability, and that I could. I promised myself I'd never live at home again.

———

In moments of confusion, sometimes people who are hard-hit begin to feel that the confusion is reality. But somehow, I never accepted confusion as my truth. Growing up in all those moments of confusion, somehow, I was still somewhat aware it wasn't right. I always believed there had to be another way.

If at the end of every single situation in your life you can name what is wrong and notice what is right—the kids are healthy, you have work, you figured out a particular problem—then you can begin to make sense of your life. You can break it down in a practical way, so that you are whittling away the confusion of a situation until what's left is rational, true, and fiercely clear.

If you're anything like me, your life can feel chaotic and messy on the best of days, even when everything is going according to plan. But when you're told that the plan has changed—your babysitter quit without warning, you're unexpectedly pregnant, or can't get pregnant, you're offered a chance to move across the country for a job you'd never imagined, you get sick, or lose someone dear to you—then life can be utterly confusing.

If you find yourself going back and forth on a decision that leaves you feeling confused, sometimes the answer is to stay still and know that you don't need to do anything until you feel clear about what it is you need to do. Just understand: Clear is not the same as easy. Clear is not the same as simple. Clear is not the same as cheap or without challenges. Clear simply means that the way to do something does not give you disruptive distress.

In moments like those, I return to a Bible verse that says God is not the author of confusion. Wherever confusion resides, God is not present. And while I may not know what tomorrow is going to bring, one thing I do know is that I want to be where God resides. I get it if you're not Christian or super faithy, but you know when something is right and when something is wrong; you feel it in your gut. How many times have you made a bad decision and known it, or tried to force something that just didn't make sense, like putting a square peg in a round hole? If God isn't your cup of tea, I have a friend who's an atheist who says, "It's not going to be easy, but it shouldn't be that hard."

CHAPTER THREE

LIFE IS THE MEETING AND SOLVING OF PROBLEMS

The day I graduated from boarding school, everything was beautiful. It was the beginning of June, and the campus was blooming with the bright greens of early summer and the smiles of kids and their families. Proudly wearing my sleeveless black dress, I felt gorgeous and mature. I was in the top 10 percent of my class and I was going to one of the top colleges in the world. I was so proud.

There were 110 of us graduating, and just before commencement, the principal gathered us and said, "This is the last time you are all going to be in a room together." We all burst into tears. For years, we had been one another's whole world, and we didn't know what would happen when we left. We knew where we came from and what we were going back to.

As my family piled into the cab for the three-hour drive back to DC, I expected to find pride in my father's face. Instead, he wanted to know why I hadn't been valedictorian, why I hadn't given a speech, why I hadn't gotten a 4.0. "If you had gotten the 4.0, I would have taken you to Hawaii." That was something he'd often said to me, but as a kid I didn't even know what Hawaii was or why it would make a good carrot. But he dangled it nevertheless. He was trying to undermine everything I had achieved. "The only reason you got into Johns Hopkins is because I made you apply there."

The weight of his perennial disappointment was heavy on me. I sat in the back of the cab quiet and dejected. The goalposts kept moving. I decided I would never live at home again, but I didn't know what life on my own would look like. But I believed that college would be a space to breathe. I didn't yet understand that life is a continuum and that while there are different phases, each phase has its own set of problems that need solving.

I got into Johns Hopkins University on a full ride. I'd also had a full scholarship at boarding school, but there I didn't need to buy anything—not toothpaste, not paper, not food. I very quickly discovered that a full ride at college meant that my tuition was paid for—and only my tuition. I still needed to figure out everything else, from transportation to bedsheets to textbooks. I also had to figure out housing and food for all the months that I wasn't in school. I was truly on my own.

My parents didn't stay for orientation. We didn't even know that was an option. They dropped me off and my dad pressed three twenty-dollar bills into my hand—more than he'd ever given me. At orientation they told us to pick up our textbooks at the school bookstore—I was surprised that the books weren't in my classrooms, but I wandered into the store with my free tote bag, following the horde of students and their parents who I noticed were whipping out credit cards to pay for the enormous stacks of books.

The woman at the cash register explained the system to me and I started pulling books. One textbook cost $200. What was in this book? Was it going to teach me the secret to life? My $60 wasn't going to buy me the secret to life or the textbook, so I went to the library, only to be told that the library didn't even carry the textbooks I needed for the class. The system seemed to be set up for me to fail.

I went to the financial aid office. The best they could do was offer me a $300 petty cash loan that had to be paid back in ninety days. I wanted to collapse in a heap, but instead I echoed my dad and told myself, *Hey, you're eighteen; you're an adult, and you're going to have to find a solution.*

I knew I needed a full-time job. The very first job I got was working at a call center. At $9.25 an hour it was the highest-paying job on campus, but they allowed you to work only twenty hours a week, and that wasn't enough money. Next, I got a job doing data entry at the hospital, which liked to hire students, for $11 an hour. Then I found a job working in a call center doing credit card servicing. I would have to get a car, but I would make $25,000 a year. I stormed through my days balancing full-time work and school my first year, during which I was called into a meeting with an academic advisor.

The Hopkins campus is a shocking bubble of beauty in the middle of downtown Baltimore. It looks like Benjamin Franklin could have lived there. Everything is made with brick and marble, and words like "legacy" are tossed around. Inside, the walls are filled with portraits of the old white men who ran everything. I took a narrow old elevator up to the advisor's office. The first time I met with him, he informed me with a degree of incredulity that I wasn't even registered for enough credits to graduate. I had no idea what he was talking about. I was registered for twelve credits, the minimum number required to attend—and that was more than I could handle with a full-time job. He told me that the twelve credits a semester wouldn't get me to the 122 I needed for my degree. This man was white, of an indeterminate age, had a full head of hair, flecked with gray, and on the wall behind him were his diplomas and signs of his success. He'd been a Fulbright scholar, he spoke fluent Japanese, and was very wise—and despite the difficult situation, kind. Now, I can see that he was a normal human, but then, I believed he was a man who held my fate.

"Well, nobody told me."

"No one is supposed to tell you; you're supposed to know."

The air leaked out of my lungs. What could I say? He was completely right. I just thought, *He's not wrong. I should have known.* But I hadn't even known to ask the question. I hadn't even known there was a problem to solve.

So many people, even as adults, box themselves out of growth and opportunities. You aren't supposed to know everything. But you are supposed to learn. You're not supposed to know entrepreneurship. You're not supposed to know how to build a business. It's stunning to think you can't do something because you don't know that one piece—and that was me in college. I felt I couldn't do it because I didn't know all the pieces.

But, at that moment, I was supposed to have everything I needed. My tuition was paid, I was a smart person who got into school because I was capable, and I was surrounded by people who—if I asked the right questions, or even just stood in the room and had the confidence to say "I don't know"—would have worked through it with me. I had everything I needed to figure out how to thrive. And yet college was not working for me. When I could attend class and stay up late enough to finish the homework, I got great grades. But these bills—to eat, to sleep, to live—weren't going to pay themselves. I didn't know what to do. I was completely crippled and anxious about how to ask for help.

All I saw were my flaws. I was a poor Black girl from a family of people who had never gone to college, at an elite, primarily white institution. It was my fault for not knowing, and for coming from people who didn't know. There were so many things my parents didn't know—they didn't know how to help me through college, and they didn't know how to plan for their own future, let alone mine.

———

Growing up poor, with immigrant parents who didn't always know how to get things done, or how to find a sensible solution, I started problem-solving for myself and my family pretty early. When I was a kid,

I learned to make everything stretch as far as possible. Nothing was wasted. Nothing was thrown out until it was beyond repair or repurposing. That was something poverty had taught me.

Years later, I called my system ROI, which usually stands for "return on investment." But when you're poor, you need to max out your investment of time, money, and energy. You have to: Restructure. Optimize. Implement. It's a method I swear by. It's how I look at everything in life.

Restructure means examining the way you think about a problem to determine if it really is a problem, and to ask what needs to be changed. *Optimize* is looking at what needs to be fixed to identify what the gaps are and whether you can fill them with what you have before you try something new. *Implement* is bringing in something new to solve the problem.

ROI is something you can keep in the back of your mind to help you problem-solve. You can ROI anything. Problems can be big questions about business or the small matter of a hole in your sock. When you're poor, you can't afford to throw things away, so you optimize. You'd look at the hole and restructure: Can I keep using the sock? How much wear is left in it? Can I optimize by stitching up the hole? Should I try wearing sandals instead? I don't just go straight to get new socks. If I can't wear this sock, can I get some other use out of it? (Socks are great for dusting.) When you're poor, you often have to go through this mental process. You can't just jump to the implementation part, particularly because implementing means you're applying something new. You often have to start by reflecting on how badly you need something. Where does it fit into your priorities? Do you have everything you need? That was how I had to look at life to survive.

When someone has a problem, they will often jump to trying a new thing. They won't examine how they're looking at the problem or try to make small adjustments.

I started creating problems the day I was born, which meant I had to get pretty good at solving them. Problem-solving is instinctual. You learned to cry when you needed food or to be changed or put to sleep.

Eventually, you learned how to eat, how to use the toilet, how to read, how to write. You solved each of these problems. You gathered information. And you figured out how to apply it. You may not have grown up knowing how to manage money, or how to pay bills, or how to do so many practical things—but you can learn. You can research everything. We show up every day to different problems and try to unpack them. How we approach those problems is either with neurotic suffering or legitimate suffering. Neurotic suffering is when you have angst over things you cannot control, while legitimate suffering is when you have stress over things you can control. But no matter what, life is suffering. Everything is just a problem to be solved.

As you probably already know, every time you get your footing, the ground shifts, and a new set of problems presents itself. Life is the meeting and solving of problems. How are you going to show up to them? In the season when it seems like things are going well, how strong are you getting to face the next challenge? Because no one's coming to save you from any of this and problems happen. Make no mistake, things will continue to be difficult. Unless you're going to take yourself out of this game, this world is going to be on fire or underwater, so what are you doing today to build a boat?

If you collect tools and resources along the way and remember to use them, you can solve the problems that come your way. Those problems will be in your own family. Those problems will be in your work. Problems naturally exist in the world. You will be dealt cards that you don't deserve, and you will still have to solve those problems. And when you've made it through one problem, you must keep your energy up for the next one coming. That is why you have to find joy in the stuff in between.

———————

My parents are probably the worst people at giving bad news in the history of humanity.

When I visited them, I noticed that my father was asking me to fetch things in the house more. Once, he left food on the stove and fell asleep as it burned. He'd had a couple of slips and falls and whenever he would get up, my mom would grab his arm to swing him up. I noticed her watching him out of her peripheral vision. These were old-man issues, but my dad wasn't old; he was in his forties. It didn't add up. Here was this big ferocious man exhibiting signs of weakness.

I came home one day from college and my dad called me into the bedroom to help flip the mattress, which he thought would help his back. My father was in bad shape, and when I asked him what was going on he casually mentioned that his doctor told him he had Parkinson's disease. He'd known for a while but hadn't told my mother, my sister, or me. He didn't accept his diagnosis and instead spent all his time trying to find a more suitable one—stress, or anxiety, or a sore back. Flipping the mattress was an incomplete solution.

It had started with back pain or feeling rickety when he got out of bed, which we thought could be attributed to years of sitting in a cab. Or not having the privilege of a new mattress. He'd ask, "Can you help me get out of bed? My legs are too stiff." At first it would take his legs a while to warm up, and he'd have a good segment in the middle of the day, but then he would hit a wall and it was like he was moving in slow motion. But then my dad started shaking. Suddenly, in his forties, he couldn't work such long hours, which meant my parents didn't have enough money. As he worked less, my mom noticed she was using more and more of her paycheck to cover not just savings and the extras around the house but also medical bills. When I came home to visit, I started to notice less food in the cabinets. My dad was halving his medication to stretch it.

By then I had found an entry-level corporate job and was not only supporting myself through college but also taking care of Maame. When she was at school her living expenses were covered, but from the time she was eleven until she was twenty-three, I was her primary provider. I was also direct depositing $50 to my mother from my paycheck, but that wasn't nearly enough to carry my parents through. To meet this problem, I needed to make more money. This was the first time I ever said that to myself.

I didn't have extra hours—school was rigorous and I was already working full-time. Where would the time come from? I couldn't borrow money from a friend even though some of my friends and their families were rich. No one was giving me money. No one was coming to help. No one was coming to save my family.

CHAPTER FOUR

SHOW UP AS IF THE ROOM IS A STADIUM

You need money, Nicole. What are you going to do? You don't want to break the law, girl, because no one's going to bail you out. What are you going to do?

That's when I thought: *game show.*

I'm funny and charismatic—I could charm a host, an audience. When I was twelve, I took an aptitude test that suggested broadcast journalism as a career. I remember thinking to myself, *I'm meant to be a news anchor. I'm meant to deliver messages to people to help them get what they need and move forward.* But what I'd forgotten and what my father hastily reminded me was that my parents emigrated from Ghana, that their life wasn't easy and they didn't have a lot of choices, but I, as their eldest daughter, had a lot of choices for my future: I could be a lawyer or a doctor.

Once I allowed myself to think getting on a game show was possible, I started reverse engineering the project, breaking it down to the tools and resources required.

I knew it couldn't be a show where I might only win a toaster, because I needed to walk away with cash. I couldn't do *Jeopardy!*, because second place gets luggage. *The Price Is Right* was too risky. What if I never made it onstage? Also, I was poor. I couldn't just fly out to California on a whim. If I had to get out there, I was going to have to hustle to make the money to bet on myself. Finally, I settled on *Wheel of Fortune*, one of the few shows where no matter what place you finish in, you get to take home the money you win. It's harder to get on *Wheel of Fortune* than it is to get into Harvard.

Back then the show had you submit an email address and they'd reach out if the *Wheel of Fortune* bus, which drove all over the country holding auditions, was in town. I half expected my email to just disappear, but what did I have to lose?

I started with this question: What were my odds of actually getting on the show? Maybe a thousand people would be at the open call. Out of those, how many of them were readers? Maybe half. Out of those five hundred, only half were probably strong spellers. Out of those, how many were well-spoken? This is TV. I estimated that would cut another hundred people, and some of those folks were probably a little camera shy—they didn't know how to be dynamic and exciting and positive. So, although I might be standing in a group of a thousand people, I'd really only be competing against a hundred other contestants. They would probably cast more than one contestant from the DC area. Out of those people, how many were good-looking? I'm young. I'm a little overweight, but I'm good-looking. I have a nice smile. I'm pleasant. And then I thought, *I'll wear my college sweatshirt. If they're casting for the collegiate episodes, I'll double my chances.* I'm Black, and they've got to have diversity. I told myself, *Girl, you're a cute, smart, educated Black girl who can spell her ass off. You're a shoo-in.*

I was going to get on this show.

People are quick to talk themselves out of something without really analyzing it. When you're talking yourself out of something, you need to ask yourself, Who told you that? You did? Really? Because a lot of times you talk yourself out of something with notions that were put in your brain by other people: I'm not pretty enough—who told you that? I'm not smart enough—who told you that? To get on *Wheel of Fortune* I did the opposite. It was the first night I ever tried this thinking, and it changed everything.

I talked myself into believing that my odds were really good and that I would be great. But I still held on to a thread of fear. I didn't tell anyone I was going to do this. I didn't want to be embarrassed if it didn't work out.

The day of the audition, I put on my jeans and my Hopkins sweatshirt and grabbed the $25 I'd scraped together so I could take the school shuttle to the train to DC and then take the Metro from Union Station to downtown. I even put a little aside to buy a hot dog on the way back.

I wrote the directions on a piece of paper and hoped I wouldn't get lost. Getting lost was almost impossible because as soon as I got close, I saw that the line was several blocks long. There were probably fifteen hundred people lined up. My numbers were a little off. Still, after all my mental cuts, I was only competing against a few hundred people. This was still worth trying, and I kept that attitude all day.

I didn't know who the casting person was or when they would start to watch me, but from the minute I walked in the door, I was smiling, pleasant, and exuding every ounce of charisma I possessed.

In the dark lobby, someone was pointing people in different directions. They gave each of us a paper that we pinned on like a marathon runner and a spelling test that eliminated roughly half the people there. The rest of us entered an auditorium filled with light. There was a small stage, a red curtain, and a set of whiteboard squares on which we played a fake version of the game.

Whenever it was my turn to pretend to spin the wheel, I put my back into it, I bounced up and down, and screamed in defeat and laughed in joy and brought everyone in the room along with me.

There were a lot of moms and grandmas, and cute young people. But people were dropping like flies. They would be playing the game and then one of the staff would say "Thank you" and they'd disappear. Soon the crowd had thinned to about thirty-five. There was one other young woman who was applying the same Nicole strategy. She was a brown girl who had on a college sweatshirt and was ready to go. Cool. *It just might be me and you. We are going to kill this.*

We kept playing until they whittled us down to a dozen. I played like the wheel was in front of me. I envisioned Pat right there saying my name, and Vanna turning the letters I shouted out. Then, all of a sudden, they stopped us. "Hey, guys, that's a wrap. Thank you so much for being here today." They called a few people down to the front. When they said my name, I hustled to where the casting folks were huddled. Every nerve stood on edge.

"We're just going to let you know, we absolutely love you guys. Thank you for coming out. If you are selected, you'll receive a letter in the mail with the date of the show you would be on."

Our little group started walking out. I doubled back to the casting folks and said, "I just wanted to say thank you so much. I don't know what's going to happen here, but this is some of the most fun I've had in a long time. So whatever it is you guys decide to do, I just wanted to say thanks for making it a blast."

I got my letter within a week.

It was a photocopied affair with the date written in by hand. I received the letter about three weeks after the day I had the idea. The letter explained that *Wheel of Fortune* would give me $2,000, no matter what I won, to cover my expenses. All I had to do was show up in Culver City, California.

I borrowed plane ticket money from my best friend Jessica's aunt and promised to pay her back as soon as I had my check. Jessica and I flew out together. I couldn't afford to do anything. We stayed in the cheapest motel (the tub was a little sketch, and the bed was so gross that I laid down a towel and slept on top of the blanket, but the room had a mirror and running water), ate fast food, and on our final night, before getting on the red-eye home, we slept in the rental car we'd parked at a restaurant near the airport.

On the trip there we were beaming and bubbly, and the flight attendant asked us what we were going to do in California. Jessica leaned toward the woman and whispered that I was going to be on *Wheel of Fortune*. As they tittered excitedly, I stayed cool. I was tamping down my hopes.

I didn't want to be overexcited, so I needed to have an alternate goal that, if accomplished, would aid in helping me reach the primary goal: to win and make a lot of money. My alternate goal was that this was my first time on a TV lot—I wanted to know everything about it. I wanted to be delightful; I wanted to be pleasant to work with. A stranger had gotten into my dad's cab and changed my life—I went from sitting in a passenger seat to being seated next to the president's children at school—so I knew what was possible. This could change my life too. So, even if I walked away with nothing more than the $2,000, I was going to feel like I'd grabbed a gem or learned something new.

I walked onto the lot giddy and ready to give everyone—from hair and makeup all the way to Pat—all my energy. I was going to ask them about their kids and their jobs, and be my regular joyful, curious self.

They film five shows in a day, so people were buzzing around for hours. I made it my business to meet everyone—the janitor, the camera guy, the caterer, Vanna.

When it was my turn to go, a woman came to the holding room and brought the three of us out into the dark hush of backstage. The space was cramped and littered with wires, which I carefully stepped over, willing myself not to trip or make a sound. Just as I was about to break through the curtain and go onstage, the person who'd led us to the stage entrance said, "Girl, we all hope you win." I was pouring energy into the world and saw the world responding to me.

Everything onstage was tinier than I expected. Pat and Vanna and the wheel itself, which is small but very heavy. I played against Wendi from Georgia and Tim from Wisconsin. I solved the first puzzle: Like Never Before. And the second: Psychic Reading. As I played, I could hear Jessica from the audience; I could feel the energy of people collectively wanting me to win—the audience, the crew, even Pat. Energy radiated toward me. I solved the third puzzle: World Traveler— and won a trip to Iceland.

I was on a roll. I was making money. A lot of money. But then Wendi hit her stride. She solved the Jackpot round with Curling Up with a Good Book of Matches and went on to solve the next puzzle: Pure Mountain Spring Water, and the next: The South Pole.

Tim had hit a bankrupt; Wendi was up to $11,200 and I had $12,600 when we entered the TV Show Title puzzle. Finally, it was my turn, and I put some Hs on the board, a W.

H _ W I _ / M _ T
_ _ _ R / M _ TH _ R

I could hear Jessica going wild. The audience was buzzing, as if they were sure I was going to get this one. I felt like they were trying to channel letters to me. But I had no idea. I asked for an S—and there was a collective gasp from the audience. Not an S on the board.

Tim spun and put a couple more letters up and then Wendi went and solved the puzzle: How I Met Your Mother. I had never watched the show.

So far I'd won $15,000 with three Ss, but Tim solved the puzzle: Crossword Clues.

Tim had $3,200, Wendi had $18,400, and I still had $12,600. Wendi won the game and then solved the Bonus Puzzle.

Still, in my own way, I had come out on top. I took home more cash than I'd arrived with and an all-expenses-paid trip to Iceland, plus I'd left a sprinkling of Nicole on everyone I had met that day.

Pat came over after the show finished filming. He looked genuinely disappointed that I hadn't won. "We really thought you had it." He shook my hand and smiled. It was great.

Afterward, two of the producers came up to me and told me, "You were so much fun to watch! We wish we could have you on every week."

One of the staff told me I had great energy. It was the highest compliment I'd ever been paid—it means you're the person we want in the room; you're a candle in the darkness, a light. Her words glowed inside me.

———————

Getting on *Wheel of Fortune* was the first time I realized I could harness the power of my energy. Also, that I could make money quickly.

You can play the odds in your favor—and that begins with believing there are things you can actually do versus thinking the odds are against you. Believe the world is conspiring in your favor. But don't be so naive as to think that the world will give you anything for free. It is both. You must believe. You must work hard. You must show up. You must walk into every space with enough energy to fill a stadium and the belief that people deserve to know you.

The hardest work of performing is getting people to buy the tickets. If you can get people in a room, then you can kick ass and be amazing and show up to meet them. That's when you get booked again. In the beginning, I booked most of my gigs because I was in the room and insistent on performing my best. So many people worry about the things they want to start. I can't start because I don't have these business cards; I don't have the right car; I'm not skinny enough; I'm not pretty enough; or any of the other things that people think they are supposed to have. But the thing that matters most is whether you are giving all of yourself to your audience. A lot of people try to measure their level of effort based on their circumstance. The measure of your effort should be based on your ethics, your moral and personal integrity. I put out a certain amount of effort because that is who I am every day. Always show up ready to do your best. Your cue to be excellent isn't how many people show up, how many followers you have, or how much money you are getting.

I've gone to keynotes where they told me there would be thousands of people and instead there were fifty—but I still showed up like I was in a stadium. If you start delivering stadium-level effort no matter the venue you are in, you will get booked time and time again. And you never know when you're going to get booked for the stadium. You don't know what the next thing is. That means everything might be wrong. Show up to feel joy no matter what. Show up with all your tools and resources and your questions. Show up like this next step is the most important, because it is. Everything might be wrong—your family can be struggling financially, your loved one can be sick, your job might be imploding—but even if everything appears to be wrong, especially during the hard times, in the thick of the struggle, know that you are enough.

CHAPTER FIVE

CHOOSE YOUR HARD

I was adulting faster than any of my friends in college. But I was also falling apart.

I never dated guys who went to school. I was working so I wasn't on campus that much and I wasn't part of campus life. Besides, the boys at school were mostly rich frat boys who weren't interested in me. And if anyone *was* interested, well, God forbid he bring home a thick Black girl. And even if those boys had been interested and brought me home, I was wrestling with my own psyche about my self-worth. I didn't know who I was or what I deserved or that I could be happy on my own. I was willing to make all sorts of insane compromises on who I wanted to be with. If a man had signs of stability—a regular job, a decent home—I would tolerate a lack of kindness as long as he was kinder than my dad.

I had no idea how to pick a mate. I thought you could do that based on paper—kind of like a résumé—the plain facts of who they were: whether they had a good job, whether they came from a good family, and if they seemed stable. And honestly, don't they always say "Love grows over time"? I also didn't realize that at eighteen you don't even know what it looks like for someone to have their life together—you think you do, but you don't. That guy may have a car, but that car could be leased; he could be in debt; you simply don't know. I didn't understand that you marry people, not potential.

What I liked most was feeling wanted. My parents didn't exactly treat me like they wanted me. I was a burden, a responsibility—an inconvenience. And my dad would destroy the joy of any place I did feel wanted, like at school, or the sport teams I joined, by making it seem as if I didn't deserve to be there or to be praised or celebrated. As a kid, anytime I won an award, he would take it from me and put it in a box in the basement. He banished my successes.

I dated the Fighter (he had a problem with violence), the Old Man (who was forty to my twenty) and, very briefly, the Athlete (. . . he was an athlete).

Several weeks after the Athlete and I broke up, I was sitting in the nail salon at the mall with a friend whom I'll call Mary. I didn't have the money for a manicure, but we chatted as her nails dried. I was feeling queasy and thought I was coming down with something. Without skipping a beat she said, "Oh girl, you might be pregnant." Now, coming from Mary O'Sullivan I laughed it off. She'd had three abortions back-to-back, and she was Catholic.

I was sure I wasn't pregnant. How could I be? I'd done everything to ensure I wouldn't get pregnant. What does pregnant even feel like? When was my last period? I was too busy to remember.

I stopped at the Walgreens on my corner that night. I felt like everyone was watching me as I walked to the aisle with the tests lined up in their tidy white boxes. There were so many different tests it was overwhelming, and they were all so expensive. I thought about not getting one, but the idea had lodged in my brain and I'd never be able to stop worrying until I was sure. In the end, I splurged on the digital response because I didn't want any uncertainty. At the checkout, I laid down a bag of chips, nail polish, and the test, avoiding the cashier's eyes.

I read the instructions twice. I peed on the stick and prepared myself to wait. I needn't have bothered. Almost as soon as I'd set the stick on the edge of the sink it showed that I was pregnant.

The blood rushed from my head and I sat down. Was something growing inside me? I called Mary, who sent me back to Walgreens for another test. I was pregnant.

I lost my mind. My brain was a firestorm of thoughts: How could this have happened? I had done everything right—I worked hard, I studied hard, I was on birth control. This didn't fit the storyline. Or maybe it did. Some part of me also heard all the societal nonsense and felt like this was a self-fulfilling prophecy. I'm Black and overweight and poor—is this just what was destined for me? No matter what, was I always going to be a statistic? Maybe everything my father had said was true.

What was my responsibility to the father? Did I need to tell him? *How did this happen?* I thought again and again. Did I have to keep this kid? What happens if I did? I knew what it was like to grow up with nothing and be raised by people who weren't equipped to parent. I wanted to convince myself that I would do better, but I couldn't promise that. And there was no one who could help. My parents? My sister at boarding school? My college friends? I didn't have a support system. I didn't even have proper health insurance. I couldn't see a viable solution. I couldn't see any options.

I will shame my whole family. My dad will kill me—and not just metaphorically, either; he might actually cause me physical harm. And then I started worrying about my sister. Who was going to take care of her if I had my hands full with a baby?

I lay on the couch and ran my hands across my stomach, then I realized that if something had begun to grow inside me it was lower down. I shifted my hands lower down my abdomen. And the thought that kept running through my brain was: *I can't have this kid. I just can't.*

Mary told me that the clinic in Annapolis was much better than the one in Baltimore. As she spoke, I began to worry about the hundreds of dollars this would cost. It felt like a billion dollars. What if I just can't pay for this? And then I thought about how much a kid would cost. I defaulted to logistics. I ROIed it.

Before I went to the clinic, I made an appointment at the campus health center to make sure I really was pregnant.

The health center was tiny—just a few small, poorly lit rooms that were mostly used to pass out Band-Aids and condoms. As I waited to be seen, I stared at the posters on the wall, all of which had to do with sex.

The nurse practitioner crowded into the postage-stamp-sized room with me. She confirmed the pregnancy as the paper draped over the examination table crinkled loudly beneath me. Looking down at my chart she asked if I was on birth control. When I told her I was using the birth control ring, she pushed her glasses up into her very big hair and asked if whoever had prescribed it had explained that it had weight-limit efficacy issues.

"No. I did not know that."

"Well, someone should have told you that with weight fluctuations efficacy can go down."

She let me take that in, then asked, "What do you want to do?"

Her tone was matter-of-fact, and its clarity reminded me that I had options. It was clear that the conversation was now about abortion. The way she spoke to me was without judgment. In that room, abortion was a viable choice—I was, after all, a student at Johns Hopkins, and no one at this institution was going to have a baby while they were a student. And no one leaves Johns Hopkins.

It was clear what I needed to do.

God is not the author of confusion, and in that moment, there was no confusion.

When I walked through the door of the clinic in Annapolis, I noticed that the recovery area was open-air. There were big, cushiony chairs lined up, like in a nail salon.

I was still in the window where I could have taken the abortion pill, but if it didn't work, I'd have to come back and have the procedure. After the failure of my birth control, I was terrified of it not working. I decided on certainty.

The hardest part was the moment just before the abortion.

Up until the day of the procedure, I'd only confirmed the pregnancy with tests. But when I went into the clinic, before they did anything invasive, they performed an ultrasound to make sure there was actually a fetus, that it wasn't just hormones creating a false positive.

The room was small. The gel was cold. The technician sat near me and ran the wand over my skin. The screen was tilted away from me, but I could see it lighting up.

"You're definitely pregnant," the technician said. There wasn't anything for me to say to that. "Did you want to see?"

Whole galaxies of time spun out within that moment. Did I want to see this kid that I was not going to carry to birth?

If I was going to do this, at least I could look. "Sure," I said tentatively.

It didn't look like a baby; it was a blob on a screen, a strange sac of cells making me very queasy—but an awareness sparked in me.

Why am I doing this? It was a real question. There was no judgment, no doubt, no confusion. Just a question. And the first answer that came to mind was because of money.

I didn't have enough money to have all my choices.

After I looked at the little glowing blob on the screen, I promised myself: I will never have to make a choice like this again. I will never have to make a choice like this that is made difficult because of money. Money will never stand in the way of my saving myself or my child. I will always be able to make the choice I need to make.

I didn't turn around and have any type of sizable funds for another decade, but from that moment on, I was moving toward that goal. I was in a position where I had to make a decision that could alter the course of my whole life, and the thing it came down to was money.

———

When I look back on my life and how I treated my body and myself sexually, emotionally, physically, I wish that I had never had sex until I met the person I wanted to be with forever. I wish I had been more particular about my partners in general. I wish I had never gotten pregnant. There are a lot of things I wish I'd done differently. But while I have a list of choices I wish I didn't have to make, I am also so glad that I'm here.

That period of my life was riddled with big decisions. Between Dad's Parkinson's, the family's financial problems, the way I cared for my sister, raised myself into adulthood, got a full-time job, and went to college, everything had pushed me to the brink.

I was constantly on probation because my grades would drop below the minimum GPA for my scholarship, so I'd go see the advisor and beg for my spot, then work my way off probation, but it was an ongoing cycle. The advisor always provided me with the full wheel of resources— counseling, study groups, tutors, and compassion. He asked me how I was doing and how my family was, and we both determined that I needed therapy.

The school's mental health office was across the hall from the advisor. It was small but friendly, and lucky for me my therapist was a Black man who had graduated from Hopkins. Sitting in his tiny office, I realized I could talk about all the things I was dealing with— the studying, how hard it was to work and go to school, and how weird it was being one of such a small number of Black kids that I was often the only one in the room. On my very first day, someone actually said, "I can't believe you got in. I thought it was just affirmative action, but you're actually smart." Everything felt like a signpost that I didn't belong. Seeing the therapist was validating, but it wasn't enough.

When I told him everything, he looked at me with an understanding that I will never forget but said, "I want to see you graduate. But there's so much going on here."

What kind of help is this? I thought to myself. Did he not understand that I needed help? But the fact was, while he could listen, teach me some techniques, and offer medication, he couldn't help me with food, money, and housing, and he couldn't change my father, or support my sister. I didn't just need therapeutic help, I needed on-the-ground logistical help with everyday survival.

Still, somehow, between the advisor, therapy, and my own sheer force of will, I stayed at Hopkins for four years. But the classroom didn't make sense to me. I wanted to learn what was practical and useful and connected to results. I wanted to DO the work. I was in a business class learning less than I did when I went to my job. I was teaching my peers the practicality of the concepts we were learning in textbooks. I could see that I was wasting time and money because I could do more. But I stayed because I was scared. But all that work, all that pressure, all that time—it was all too much.

By the second semester of my senior year, it was evident I needed more time to graduate, and once again I found myself sitting in the advisor's office. At this point he knew me really well. He knew everything I was accomplishing at work. He had heard my dad yelling at me over speakerphone in his office. He knew I was on my own in life. Finally, he looked at me, removed his glasses, sighed deeply, and said, "You're doing too much. Do you know you can be successful without a degree? You have so many other skills. You're brilliant at sales, business, speaking, and writing. Why are you trying to make this happen?"

"Because my dad said," I told him through tears.

He shook his head.

He was telling me that school was just *one* option. I didn't have to pick that option. But I was stuck thinking it was my only option, thinking I didn't have any other choices, even as I forged a whole other path for myself in the corporate world.

I was testing to get my securities exchange licenses—Series 6 and 63. I easily passed and started working for the largest financial firm in Baltimore. The semester before the rest of my class was going to graduate, I took a leave of absence, telling myself I could go back next fall, when I had more money.

Still, the shame of disappointing my father and my family tore at me. I slipped into a depression and suicidal thoughts gathered like storm clouds before a hurricane. I just wanted to turn away from everything, escape my life, walk out some secret door. Avoid the sure-to-come judgments, and rest. I was exhausted. That feeling grew and I started imagining how I would hang myself.

But I couldn't do it. I wasn't just responsible for myself; I had my sister too. And that kept me alive and working. In the years after, I quickly learned that degrees are hardly prerequisites for success. Yet I haven't talked much about not graduating, because where entrepreneurial white men are celebrated, Black women are ridiculed. And, frankly, much like Zuckerberg, Gates, and Jobs, I don't need a degree.

The degrees, certifications, and all those things are points of pride if *you* want them and want to use them. They're even better if you can afford them and are able to build a life financially after getting them. If not, and you don't believe in your ability to work and create and do (even with the degree), they don't mean a dang thing. Defining your educational path so that it will *actually* be used meaningfully is so important. Degrees are valuable and something to be proud of—graduating from college is an incredible endeavor. However, we've been bamboozled into thinking we're less than if we don't have the stamp of approval from an institution, a man, or a job. But nothing is missing.

At first, when I'd arrived at college, I thought I was missing a piece of the puzzle and that if I could acquire that one piece, I'd be successful. What I discovered was that sometimes you need to learn the missing piece, but other times you need to be able to recognize when you're not in the right room. Knowing where you're *not* supposed to be is just as important as knowing where you *are* supposed to be. But when I was eighteen I didn't know that, and so I spent several years trying to do something that didn't make sense for me. Maybe I could have started my business sooner, in my early twenties, like Henry Ford or Walt Disney, but here I was, still in the room screaming out "What's the game plan?" when there was no game plan for me, especially on the traditional path society (and my parents) expected. I needed to leave. I realized I didn't know exactly how to do this thing, but that there were other things I could do. So, I started playing with some tools I had. I went from asking "What don't I know?" to asking "What *do* I know?" That was the shift. I stopped standing in front of my table of tools and not doing anything. From that moment on, I began to show up, try things, gather all the information, and use it to solve problems. That changed everything for me.

———————

Sometimes you have to do something hard and you will have to choose the particular brand of hard it is going to be. Sometimes you have to choose the hard thing in order to set your future self up. Maybe that's choosing whether to take the shorter walk uphill or the longer walk on a flat path. Do you want to stay in a job you hate, or do you want to be an entrepreneur? They're both hard. Do you want to have another baby, or do you want to always wonder if you can? It's just hard. It's uncomfortable to have a conversation with your teenager about sex, but do you want to be a grandma early? Do you want to work a side hustle now so you can afford the down payment on a home later, or do you want the difficulty of not being a homeowner down the road? Starting something is hard. But so is moving forward. There's no getting around it. Life is always hard. Life is suffering. You meet and solve hard, hard problems—that's life. This difficulty gives us grief because we're struggling to accept the fact that life is difficult. But the minute you accept that life is difficult, then you can start getting on with the business of finding joy, coping with life in a healthy way, and making it meaningful for yourself. That's the best you can have—a meaningful life.

The privilege of choice is an incredible gift. Don't minimize the flexibility and privilege of having the choices that you have. And don't dishonor them by not exploring them fully when you have them. But also, recognize that if you have to make hard choices, which a lot of us have to do all the time, that you can choose hard and still honor your future self by saying, *Look, I might be choosing hard now, but*

I'm also going to make choices so that I don't ever have to do this hard again.

Today you may have all the choices you will ever have, and tomorrow something might happen—sickness, pandemic, a car accident—and you may have fewer choices.

Make good choices.

CHAPTER SIX

YOU ARE ENOUGH

I had a dad who was a fierce atheist who believed people who go to church are fools, and I have a prayerful mom who believes God is everything.

Once, I walked into my parents' home and felt drops of water flicked at my face.

"It's holy water."

"Mom. Hi, can I get a hello?" I said and tossed my keys on the ironing board.

"It's been blessed. Drink it." She pushed a glass into my hands.

"Mom, I'm not even thirsty."

"You have to thirst for the Lord."

Although I was a believer, it took me a while to find my spiritual home. I've always liked religion as a concept. I liked the value systems and structure—why should I make it up when someone's gone before me, made all the mistakes, and has information to share? Like my mom, I was always prayerful. I had no problem speaking to God, but the fire and brimstone thing was wrong for me. I believe that bad things will happen if you do bad things, but I don't believe in a God who throws people away. That fundamentally doesn't compute for me. Why would God preach forgiveness for us but then not be capable of it himself in an ultimate way? That's where things don't add up for me.

I've been on a journey looking for a faith home. I didn't want to be Zoroastrian or a Hare Krishna. I didn't think I fit the type and I never looked good in a robe. I wanted religion, and I knew I wanted something more conventional. But the brand of Christianity I'd grown up around wasn't right for me either. Ghanaians are super religious. When you go to Ghana, the businesses have biblical names, things like Psalm 23 Market, or the Lord Is My Savior Barbershop.

In my teens and twenties I was seeking out religion. I considered Islam—half my mother's family is Christian and half is Muslim, and I really loved the ritual of the faith, and how that lends itself to keeping your spirituality and your values at the forefront. If I have to stop and pray five times a day, I'm stopping to recalibrate myself with God—that is beautiful. I also really liked how the language of faith is integrated into everyday speech. When you greet people, you say "assalamu alaikum," peace be upon you, or another common expression is "inshallah," God willing—again, keeping the faith at the forefront. As a child I'd witnessed the prayers and covering of heads, the ritual, and again thought it was a beautiful practice, but I wasn't sure Islam was right for me.

I looked at Judaism very seriously. Ever since I fell in love with redheaded Avi Rosenthal in kindergarten, I thought I would be Jewish. My first introduction to other religions came when Avi explained the yarmulke he wore to me. Avi was the love of my life, but it just wasn't destined to be. He was very into sailing, and as a child of a taxi driver, I was never going to have a boat. I studied ancient Israel in college, and I often dated Jewish men. But no matter what it is, I have a clear and distinct type: I like a Moses-looking gentleman.

The Jewish faith is beautiful and seemed like a happy medium between Islam and Christianity, with roots that felt familiar. I liked the sensible practicality of it. Plus, in Judaism everyone is flawed. You'll get to heaven if you try your best. No fire. No brimstone. They don't even believe in hell; it's too dramatic.

Most of all, I was drawn to the sense of togetherness that Judaism breeds. I loved the idea of the synagogue and how the community is rooted in it—from services to school to activities. I loved that Jewish people are extremely family-oriented. Ultimately, though I was seeking religion, I was looking for family.

When I met Josh, I realized that I might actually marry a Jewish guy. I was twenty-two and had taken a corporate job in finance, but my understanding of love hadn't evolved much since college.

I almost didn't go on our first date, but I was talking to my friend, a gay neurosurgeon from Queens, who was very clear that I had to go. "Oh no, he is the holy grail of husbands, you need to go on that date—he's a Jewish lawyer!" Our first date was at Sofi's—a great crepe café that was warm and bright. Josh was in fact a Moses-looking man, a lawyer, even-keeled, and seemed kinder than my father. He hit all my marks. He made sense.

We met on the hottest day in Maryland in July. It was humid. The temperature was ninety but felt like 104. He was new to town, which was clear when he parked half a mile away and decided to walk to Sofi's in a wool suit and didn't even take off his jacket. He had a killer smile, cute dimples, blindingly blue eyes, and was sweating profusely. To hear Josh tell this story, he was going to win me over as he talked about sports, video games, and how video games made him appreciate sports more. What I can tell you about our first date is that we talked about all the things you're not supposed to talk about on first dates: politics, religion, and money. And we laughed a lot. Unlike some of the other guys I'd dated, he was wicked smart, with a sarcastic wit that I got. He may not have remembered to pull my chair out, and he may have insisted on splitting the tab, but he was the nicest guy I'd been with thus far and that made him stand out.

It wasn't hard. I didn't realize then that, as in any relationship, the hard was to come, and what really mattered was how we would handle it together. And things got hard. Very hard.

I have to admit that from the beginning there were signs that we shouldn't have gotten married. But much like the rest of my life, I made what I thought was the right call for the season I was in based on the data that was in front of me. And I wasn't wrong. It can be both.

On the way to our third date, we stopped at his parents' house for a minute. He didn't introduce me; he had me wait in the car while he ran inside. Then we went to Brookside Gardens—everything was lush and verdant and humming with life.

I'd never seen anything like it. A garden should feed you, but this place was filled with plants that I couldn't eat. It was hot and we walked miles and miles, but I was wearing the wrong shoes—sandals, not sneakers. The garden was quiet and peaceful, and every time we crested a hill, I expected to see tombstones. We didn't find graves, but we saw an infinity of pergolas and water features.

Despite my aching feet and the cemetery vibe,* it was the type of date that signaled he wasn't just trying to get into my pants—we weren't going to a bar or a club where one thing might lead to another. We were walking around, literally smelling the flowers, when he told me that there was no way he'd ever be able to pursue a serious relationship with me unless I lost thirty pounds.

I kind of teared up with worry that this man, the most normal person I'd dated so far, might not want to be with me. So I took his words as constructive feedback, as in how great it was to be with someone who cares about my health and well-being. This was just a problem that needed fixing. I had always been told and shown that happiness was a moving target, and that if I could just keep chasing it, then one day I'd get there.

---

*   Listen ladies, if you like a walking date, I support this. If you want to take long strolls on the beach, you do you. "Romantic" to me is sitting around talking stocks.

I started learning Hebrew, going to synagogue, and studying with a rabbi. According to rabbinical law, you have to be rejected three times before you can start the conversion process. It's a form of proof of sincerity; it's also incredibly awkward. I walked into each synagogue so they could get to know me and then reject me. The fourth rabbi, a woman, was the one who would convert me. I studied; I read; I learned about the history of being Jewish.

The room where I had my final interview was vast. Beneath the twenty-five-foot ceilings, I could hear my footsteps on the carpet and feel the four sets of eyes on me.

"Have a seat there," my rabbi said, gesturing to a chair in the middle of the room.

The four rabbis doing the questioning loomed in the distance. I perched on my seat, worried that if I did something wrong, they would reject me or that God would strike me dead. I'd been working toward this for a year. Josh and I were planning to wed in a couple of months—would a rabbi marry Josh and me if I failed my conversion interview?

There was no hello, no small talk or niceties. They asked questions and I answered them. Back and forth we went.

"Are you here of your own free will?"

"Yes."

"You know, this is a lifelong commitment to God, you're not just doing this to get married?"

"No. I was considering this before I met Josh. It was great to have guides in the process, but this was something I planned to do."

"Will you raise your children Jewish?"

"Yes, if I'm Jewish and have kids, I'd raise them to be Jewish."

"Why would you want to become Jewish? You know we are the most oppressed people in the entire world. Every generation we have been persecuted."

Almost involuntarily I said, "I'm Black." I wanted to laugh; I wanted to say: *I'm Black and a woman. I wear my oppression everywhere I go. Adding Jewish to the pile wouldn't be so bad. At least I can keep that secret. No one is going to look at me, and think, "Well, she's definitely Jewish."*

There was a synchronized shuffling of papers.

I wondered if I had just made a terrible mistake. I thought of my mother- and father-in-law-to-be and Josh sitting outside the interview room waiting for the approval to become Jewish.

"Well, you would be both. Right?"

"I think I can handle it."

There was a long pause. Finally, my rabbi said, "All right, Nicole, now we have to discuss," and motioned toward the door.

I don't know what they talked about in there. They made me wait just long enough that I began to sweat and then they called me in to tell me I'd been accepted into the faith. It was time for my mikvah.

The rabbi led me down to the locker room. She made me take out my contacts and the whole world went blurry. She stood by as I disrobed and then I followed her to the ritual bath. It was a subterranean spa—gray tile, soft light, and a dipping pool filled with natural water from a free-flowing source, as per rabbinical rule.

The water was warm and a little salty.

The rabbi asked me more questions that all amounted to: Are you sure you want to do this?

At this point I'm stark naked in front of a rabbi, we dippin'.

I told her yes and she reminded me to open my eyes underwater.

Every nook of me had to be converted.

I wondered what would happen if I kept them shut; would that mean I was still a little bit Christian? I did not test the theory.

I went under. I opened my eyes. I emerged.

Once I'd blinked the water out of my eyes I could see the awe on the rabbi's face. But, as much as I wanted to feel different, transformed, everything still felt the same, only wet.

The next day I thought to myself, *Do I feel different?* I didn't. But I did immerse myself in the practice of Judaism. I had a front-row seat—going to synagogue for high holidays, being with the family on Passover and Shabbat. Josh's parents are conservative, which meant a nice happy medium of the formalities mixed with the more casual things—we would eat out and have dinner even though it wasn't kosher, but we wouldn't order pork. Josh and I tried keeping kosher, and I learned to make a mean challah—that braid is not easy.

I was learning Judaism as a culture, not as a religion. So, I understood why we love Adam Sandler and why Sammy Davis Jr. will always count. But I struggled.

———————

Josh and I had been planning a bigger, more formal wedding after my conversion, even though we had already been married in the eyes of the law since our courthouse ceremony. The day before our wedding, I was coming out of the hair store where I'd been trying to figure out how to do my hair when Josh called to talk about his parents' doubts about me. Despite our courthouse marriage, we hadn't yet been married before God and family, and they seemed to feel that it wasn't too late to call the whole thing off.

I backed up on the sidewalk until I found myself on the steps of a church, crying. I was sick about being publicly rejected, about the humiliation of not being good enough. I felt as though I wasn't wanted as I was. But I thought that if I could change enough, I would be wanted. That was not the case.

Ultimately, I failed as a Jew. I failed at organized religion. I had been treating religion like a weight-loss plan. Testing out keto, the South Beach Diet, Atkins, trying to figure out what I needed. So far, no one program felt entirely right, but my faith grew. Gradually, I returned to my Christian faith, but it was defined less by the church and more by my relationship with Jesus. Whenever I felt alone, my faith showed up—and it showed up in a Christian way. Whenever I was alone, Jesus was there. Even if I was trying to be far from Him, He was around.

God was pursuing me and He was using the language of Jesus, and I understood it. It made sense to me. It was graceful and forgiving, and it made me grow. I was constantly being asked, *What are you doing to pursue being better?*

Of course, not all Christianity is like that, but with Christianity I felt like I could immediately start talking and I could feel God showing up. I didn't need an intermediary. I didn't need structure. I definitely didn't need words from someone else that I had to say every day. I needed a place I could go and be messy.

I started communicating with Him directly, and not just in the form of the Lord's Prayer, which I said when I was younger. I communicated in a conversational way, where I was listening for answers and looking for results. If God is an example of the perfect parent, then why wouldn't I talk to Him? When you have an issue, you go to your mom. If you crash the car, you call your dad. I wasn't going to God to clock in for a job; I'm going to Him for advice, support, and love. I started thinking about my faith as a relationship versus an obligation.

Friend, you deserve to be in places where you are wanted. You must be willing to leave if you are not wanted just as you are. Finding the space where you are wanted is nothing more than a problem to solve. You know how to solve problems. But first you must believe you are enough.

In some ways my search for religion and family had been a failure to recognize that I was already enough. I couldn't see that I had everything I needed—from my body to God.

CHAPTER SEVEN

OWN YOUR NARRATIVE

I entered a season of change. In order to change, I had to question. Questioning is the birth of all my work; it's examining my thoughts to determine if I have to do things the way I've always done them. Questioning is the first step in ROI—restructure. At the core of every change I've ever made is this question: This is how I've always done it; who told me it had to be done this way? If I can't find the answer, then I start thinking, *Well, let me figure out how I want it to be*.

For the first time in my life, I was really looking at my wellness and deciding how I wanted to live. I became a weekday vegetarian. The first few years of marriage didn't ease the challenges, so Josh and I started seeing a therapist, and things began to shift. It turns out therapy is like getting your eyebrows done—it doesn't feel great, you have to keep doing it, but the results are life-changing. I was also learning about people taking the natural-hair journey—growing their hair back without chemicals. I was twenty-six and didn't know the first thing about natural hair. I didn't know how to manage my hair; the stress of the wedding, of my job, of my quest to lose the thirty pounds Josh had asked me to, and of everything else had caused my hair to start thinning. I was working my corporate job. I also had a side hustle babysitting a five-month-old for a couple of musicians to make extra money to give my parents. Josh told me we didn't have enough to give my parents $150 a month—and I didn't question him. I trusted that he was making good decisions for our family.

My hair loss was a symptom of a much bigger problem. For the last two years I had put myself, my health, my happiness in a little box and tucked it away, putting everyone else's needs first, and the result was written across my hairline.

As a little kid I was unaware of my hair—it may have been frizzy, or tangled, or pulled into a tidy ponytail, but no matter its state, I was blissfully oblivious. Once in a while my mother would pull me into the bathroom and spread some white cream on my hair, parting each section, smoothing the cream down while telling me to sit still and let her know when my scalp started to burn. (That just doesn't make sense. I was being taught beauty is pain and that anything good comes from struggle.) Then she'd rinse and shampoo and rinse and shampoo again and comb my hair back into a ponytail or braids and off I'd go.

When I was nine, I was getting ready to go to a soccer game when my mom announced, "I have to do your hair because you're not going to the soccer game looking a mess."

We went into the bathroom: smear, burn, rinse. And when she was done and I looked in the mirror, it dawned on me that my hair looked different from before. It was flatter, slicker, and instead of bouncing up it stayed down.

I went to a game, and my soccer coach, a Black woman, casually asked, "Oh, did you get a relaxer?"

What was a relaxer? I knew only that my mother had done my hair and it didn't look the way it had when I woke up that morning.

"No," I said.

She rolled her eyeballs over me. "Yes you did."

She must have been looking at me thinking, *Girl, you lied about your relaxer.* But I wasn't lying. The truth was I didn't even know that what my mother was doing was relaxing my hair, taming my curl. Until that day, I didn't even know when my hair was in its natural state and when it was altered. But, after that, whenever I had a big event, I'd ask my mom to do a fresh relaxer. I had been putting chemicals in my hair for twenty years and didn't know how to do it any differently.

A lot of time in the Black community is spent talking about our right to have Black hair in its natural state, because for centuries the prevailing narrative was that Black hair not being in its natural state was somehow better or more desirable. Our hair has been subdued and straightened into looking like something that it is not. It was telling someone else's story.

That cost us our sense of self-worth; it cost us the love of our authentic selves.

Here I was, a whole adult, and I didn't know how to fix my hair-line. And no one was coming to save me; I had to do whatever I could to heal myself.

I started transitioning: I stopped relaxing my hair so that the bottom was straight and the hair close to my scalp was curly. My hair was grow-ing in curly and healthy, but the straight parts were breaking off. It was a mess, but I wasn't ready for the big chop. What would happen if I cut off all my hair and started over? I researched natural hair. I walked the aisles of pharmacies and bought any products that *might* help. When nothing did, I moved to the aisles of grocery stores and made my own concoctions using olive oil, Crisco, and mayonnaise as conditioners. I bought a Craigslist-spectacular vanity that I spray-painted white and filled with products, and then I developed a system for testing each product to see how it worked.

And then one day, in the parking lot at Lowe's, I looked at myself in the visor mirror and decided to blow everything up and start from scratch.

I didn't want to go to a hair salon where I'd be asked a lot of questions or forced to fend off other people's opinions—some Black women are very resistant to your cutting your hair down. I remembered a new barbershop on Harford Road, next to the Jamaican place with delicious food. The smell of curry hit me as I walked into the tidy brick building. The barbers didn't want me to look too much like a man, so I had to wait forty-five minutes for Toya. The '90s music was bumping, men cycled in and out of the chairs, and I sat there feeling like an island. I felt like the only woman in the world ever to do this. Toya wore a T-shirt and had a septum piercing and her own chair at the barbershop—she was cool. I told her everything and explained that I wanted to cut all the relaxed part of my hair off.

"It's gonna be really short."

"That's fine. Just leave me enough to braid." I was terrified and wanted the option of putting in braids if it was unbearable. "And don't shape me up too tight."

"I got you."

She began picking my hair out, misting it, and then she pulled out her scissors. I didn't know I was holding my breath until the first clump of hair hit my thigh. It felt like it weighed a hundred pounds.

I listened as the blades sliced through my hair and imagined how regal I'd look. Visions of Grace Jones and Nina Simone danced in my head as Toya pressed the clippers to my neck and shivers ran up my spine.

When Toya held up the mirror for me to see the back, I stared at my reflection. I did not see a queen. Why did I have to wait so long for her to cut my hair? The cut was not transformational. I was no different. My hairline was still thin. My hair was just an undefined mass. Toya was talking about how my curls would pop when I washed my hair. I didn't know what that meant. I didn't know what products to use. All I knew was that I didn't die. I was still here to figure out how to do it.

On the way to the car, the air on my skin made me feel exposed. I slid behind the wheel and pulled down the visor to look at myself.

It wasn't perfect, but it was done. Honestly, my hair looked nightmar-ishly bad, yet it was still better than that weird, tangled tension I'd felt before. At least I had done something.

I noticed how light my head felt. I felt good. It was as if I'd never seen myself just as myself. I looked at my reflection one more time. People are always talking about how haircuts can change your life. Maybe you got your hair cut and met the love of your life or took a new job. My haircut made me a multimillionaire. That first clip changed every-thing.

But before I realized that everything was different, I had doubt. At home, I spread out a cornucopia of natural hair care products on the bathroom counter. I didn't know what would work. This was going to be a long process of trial and error. I turned all the lights on and started taking pictures to upload to the Internet for my friends to see. It was where I was going to collect my proof that this experi-ment was working. I needed proof because I didn't have belief. I didn't believe in myself enough to believe that my hair would grow back. I was afraid I had damaged it so much that I deserved to be punished. *It's not going to work. It's not going to work* kept running through my head.

Josh walked into the room as I was snapping pictures. He gestured to his head.

"So, what is this . . . ?" His voice trailed off; he seemed unsure what to say next.

I explained that I was going to share a record of my natural hair experience.

"That's stupid," he said. "Why would anybody care about that?" Then he walked out.

"Because I'm a beautiful Black woman!" I screamed at his back, though really I was yelling out the affirmation I needed to hear.

A part of me was critical of the way I looked while I was going natural. I was scared to let go of my weaves because I believed I looked prettier with them. I had to tell myself I can always go back.

But even with that uncertainty, I understood that I needed to know how to love myself in my natural state. I could not be forever reliant on something I don't create, own, or hold in order to feel complete. That just can't be enough. There's nothing scarier to me than not being able to figure out who I am independent of everything and everyone else.

I needed to know what my own hair looks like, and I needed to know how to manage it, without anything extra, because I didn't know what the future would hold. I didn't know if there would be a global ban on hair extensions and I wasn't about to be some bald chick. What if in the new world order there are people walking around with bags collecting all the weaves in the room? What would I look like underneath?

After the big chop, I was terrified to go to work. I was no longer the straight-haired, wig-wearing woman my colleagues believed I was. I felt like an imposter. A bald fraud. But this was me. Besides, they couldn't fire me for cutting my hair.

Standing in the elevator I felt naked. Walking through the halls I felt naked. Sitting in my cubicle I felt naked. I was baring myself for all these people to see.

My office was a white space with white people who thought natural hair was interesting—as long as it was loose, curly, undefined, and big. But there were a handful of Black women too—we all knew one another and kept a mental count of who was in the building. At first no one said anything. What could they say that wouldn't be rude or a lie? But after a few days, once it was clear I wasn't just between hairstyles, the other Black women with their glossy hair extensions, braids, and wigs started stopping me in the break room, the elevator, and the hallway. "I see that you're not doing what you normally do. What's this about?" they'd ask. "Oh, are you going natural? I'm going to do that someday," they'd confide. I could tell they were genuinely interested because we'd be standing around talking for way too long. Once they saw my edges growing in thicker, my hair growing out, and my new styles, they wanted to hear about what I was doing and what I was using. I started giving out the link to where I'd begun to chronicle my hair journey online.

I started my first business the moment I cut my hair. In the beginning, I didn't have money or experience running my own business, but I had a passion for finding solutions, years of corporate experience, and a deep desire to help people be confident in their own skin. I was getting a lot of questions from people, and while I didn't have all the answers, I did have a lot of information about what did and didn't work and that information seemed to be helping people. That's all you need to start: passion, drive, and desire. It's those human elements that are going to get you going and keep you going.

Almost immediately, brands began reaching out to me to try their products and write about them. I said yes. But I don't do free, so I also said, "That's called advertising: you have to pay me." From my day job I knew there was a budget for that kind of outreach. So, even when my readers numbered in the tens, I was embarking on entrepreneurship.

People always ask about a breakthrough moment on the path to entrepreneurship, but for most of us, entrepreneurship is a quiet hum in the back of our brains, not a loud roar. It's the thing that makes you think *Why did they use that font?* when you're standing in the grocery store, and it's the way you master the most efficient way to get children into a car. Chances are, that hum of entrepreneurship has been there all along; you just need to decide if you want to turn toward that sound and explore it.

The first time I remember hearing that call I was in grade school. Our campus ran alongside a major road and all kinds of litter would accumulate at the edge of the playground—Styrofoam cups from McDonald's, candy wrappers, aluminum cans. Not only was it dirty but it was also bad for the planet.

I got all my classmates to play a game I called Trash Bag Brigade.

I brought in a menagerie of plastic bags we had at home (we saved every bag from everything we'd ever bought) and handed them out. We spent the next recess picking up trash. I was the CEO and after that first day, I didn't pick up trash anymore—I supervised. But my first business failed in a week. One of the parents complained. (Mind you, this school cost tens of thousands of dollars a year in 1990 money, and here was this little scholarship student whose dad was a cabdriver rounding up children to pick up garbage during recess.) Almost as soon as it began, a kibosh had been put on the brigade. The headmaster called my dad, who then lectured me about being a ringleader, telling me I shouldn't manipulate the other kids. I sat there thinking, *If I am a ringleader, I am a ringleader for good.* I saw a problem and had found a solution.

Society will try to tell you who you are and what you deserve, but you are not a label, a checkbox, or a stereotype. You are the author of the story you tell yourself. If you aren't where you want to be, you can restructure until you get there.

We spend so much time building things up and avoiding them—I don't want to do the assignment, I don't want to quit the job, I don't want to make that change—that we turn our psyches into pressure cookers of anxiety. No matter what is inside your pressure cooker, it just feels good to let some steam out. Just doing something, anything at all, will feel better, even if the thing is terrible.

Entrepreneurs are problem solvers. Any endeavor I've ever started has been a journey of finding answers. Whether it is picking up trash, or making extra money on *Wheel of Fortune*, or experimenting until I had the information I needed to heal my hair, I've always started with a question I had to answer for myself, and it has always resulted in my taking people along on a journey to figure it out. Other folks have questions too, and sometimes the answers you discover can help them. If you're surprised by the questions people ask you because the answers seem so obvious, that's a sign that you know something they don't, and that that should be the business. When

I began my hair blog, I started finding answers to questions I knew I wanted, and it didn't take long to realize that other people wanted them too. I had no idea where it would lead me, but by taking the first step I was able to discover new possibilities. I was rewriting my story.

CHAPTER EIGHT

YOU ARE WORTHY WHEN YOU WAKE UP

I grew up with parents who were entrepreneurs. My dad made his own schedule. He worked his own hours. His cab was his office and his passengers were his clients. So, I grew up in the passenger seat of a rolling consultancy. But I also saw what went along with that—the high stress, the crazy hours, and ultimately, he was still ruled by a little dispatch box that was telling him where to go, what to do, and when to be there. My dad was always talking about paychecks and bills, and it seemed like nothing ever came together for him. So, I'd always put the corporate world on the highest of pedestals. My end goal was to get that corner-office corporate job—and after college I got it. No more entry-level. I was officially on the corporate ladder.

I'd begun working for an insurance company and was making a decent salary, more money than my parents had ever seen combined. I loved my office. I loved the place at the bottom of the building where

I could get a breakfast sandwich. I loved the regularity of my job, the structure, and I was proud of my work. I used to joke that they would bury me under the building. For the first time in a long time, I felt like I could rest.

I loved my wide cubicle in agreeable gray, and always wanted it to be a place where people felt at ease. I had a Zen garden, a set of swinging magnetic balls, stress balls, and a candy dish filled with Life Savers. And I had a rearview mirror affixed to the corner of my monitor, so I always knew what was coming.

But there were still surprises.

A few of my coworkers had jumped ship to a competitor, a new division of an established company. I thought they were insane. Why would they leave the number one player in this space and go to this new business? The unknowns of a new division made me nervous.

But my peers weren't thinking the way I was. They were not waiting for a promotion; they were thinking about where they could go to drive their careers. That was counter to my dad's advice—stay until you're kicked out. And counter to what my mother had always done—turned down promotions to avoid the chance of failing.

Then one day Laura Lerner called. Laura came out of the womb as a sixty-five-year-old woman. She made herself soup, lived in a cottage near the water, was a runner, and was one of the kindest, most unassuming, most harmless people I'd ever met. She was just a little older than I was, and a rung above me on the corporate ladder. I loved working with her. She was a hard worker who would bend over backward to do what was right to take care of people.

Laura told me she was leaving the company.

"How are you leaving? What are you talking about? You have a great job. Where are you going?" Not only would I miss her (I didn't yet understand that people in the corporate world are temporary), I was also mystified. I still bought into the outdated idea of pensions, loyalty, and staying with a company for forty years. Who leaves? We were going to be buried under this place, weren't we? Laura did great work and was always looking for a promotion, and she got small promotions, but that wasn't enough. If this wasn't enough for Laura Lerner, and I was at least as good as Laura, I needed to question what was good enough for me.

When she told me she was going to a competitor's new division, I almost dropped the phone. As she told me about the move, I stared at the world map on my cubicle wall, looking at the pins in all the places I'd traveled to. What else was out there?

Quiet and unassuming Laura Lerner had seen something new and then asked for what she wanted. That changed everything. Laura had been doing the job I hoped to be promoted to, but if she didn't want that job, did I?

When Laura said, "You should come too," I didn't know what to say. She pressed on: "I know it's risky. I built a lot here. But you know, a couple of other people from our company have already gone there to start things and it sounds good."

I was worried for her. What if it didn't work? What if she wasn't okay? But she seemed to believe she would be fine—and her whole approach was educational to me.

After Laura left, for the first time I thought to myself, *What if I left?* Despite my desire for stability, I sat in my cubicle thinking about Laura and the other people who had left and how happy they were. The idea of a new frontier sat in my brain and niggled until I realized that if I stayed where I was, I would have nowhere to grow. My biggest fear was that the new division wasn't established. If I went there, it would be the first time I was leaving stability to go try something. I took the risk. In my unwitting first step into full-time entrepreneurship— because belief in better is the true first step—I started looking at job postings.

Laura and I stayed in touch, and when I applied, I let her know. From there things moved quickly. It was as if they'd been waiting for me to reach out. They wanted all the people they could get from our competitor company to develop this product.

The day of my interview I was racked with guilt. I was doing a virtual interview from my current employer's office. I found a windowless conference room—I couldn't be in a fishbowl committing my act of betrayal. In case anyone wanted to know what I was doing, I prepared a ridiculous alibi, but honestly, I was on break; nothing was wrong. But that's how nervous I felt at the prospect of changing my life. At the appointed hour I slunk off to the conference room, where I sat in worry and talked to the hiring manager, afraid the door would click open at any moment.

The interview went well, but there was a pit in my stomach as I thought about telling her that I hadn't finished college. I already suffered from imposter syndrome; I couldn't compound that by not being up-front about my degree.

"I just want to call out that I haven't completed my degree. I have one more year left."

At this point I hadn't been in school for a few years and she sounded surprised that I'd brought up the degree. "Oh, are you thinking about returning?"

"I don't know if that's required, but I wanted you to know."

"That's not really required for the role, but if that's something that might come up in terms of time . . ." Suddenly I realized she was thinking of it as a detriment in terms of my energy.

I quickly told her I wasn't planning to go back anytime soon and she assured me we could always have a conversation about it down the road.

She didn't care about my degree; she cared about results. And my data and stats demonstrated the work I did.

The offer came over email. I nervously checked the mirror on my computer to make sure no one was coming and read the letter on my phone. I was wildly excited; they offered me $10,000 more than I'd been earning. I texted Josh right away. I wanted to know if he thought I should counter.

I used to always be so grateful to take whatever was given to me. That came from my dad—never look a gift *house* in the mouth. If you're lucky enough to even get someone to give you a handout, just shut up and take it, because you barely even deserve to be in the room. Be small, don't be noticed. If you speak up, they might take the thing you already have. My mom wouldn't report repairs in our apartment until they were really, really bad because she was worried that if she reported problems, they would take away our subsidized housing.

Josh wrote me back and asked, "Are you even sure?" I wasn't. It was hard for me to ask for more because I didn't feel like I deserved it. But, for the first time ever, I asked for more money. This was monumental, and so was the result. Just by countering, I got an extra $25,000. I possessed the power of making money just by opening my mouth, which is something I hadn't done before. This was an extension of what I'd learned on *Wheel of Fortune*, that I could harness the power of my energy and make money. I'd taken a risk and with the bonus potential I'd more than doubled my salary.

I looked at the pictures I kept on my desk—Josh and me on our wedding day, and a picture of my sister and my parents. What if the whole thing closed? What if I didn't have a steady paycheck? Would I be able to get another job? And if I didn't, what would happen? So many people were counting on me—my parents, my sister, even Josh. I started doing calculations. I figured out what my paycheck would look like, how much we would be able to save each time payday came around. We'd finally be able to pay off the credit card. This money was going to change our lives.

At the office, I printed out the second offer letter; I needed to feel something in my hand, to make it real. I kept looking at it. I'd pick up the paper and read it again and pop a back-of-the-mouth smile that was just for me. I raced home that night and ran upstairs to where Josh was already at his computer gaming.

I burst through the door, waving the letter in my hand.

"Good job."

"Do you know what this means for us?!"

When I told Josh, he was very low-key. He was glad I was making more money, but that was all he said. There was no booming whoop of excitement, no rush to go buy a bottle of champagne. Of course, back then, I didn't expect those things, but I did think we should celebrate.

So that evening we drove to Pei Wei. I cried happy tears over my shrimp pad Thai.

————————

To be clear: Your worth has nothing to do with money. If you focus on the money, you'll miss the meaning. And it's so natural to focus on the money because we're trained to do that. The money was immaterial. What I learned was that I acted differently and got a result that affirmed what I wanted.

I am a person of possibilities and potentials. But, up until that point, any job I'd gotten had been out of necessity. This was the first time I switched jobs because I felt like I deserved more. This was the first time I moved because I felt called to, and because I felt that my gifts would matter here. This move unlocked a whole new mental level for me. I had never thought before that I was allowed to want more than what I'd been given. And when I realized that I was allowed to define my own worth, even if it was within the parameters that society had written for me, it changed everything. That's when I understood that the whole rule book was trash. Once you realize that, you are able to do more. That's the truth.

A lot of people, I used to be one of them, think self-worth is defined—that you get it when you achieve a certain level of life. You might think you are worthy if you have the right job or the right home. You might not even allow yourself to reach for something because you feel your self-worth hasn't been validated by some external force. But that's false.

Your worth isn't defined by a destination. It's also not defined by what you do between lifting your head up off the pillow in the morning and laying it down again at night. Here's the twist. Your worth doesn't increase or decrease. Some people think your worth can only increase if you hit a goal, but it doesn't. It also doesn't decrease. You are just worthy. No matter what. You inherently have value.

You are worthy when you wake up.

Yet we tell ourselves we're not worthy all the time, in a million different ways. If you wake up saying that in order to display your worth to yourself you want to eat well, exercise, and show love to your children and then you decide to do drugs, not honor your commitments, and neglect your children, then understand that the reason you question your worth in that moment is because you aren't affirming what you're saying you're worth with actions that support it.

Once you understand that you are worthy, affirm that with action. You can keep saying your affirmations in the mirror all day, but they don't mean anything if you don't follow them with an action that proves to your whole body, your whole self, that what you are affirming is true.

CHAPTER NINE

KEEP TAKING STEPS

Once I went natural, whenever I saw people who had it all figured out, I talked to them. I asked them how long they'd been growing their hair so I could gauge my progress. I wanted to gather all the information. Everyone I saw was an inspiration. A promise that mine would get there too. I'd started asking people if I could take their picture and talk to them about their hair-care routines, which is why I needed business cards. It was weird to photograph someone and not have something to give them.

At night, while Josh slept, I sat at the dining room table making my business cards. I had spent hours bent over my computer, formatting and reformatting the cards. They were simple. Naptural Nicole. My name. My email. I printed them in blue on white paper so thin that I kept mangling it with my too-big yellow-handled scissors. My fingers cramped into claws, but eventually I found a rhythm navigating the long blades. By the time the sky was that deep, quiet blue-black that makes you feel like you're the only one awake, I had a modest mountain of tiny slips of cards, just a few inches big.

As I cut, I thought about my mom's stall at the market in Ghana. I thought about the company my mother kept. She was caught up in the entrepreneurial spirit—and so was I. I have an uncle who is the widest distributor of skincare products in all of Africa. I remember being small and sitting with my mom and my uncle's wife in their tiny apartment while she bemoaned how the business wasn't taking off. My mom was there helping cook while they barely had anything—they were broke with a bunch of kids and he was never home because he was always working as a chemist trying to figure out how to create products for Black skin. And when he was home, he was hidden in his chaotic base-ment office, surrounded by stacks of paper, boxes of product, boxes of packaging. It was a classic entrepreneurial mess. He was a classic entrepreneur. There was a problem he wanted to solve: very few beauty products designed by and for Black people, but he had to keep exper-imenting to find the right formulas. They became my parents' richest friends, but it took fifteen years.

I remembered Auntie Efua's enormous industrial mixer dominating her foyer. Auntie Efua made bread. For years she made it in her house, and when we stepped into her home we entered a makeshift bakery, a world of entrepreneurial vision. Plastic sheeting carpeted the floor around the mixer; the thing was so big that I couldn't even wrap my arms around it. Bags of flour were stacked against the wall, pans and giant mixing bowls were everywhere, and there were piles of plastic bags and twist ties on the counters. And the smell of Ghanaian sweet bread swirled through the air. She'd started by selling the loaves at the soccer games. Seven years later when Mom said we were going to visit Auntie Efua, I expected to pull up at her home, not her warehouse. She called her business Effie's. She'd built the whole thing up, but she wasn't baking the bread anymore. Now there were big machines, conveyor belts, and a staff of twenty running around in hairnets, and Auntie Efua was in the back monitoring shipments, making sales—

running the show. Now, Effie's is the Black Wonder Bread. You can find her bread in any ethnic market, or in stores in Ghana. As we left the warehouse, I noticed a big delivery truck with the company's name and logo printed on the side.

When Mom and I got back in her car, I felt the heat off her body. I don't know what she felt—jealousy, regret—but I could feel the churning. I imagined she was thinking, *This could have been me. That should have been me.* She wanted it for Auntie Efua, but she also wanted it for herself. I wish I could have told her then, *You can do it.* But the truth is, my mother didn't have the necessary belief to do something.

How much belief must Auntie have had to take the risk of buying such expensive equipment and turning her foyer and kitchen into a bakery? That's the basics of entrepreneurship. At each stage, you want to do a little bit more; you have to take that one risk to buy that thing, or invest in that thing, or quit your job, or go to that place. Whatever it is, it's going to be scary and it's not going to make any sense to anyone else, but you must take that risk.

As I set the scissors down, the cards fluttered. I was tired and the farmers' market opened in a few hours, but now I had something to give the people I met.

Josh and I went to the Baltimore Farmers' Market beneath the overpass most Sundays. We'd walk past the brightly painted pillars, our empty glass milk bottles clinking in a tote bag. There was a riot of color—flowers cascading out of their pots, vegetables piled in baskets, fresh bread stacked in pyramids, and so many Baltimore beauties with natural hair.

A woman with an armful of lilacs walked by me, her hair in tight curls.

"Hey, my name is Nicole. I have a little blog about natural hair. Your hair is incredible. You look beautiful. Could I ask you questions and feature you on my site?"

She gave me a smile but shook her head no.

We got in line for fried fish sandwiches. Josh held our spot as I darted off to talk to a gentleman with short twists. He didn't want to be photographed. A woman with a gorgeous silver Afro who raised her eye-brow when I said "blog" and "Tumblr" sweetly said no thank you. Then I saw a pair of women dressed in blues and greens. Eula had long twists she'd been growing for four years and Mia had a lovely Afro puff she'd been growing for two. We talked for a while, I photographed them, and then I took out two of my thin cards.

Josh was hovering by the dairy stand—our fresh bottles of milk in one hand and our fish sandwiches nestled in their red-and-white paper trays in the other. His eyebrows jumping with impatience.

"Come on, Nicole," he groaned and rolled his eyes.

Finally, I pulled myself away from my people.

I slipped into the car, giddy. I was finding people who were like me. Who fed my soul. Nobody wants to feel like they're alone in the void. That's why we're always looking for community. It's why we're always looking for people to interact with who share our thoughts and ideas, especially as we're trying to grow.

A hair blog may not have been broadcast journalism, but I was noticing that if I had a message, I could deliver it to people. I could connect with them.

I went to sleep with this idea of connection in my head. In my dream, I climbed onto one of those rickety stages, the kind that get set up in hotel ballrooms for corporate events. There was a modest crowd and I was giving a speech. There was no podium, just the audience and me, and they were leaning forward, listening.

Although it didn't make sense, I was certain that God had showed me that I was going to be onstage. I just didn't know how I would get from A to B. So I kept taking steps, doing the next right thing. The focus was helping people. I wasn't entirely sure how, but I did know I had to start.

One of the ways I had begun to help was by performing random acts of kindness. I discovered the Hey Stranger Project, which was started by Rachel May, who went around doing nice stuff for random people anonymously, with no expectation of anything in return. She would leave a note in a magazine at a doctor's office that read: *No mat-*

ter what it is, you can handle it, because you're already handling it. And I hope that this reminds you of how important you are. Rachel would do tiny stuff like that, an everyday micro gesture of altruism. Micro-giving.

I started to think of the world on a good/bad axis. If I can do good, kind, generous things, I can tip the axis toward good. I realized that I didn't have to be what I call a transactional survivalist—where I plan things to get food or gather people for friendship and entertainment, which they then reciprocate in a doing circle. I can show up in the world as an independent self and just do things. I could put something out in the world and leave it and just see what happens—the good intention was enough. You don't necessarily need transactions; you can actually be sufficient. You are enough.

I sent Rachel a message and she sent me an envelope of Hey Stranger cards. I left them in airplane seat pockets and bus windows. Josh called it glorified littering, but for me it was transformational. I had been living in my own bubble and suddenly, I started seeing people.

Soon I began personalizing the cards. Once I saw a guy getting out of his car at the grocery store and he did this big, committed yawn. I left him a note that said: *I just saw you yawn and it looked like that was really rewarding, and I just want to let you know you made me smile. Have a great day.* I left notes in grocery carts that said: *Hey, Mama, you're doing great today. You're about to go grocery shopping; I know it's not going to be easy, and I just want to let you know you're a champ.*

It started off with the cards, and then, when I started my new job and started making some money on my blog, I began popping into grocery stores and tucking some cards into baby formula or bags of diapers. When I traveled for work, I would put a note in my room for the cleaning staff that said: *I really appreciate what you do; it made my room very comfortable, and I'm thankful for that.* I put notes on the back of my restaurant receipts, saying thank you and mentioning one specific thing they did. Whenever I paid the toll at the Baltimore Harbor Tunnel, I paid for a few of the people behind me. Occasionally, I'd see people sleeping on the street and leave a couple of dollars with some water and food so that they'd wake up knowing someone had cared for them. It wasn't that I had a lot, but I had more than enough.

The practice was even rubbing off on Josh, who was kinder to strangers and making more eye contact with cashiers and servers. I noticed that most people's inclination was to gloss over the person in front of them. I would start my day with the thought, *If there's something I can do for someone, God, help me do the right thing for them.* If I saw someone who seemed kind of sad, I'd ask them, "How are you doing?" And then I would listen and respond. I made sure I *saw* everyone I met; I made sure I was fully present.

That wasn't who I'd been, but it was who I wanted to be. I often felt like that type of joy, or that type of kindness and generosity, was reserved for different people—happy people, rich people—as if there were some milestone you had to reach before you could have that freedom of generosity. But I quickly learned that wasn't true. And, in the context of helping others, I knew that I was enough.

The Bible talks about being the hands and feet of Jesus—enacting his compassion in big and small ways. And just in doing those things, I started looking for ways to help. That was the shift. My brain was being rewired to look for ways to help.

So many of us think the answer to our success or happiness is in something else and that it will arrive neatly packaged in the shape of a partner, a job, a paycheck, or a big break. Just because no one knows you exist doesn't mean you're not out there being great. Don't let anyone Columbus your existence. You keep taking steps until your presence is undeniable. A lot of times people think things are black-and-white, rags or riches. They think someone suddenly chucked her job to the side and forged her own path. It isn't like that; it's tiny baby steps. It's a million big breaks.

The answer is in the doing. If you're wondering if you can, the answer is in the doing. If you're wondering if it's good enough, the answer is in the doing. If you're wondering where to find the joy, girl, you better find the joy in the doing. Don't sit here and tell yourself you're not allowed to be happy while you do things. This grind-and-hustle culture will have you convinced that if it doesn't look like pain, sweat, and tears, it's not worthy. That's crazy.

Most of us don't enjoy feeling like we're scrambling or standing still. We enjoy making progress. But we are often paralyzed by perfection or let safety stunt our growth. Seek progress, not perfection. Success is built with small, sustainable wins. Aim to be a few steps further ahead tomorrow than you were today. This world is designed to distract, divide, and deter you from your goals. Any negative thoughts you have fall into one of those categories. If you're able to categorize your negative thoughts, you're able to apply them where they need to go—sometimes that's in the trash, but other times it might be a matter of asking, Why is this working on me that way? What do I need to grow? Where do I need to grow from? Ignoring your problems keeps you from doing the exploration in those areas so that you can move forward. It's an impediment to growth, an enemy of progress. It keeps you from doing. It keeps you from the next level.

CHAPTER TEN

BLACK WOMEN ARE EVERYTHING

The signs, printed on computer paper and taped up, lead me to the basement of a small church in Hyattsville, Maryland. It was a low-slung '70s building, and I could tell it was a well-loved place that the church members took care of because it was their home.

I walked in and there was a glorious mishmash of plastic folding tables. Some were buried under foil trays filled with food. Others were covered with flyers, jars of homemade hair products, and lush cupcakes. Someone was talking to people about insurance as they trickled in. It wasn't a hair event; it was more like an after-hours flea market.

All the windows were high up and the only light came from terrible fluorescent strips that ran along the ceiling. The room was too big for the crowd—maybe there were forty people spread out on the rows of folding chairs. (Churches always have a lot of folding chairs—if nothing else, they want to be ready in case people do decide they want the Lord that day.) The chairs were filled with Black women—mamas, aunties, and grandmas, and the occasional college girl.

I walked down the middle aisle toward the front of the room, stepping over a raft of power cords. There wasn't even a stage—rickety or otherwise—there was just a microphone, which had probably been brought down from the altar where the preacher used it for services.

I saw Josh at the back. Everyone was eyeballing him 'cause he clearly didn't have natural hair. Someone asked him if he was lost. He found a seat at the edge of the audience and tried to disappear.

It felt good to hold the mic; that wasn't something I'd ever done. As I shifted back and forth, drawing close to one side of the audience and then the other, I reminded myself not to trip over the cords.

I didn't have a plan. I simply started talking about my hair journey. But here I was, in front of a bunch of Black church ladies, who will let you know if you're good at what you do because they only know one way to interact with the speaker onstage—and it wasn't quiet listening. If I ever had any fear or insecurity or worry about whether it was working, these women eradicated it.

I told stories about getting my hair relaxed, about the excitement of upgrading from synthetic wigs to real hair wigs. I told them I would need to buy stock in combs because I was bound to break them on these curls. As I spoke, heads tilted back and the room filled with laughter. I wasn't intentionally telling jokes; I was telling the truth, and people thought it was funny. Not only does this feel good but I'm making them feel good, and they're getting answers about their hair and their beauty and their confidence.

"Mm-hmm. That's good."

One woman in the audience asked, "Why did you start doing this?"

I paused. I cocked my head to the side and thought about it. I'd never done this before. I didn't have any stock answers; I just spoke my truth. "Well, honestly, what was wrong with my hair?"

"Come on, tell 'em," someone called out.

"Well, there's nothing wrong with our hair to start with. Why did we start changing it when we didn't have to?"

"That's good, that's good," I heard. I could see one of the vendors in the back step out from behind her table to come closer. The temperature in the room seemed to rise.

"Shouldn't I know how to manage my hair in its natural state, without any products or modifications, because what if I don't have those?" I was asking questions out loud that many of those women had asked themselves.

"That's right."

I kept on going. I started finding my own voice because I was having voices yell back at me. Women of all ages were telling me what was good, what felt true to them, and when I spoke, they saw me. "I see you, Sis," a woman called out.

When we build businesses or deal with problems in our marriages or struggle with challenges, we often do it in a vacuum. That is not good. It is like playing racquetball alone. When you're playing with yourself, and the ball just bounces back to you, how can you know how good you are? How can you understand your game unless you have an opponent? Or a coach? How do you know how good you are if you don't take it out into the open and compete?

Up until this point I'd been doing it by myself. I'd been talking about natural hair one-on-one with friends and coworkers and researching so that I could answer my own questions. But standing in this church basement, in front of people, I realized that the things I was experiencing were shared. That's when I knew I had something.

As the questions wound down I pointed out Josh. "That's my round, white Jewish husband over there. He's not the police."

Everyone busted out laughing. He smiled dopily and waved. Then he was out of his seat, walking around, handing out my homemade business cards.

All these women were coming up and speaking life into me.

In case you don't know, Black women will holler across the street to tell you you look good. They will scream out of their cars and tell you that you look good. It doesn't take much. They simply state the part of your body that looks good. *Come on legs. I see you.* They can do it in two words: *Yeeees. Yellow.* And you start swishing your hair with pride. At some of my lowest moments I've reminded myself, *Clap for your own damn self.* I remind myself to praise myself the way other Black women would praise me. But the truth is, what's amazing about my community is that I've always had people cheering me on, and doing my job means I get to cheer on others.

There's something I have to tell you: I WOULD NOT BE HERE WITHOUT BLACK WOMEN. I WOULD NOT EXIST WITHOUT BLACK WOMEN. BLACK WOMEN ARE EVERYTHING. The ones who raised me, the ones who call me out, the ones who tell me what to do, and the ones who came up to me after that first talk.

That night, one grandma said, "You gifted, honey."

A charge ran up my spine.

I looked up at the fluorescent lights, then at the plastic folding tables, the foil trays of food, and the ladies waving their hands in the air, and I had the feeling that one day I'd be telling the story of this evening in this church basement in Hyattsville. Something had begun.

When we got in the car, I was floating, and Josh had a contact high. He was looking at me differently, like he'd seen something entirely new in me. "Oh my god, they really loved you in there. You killed that room."

"Thanks."

The very person who shouldn't have had to be convinced was convinced. I was witness to his transformation. I had made him a believer.

I started getting this frisson of excitement from doing exactly what I had been called to do. I was taking the next step, which is how I found myself on a rickety stage one step closer to what I'd envisioned. I was beginning to practice my purpose in small ways.

There's so much jargon and marketing around clarity of purpose, as if purpose is a thing you land on. Some people might define *purpose* as being this grand meaning of life, something that explains what you're here to do. But I'm not a big proponent of teaching this. That definition can make people feel bad if they haven't locked into that one thing. Of course, if you happen to land where you are uniquely in your purpose for a given season then you can feel a palpable joy, a light energy that pours into everything you do. But, for most of us, purpose is dynamic and shifting. It is the journey, not a milestone or a finish line. The process of searching for it is where the real value comes from.

We often romanticize having purpose, thinking of it like a singer who has some natural gift, and when they use it, they and those around them are filled with joy, light, and energy. When they sing they can feel it, and they can do it anywhere. The question then becomes, How do I get this thing to pay me? Or, how do I do this in a place where more people can hear it? That notion of purpose is a lie—and oh, the money made off that lie. For most of us, standing in our purpose is not like that.

Just as you can practice micro-giving, you can also have a micro purpose. Some days your purpose might be to help your daughter get through her homework. Or to fix the leaky faucet, or help create your community garden, or fix whatever problem life has set in front of you on that particular day. You can have many purposes along the way that lead to your larger purpose.

If you can find your purpose in the moment, if you can do the next right thing, that can be sufficient.

I unlocked my business when I realized that all my work came back to my taking people on a journey of exploration and figuring things out. A lot of people think, Oh well, this industry/field/product is saturated, but no, there will always be somebody out there who's looking for you to help them.

Many of the content creators I followed had been chronicling their hair journeys for three or four years, or their hair was already really long, and I noticed that there wasn't anyone who looked like me. I could loosely follow their suggestions, but I still had to do a lot of tests myself. I saw a gap that could be filled, and I had a vision for how I could fill it. While I was trying to grow my hair, I tried new hairstyles, products, and systems, and shared all the information I gathered and answered people's questions. Try new things, see if they work, share what they did or didn't do. That's literally the recipe.

What I was doing was sharing the ROI system. Restructure. Optimize. Implement. Restructuring the way you think about a problem and examining what needs to be changed. Optimizing what already exists, what can be fixed or improved with the tools and resources you already have. Implementing something new to solve the problem. I had ROIed my way onto *Wheel of Fortune*; I had even ROIed my faith. I just kept looking at the problems I faced, tweaking the way I thought about them and using all my tools to solve them, and then acquiring new tools and resources as I needed them. I had used ROI to heal my damaged hairline, and sharing what I had learned helped other people.

People told me they had used a hair mixture I'd recommended and that it had helped. Or they'd report that they'd tried something and it hadn't worked but they were thinking about tweaking it and wanted to know what I thought. I'm not an expert on hair, but navigating the questions together brought us closer to a solution. It also provided communion.

I started sharing my answers for everything that I was trying to figure out. I always tried to fix everything myself. One day I posted updates on the saga of fixing my HVAC system. I started, as one does, by googling, then I crawled onto my roof and replaced the capacitor. Problem solved. One of my very first followers had been watching, and a few weeks later she messaged me to say that her AC was acting weird and that she was going to try to fix it herself. We went back and forth until she figured out that it was her capacitor, which cost her about $15 to fix, instead of paying an HVAC guy $1,000.

Sometimes we think everything has to be big—we have to open a company, invent something new, revolutionize our industry, or cure cancer. But it doesn't have to be so dang big. I saved this woman $1,000.

The biggest thing I did wasn't showing her how to fix her capacitor, it was taking the time to chat with her. It was giving her the belief that she could do it. That was the game changer for me. It affirmed the many ways I could change people's lives. For the first time I had a platform, a way—albeit modest—to amplify what I was learning to a community of people.

Being part of something is better than being part of nothing. I'll take it any day. I would rather have something to live up to than realize I don't belong anywhere or to anyone.

My dear friend, let's call him Jan, is a biomedical engineer working on a cure for cancer. I asked him if it was frustrating to have $250,000 in student loan debt and be working every day in a lab trying to cure cancer and know that he may die before ever actually discovering the cure. He said, "No, it's not frustrating, because I know I'll leave behind a book of work that will help the next person who could literally do one experiment and cure cancer." He is content to play his part because his part is essential—he can discover information and share it.

Jan doesn't view himself or his work in isolation. Instead, he recognizes his place in the larger community. Whenever I have suffered the most, I have been isolated. If you're surrounded by people reflecting to you who you really are, it is harder for negativity to worm into your ear. That's why abusive partners often isolate their victims from their friends. Or maybe you've noticed that when people are suffering from depression, they isolate themselves—either from social situations or through substances.

Community is integral. Don't underestimate the power of asking—for help, information, or support. Having a community helps minimize your learning curve. It has literally helped me pick out the right insurance policy, the right neighborhood, the right shampoo. When you are part of a community, you are seen. You are counted. That is so much better than going it alone. Even in the toughest of circumstances or the newest, the most familiar faces will always be "home." This is something Black people can speak to: You go into a room or a restaurant or a new job and you look for the other Black face just to have that connection for a moment. It's like finding a little piece of home. I realized that I needed that home, that support, that love, that guidance while I was branching into something new, and I found it in Black women.

CHAPTER ELEVEN

WAY MAKER

"Josh, we need to stop." I could practically hear his eyes roll as he pulled over. We were on our way to Sofi's, the restaurant where he and I met for our first date, and I wanted a good dessert to counteract the mediocre phó we'd had for dinner.

On the ride there we analyzed our dinner. The noodles were a little dense. The soup a little thin. *Was the bean sprout-to-broth ratio off? Did you taste MSG? Can you taste MSG? The soup's not good? Are we purist soup people? What is soup perfection actually?* Being married to a Jewish man made sense for me because he's willing to be analytical about mundane nuances.

Baltimore is a little big city. During the day Northern Parkway is buzzing with traffic, but it was almost nine o'clock and the night was quiet and still. I saw something bouncing up and down on the corner. I thought it might have been a puppy and yelled at Josh to pull over.

Before I met my Jewish husband, I had a Jewish dog. He was an eleven-year-old black Chihuahua named Morton Goldstein. Once, I lost him for twenty-four hours. The morning after he'd gone missing, a kid called to tell me they'd found Morty but that his mom had said he couldn't keep him so he'd let him go in the park. But hours later, my phone rang again. This time it was a park ranger who'd found Morty wandering around. After that, I made a covenant with God that whenever I see a stray dog I would stop. No matter what, no matter where, I'll pull over to see if I can help. For seven years this was the rule I lived by. During that infamous "Summer of Strays," as we called it, we had a new dog every couple of weeks. Josh hated this rule.

As we drew closer, I realized the bouncing figure wasn't a dog at all. It was a small child with a fur-lined hood on her coat, jumping up and down beside a woman who looked older. She was wearing a lot of the life she had lived on her face and was holding a sign that read I'M HUNGRY. PLEASE HELP.

Josh rolled down his window and a cold wind blew in. The woman said hello and he went to give her a dollar. I leaned over Josh and said hi. I elbowed him and pointed my jaw at the little girl, and he pulled out another dollar. The girl reached up with her little mittened hand.

"Now what do we say?" the woman prompted.

"Thank you," the girl squeaked. Her hair was pulled into two puffs, and there was a big gap in her smile where one of her front teeth should have been. She gazed up at me, her eyes big brown saucers. They started to water and I didn't know if she was sad, tired, or just cold.

"Okay, well, you guys stay warm. Have a good night. God bless you," I said.

As Josh drove toward Sofi's, something within me shifted.

In Belvedere Square there was no bustle or glow. The parking lot was empty, the bright blue and purple neon lights of Sofi's were off; everything was dark.

I like doing my research—I like knowing exactly where a restaurant is, what you should order, and when it closes. When I was twenty-eight, I wanted order, predictability, and to enjoy dates with my husband. But, for some reason, that night I hadn't even checked Sofi's hours.

"She seemed older, didn't she?" I was thinking out loud. It was only when Josh said "Yeah" that I realized I'd actually spoken. The questions kept churning. "Do you think the baby's okay?"

"I don't know," he said.

"Do you think they'll still be there? What's she doing out with a baby in the cold like that?"

"Nicole, I just want to get home."

"Okay. I can probably throw some cookies in the oven." But the whir of my brain would not stop. I couldn't stop thinking of the woman and the little girl.

As we approached the corner of York and Northern again, I thought, *Please God, don't let them still be on that corner. Don't let them be there. Because if they are, I'm going to have to do something.* But I just wanted to go home and find a snack and sit on the couch with my husband. I willed myself not to look at the corner. I was like Lot's wife trying not to look back at Sodom. I would have turned into a pillar of salt.

There they were.

I tried my best not to make eye contact. Josh drove by but I could still see them in the side-view mirror. Before we'd made it to the next stop sign, I was hitting his arm hard again and again.

"We have to go back. We have to go back," I said, emotion knotting in my throat.

"It's going to be hard to make a U-turn," he grumbled.

"I don't care," I said. "Go back. Go back."

I didn't know what I was doing. I didn't know what I was going to say until I rolled down my window and asked, "Are you guys hungry?" The woman nodded. "Could I maybe get you some dinner?"

"That'd be really great."

I invited them into the car and while Josh drove to the sandwich shop, I chatted.

"Oh, is this your daughter?"

The woman gave me the side-eye. "You didn't think she was my daughter because I look old?"

"No. No. No. I just didn't know."

"I got two more at home."

"We should pick up some food for them too."

The bell on the door of the sandwich shop rang and someone emerged from the back, stuffing their hands into a fresh pair of gloves. We were the only customers.

"Get whatever you want," I told the woman as she slipped up to the counter. I held back behind the metal bar meant to guide the line.

The little girl was so tiny she couldn't see over the counter, but she was trying to catch a glimpse of the food, pushing up onto the toes of her worn boots. I could see the tip of her big toe through the hole on her left shoe.

As the mother was ordering, she kept turning around and asking me if she could get chips or a drink and I kept saying, "Yes. Get whatever you want." She thanked me repeatedly.

The doorbell dinged, a gust of cold air pushed in, and there was Josh, filling the doorframe. He came to stand beside me on the small reddish-brown tiles, discolored with stains. A refrigerator hummed on and off. Behind us was the soda fountain and every few minutes the ice machine rattled the cubes around.

The girl turned around. She had this half smile, as if she was amused but not exactly sure what was going on. She was dirty, her coat was smudged, but her face was a light. She was really small—a new, new person who had just started conversing and having opinions and really engaging with the world. I got down low, so I was looking right into her bright eyes.

"Hey, what's your name?"

She looked right back at me. "Aaallly," she said, drawing out her name slowly in a sweet, babyish voice, as if she hadn't said it very often.

"Hi, Ally, I'm Miss Nicole."

I felt this connection, like we really saw each other. All I could think was, *I have to do whatever I can to help this little girl. I don't know what that means. I don't know what it looks like, but I need to help her.*

"I see you lost a tooth," I said.

The mother turned from ordering foot-long hoagies for everyone in the family. "The dentist had to pull it. She's gonna lose the other one too."

"Wow, you're a brave girl. If you're super brave, I'll get you something. We can pick out a toy." Her eyes, which I didn't think could get any bigger, widened.

Her mom repeated it back to her, "You hear that? If you're good at the dentist, you can get a toy."

It was as if Ally's whole being leaned into her smile, turning her toasted-pecan face luminous.

Out on the sidewalk, as the wind whipped through my coat, the woman thanked me and turned to walk back.

"Hey, uh, could we give you a ride?"

Josh shot me those eyes that said, *Nicole, what are you doing?* I shrugged my shoulders and gave him a *Please. I'm sorry* look, and Ally and her mom got in the car.

"We live right around the corner," which in Black speak could be right around the corner or four and a half hours away—but Josh didn't know what that meant so he calmed down a bit. For a split second I worried that we didn't have a car seat, then I thought about where Ally had been twenty minutes ago.

They lived in an apartment in a small brick row house in Baltimore. When we pulled up, I expected to say good night, but Ally's mom was fumbling to get her out of the car. Her hands were full of thin, clear plastic bags each holding a foot-long sandwich and another bag full of chips and cookies. So, I helped Ally out of the car, but the mother was beelining it toward the building, so I held Ally's hand as she toddled up the concrete steps with weeds sprouting through the cracks. I expected to say goodbye, but then I remembered the two older girls.

I crossed the threshold and was hit by a wall of heat. Ally dropped

my hand and ran inside looking for a toy. Their dog met me at the door
and reminded me that I didn't actually know what I was walking into.

The situation was much worse than I thought. Yes, I'd seen them
on the side of the road—I knew they didn't have money. I knew they
needed food. A lot of people think that if you're asking for food you're
sleeping under a bridge, but they don't recognize that there are a great
many people who just don't have enough. I related to that. Oh, they're
poor, like me, I realized. When I was a kid, I didn't always know where
food was going to come from. I thought it was normal to hear mice
in the walls. I spent years sleeping on a couch, and I would try to fall
asleep quickly so that I wouldn't wake up while the roaches crawled
over me.

Their life of lack was familiar. It didn't scare me. I didn't have to
run from it. I stepped inside and stood near the door, trying to be as
respectful as possible. They didn't know me or where I'd come from.
Standing near the front door, I had walked right into a makeshift master bedroom. The place wasn't super clean and there was a muddle of
furniture and all manner of worldly goods pushed against the walls and
edging so far into the living space that there was only a narrow plank of
floor to walk along. I couldn't figure out where a little kid would play.

Their mother called out, "Krissy, Day-Day, come out here and say
thank you to the nice lady. She bought us food."

Out shuffled these two teeny-tiny people. Their clothing was ill-
fitting. Krissy was very narrow but long, and her pants were high waters.
Daya had her hair done. She had self-installed hair extensions and was
experimenting with hair bleach—instead of fading into a natural brown,
the ends of the extensions had turned a brassy orange. She was at the
age where you start caring about the way you look, but you're only working with what you have. They were pretty girls, but they were wilted
flowers, a little slumped over, like they were trying to make themselves
small. Plus, they were doing the whole annoyed-teenager thing where
you can see they are irritated, but you can't tell what the problem is.
Maybe it was just that their mother was making them awkwardly talk to
me, a complete stranger. They kept a solid twenty feet away, and when

they said thank you, their voices were flat and their eyes were aimed at the ground.

I felt old and awkward. I was grasping at straws for something to say. Finally, I managed, "Uh, do you guys like makeup and hair and stuff? I have this little blog thing that I do and if you like, I have some stuff I could bring you."

Daya's head popped up. In that moment I recognized her. Even if her body reflected a lack of belief, her eyes had the fire of a fight. I knew that she was like me, a survivalist. She saw this encounter as an opportunity to take a couple of steps in the right direction.

"Well, I can bring some makeup."

"Sure," Daya said. Krissy still hadn't looked up, but I could see the way she was listening and that a half smile had snuck across her lips.

Their mother reminded them to thank me. "Thank you," they chimed and then stood around to see if they were going to be dismissed. Their mom told them what sandwiches she'd brought and Krissy took the bags to the kitchen.

"You know I don't like cold cuts," Daya said. I could feel the attitude and anger jutting out of every bone in her body. I imagined the shame she might feel in front of a stranger, me, who had bought food for the family.

Their mother started fussing at how she was talking in front of the company, so I changed the topic. "Is there anything else you need? Because I don't live too far away."

"Well, we really could use some groceries."

Although they all thanked me, their voices pitched up, and I was pretty sure none of them expected me to follow through. But they didn't know me. Their doubt was a challenge.

"Well, I'm going to get going. I'll see you guys. Is Wednesday okay?"

"Yeah, that's fine." The mom gave me her phone number and I gave the girls my business card, even though they probably didn't have a computer or Internet. I offered them the thing I had. I wanted to leave something with them, a little piece of evidence that I was there, that I saw them, and that I was coming back.

When I pushed through the door, the night air was cold and fresh and the busy smell of their home with all its people, the dog, the heat, the old-building scent disappeared.

I shut the car door behind me quietly. Josh started shifting the car into gear, but I put my hand on his to keep him still a moment longer. I felt pangs of urgency. There was a situation in there, and I don't like to see a problem and not do something about it.

"I told them I'd bring them groceries." I felt his eyes on me. "So we have a choice right now. I know what it's like to have people promise you they're going to help and for those promises to fall through every single time. Here's the truth: We can walk away and never come back, and we wouldn't be the first. They wouldn't even remember us after a while."

Josh looked at me with his big blue eyes and said, "Nicole, you can bring them groceries."

"But if we say we're going to come back and we do, then we can never, ever leave."

"Okay."

Josh had no idea what he was agreeing to, and honestly, neither did I.

———

When I tell people that story they are shocked. *Boy, you did a good thing that night.* I think the appropriate response is, "Boy, that was a little bit stupid." Everybody's a little stupid sometimes—they eat the hot dogs at 7-Eleven that have been there for twelve hours, they go on that second date with the guy who never should have been a first date, or they wear a pair of pants without their favorite Spanx. We've all had our moments, and this was a different type of stupid—it wasn't smart, but it was oh so right.

I can't explain this. I can't explain why I said "Let's just swing by Sofi's" without checking the time. That's just how God works. God is a way maker. He moves and ordains our steps and sends us in the right direction—even if we don't necessarily know why that direction makes sense—because there's some place we have to get to, and we are going to get there whether we like it or not.

In the beginning, the plan wasn't to be their mom. I never saw myself taking in three kids. I had specifically said I wasn't going to have any kids until I was thirty-five. When these girls came into my life, I just wanted to help. I thought I was a mentor. I did it because it was the next right thing to do. Because I believe in leaning into opportunity, and it was an opportunity to impact their lives. What I didn't know is that it's these exact types of moments, when the unplanned meets the well prepared, that change your whole life. I just didn't know I'd been preparing the whole time.

I leaned into doing the next right thing that night and every day after, and what I discovered was that I kept landing in a place that was so wildly beyond my expectations, so amazingly, surreally good for me, that I couldn't even believe I had arrived there.

PART TWO

CHAPTER TWELVE

THE FIXER

A week after I met the girls, I was taking Daya to one of my natural hair events and picking her up after school to take her to Sonic for a slush—I was a big sister, a mentor, an alternate adult to talk to about school and life. Daya is the eldest of the three, and at fourteen she was at that age when she was at risk for all the trouble teenagers can get into. At first I saw her once or twice a week, but those initial days with Daya were a revelation of what she was facing. I thought I was taking a girl out for an icy treat and giving her advice on college. Really, I was going into a war-zone recovery effort.

I'd ask Daya about school and she couldn't tell me the kind of information I needed and if I don't have the information, I'm going to go find it.

Her school easily could have been confused for the Baltimore city jail. There was no basketball court, no murals on the walls, no color. I'd been driving past this building for years without even realizing it was a school that held the neighborhood's children. It was a forgotten building with hardly any windows and most of the heavy metal doors didn't have handles so I couldn't figure out how to get inside.

When I finally found an unlocked door, I was greeted by a huge security guard, Mr. Jackson. Despite his warm smile, he was imposing in his blue uniform. As I waited to be buzzed inside, his deep voice rolled down the hall toward a group of boys who needed to keep it moving. I knew right away that he was the guy who was called to break up fights or calm down a room. He had to play the disciplinarian, getting the kids used to policing, which is what the world was telling these kids to expect.

I walked up to the receptionist in the lobby. Everyone knows a lady like this—the one who came with the company, who knows where all the bodies are buried, who is not worried about rising through the ranks but knows absolutely everything. If there's any question about why Johnny is in the principal's office, when the printer will be fixed, where the Band-Aids are kept, or why the cops are parked outside, she has the answer.

In her seventies and put together, Miss Moore flicked her eyes at me skeptically when I gave her a bubbly hello and told her I was Daya's mentor and that I was here to meet her teachers. The way she dismissed me, I could tell she'd seen this before—a do-gooder mentor who shows up once or twice and then disappears.

Without looking at me she jabbed her finger toward a clipboard. "Just sign your name, then you can walk down the hall." There was no form to fill out, no need to show ID; they didn't pat me down or check with Daya's mom—they just let me waltz right into the school.

"Thank you, Miss Moore," I said with honey in my voice. Instinctively I knew that part of being able to help Daya was going to be winning over this woman.

I walked around and met all her teachers so they could see my face, so they knew Daya had a person. Kids need to know they have a person, and letting everyone know that someone is watching out for them is also a way of protecting them. I wanted everyone to know this child belonged to somebody.

In this school, teachers are overwhelmed, overworked, and underutilized. God bless them. Daya's mom had never been to her school. Everybody was dismissive. Everyone lacked belief. Well, to me, that was fuel. If you don't believe I can do something, watch me show up more than ever.

I told all the teachers that if there's ever anything they need to let me know, I'd be happy to help. I made a big show of saying goodbye to Miss Moore before I left the gray, lightless building.

I worked remotely and had a flexible schedule so I went to Daya's school many times over the next couple of weeks and saw that Miss Moore did everything for these children during these hours. She played grandmother and nurse. She listened to troubles, proffered a piece of candy when something ought to be celebrated, offered tissues for runny noses, cleaned cuts, got water for thirsty kids because they couldn't drink from the school water fountain, which was broken. I would sit and wait as she tended to the stream of children and their needs. As I waited, I earned her trust. Plus, every time I signed the sheet, I gave her all the sugar: *I love what you did with your hair. I love that blouse. I appreciate you, Miss Moore.* One afternoon I arrived to have lunch with Daya in the cafeteria and actually got a tiny, tight half smile from Miss Moore. I was pretty sure she was warming up to me, albeit slowly.

When I started mentoring Daya, I thought I'd see her once a week to check in on homework and drop off some food. But I told her and her mother to let me know if they needed anything, and almost immediately I was seeing Daya three times a week. I never imagined her staying with us, but some situations arose where my house became the safest place for her to sleep for a time. I was just there to support where I could. I made it work. I gave up my free time because it felt like time well spent.

Soon, I started picking Daya up from school every day and she'd spend a few hours at our place doing homework and having dinner. She could use our Internet and supplies—things she didn't have access to at home—to do projects, and I was always there if she needed help. One afternoon she pulled out her reading assignment for English—instead of a book, she had photocopied pages of the class novel.

I didn't understand.

"Oh, we only have one book for the class," Daya explained.

"You're only reading one book this semester?"

"Oh no," she corrected me. "Our teacher makes everyone copies of the pages every morning."

Fury colored everything around me. Daya was already in a school where no one knew anyone who went to college; the school didn't even administer the SAT, and they certainly didn't prep the kids for it, and now they were saying these kids weren't even worth an actual copy of a book. These kids didn't know any better—they thought it was normal to read from a printout, which is why they were being taken advantage of. They were being told, Your classroom is only worth one book; you're only worth being yelled at in the hallways; the setting for your education isn't bright and light and colorful, and it takes place in a dark, windowless cave—but none of that is normal; that has never been normal.

Just because something is normalized doesn't mean it is normal.

I wanted to make banners and stand in front of the school telling all these kids how much they were worth.

The next day I barreled down the hallway to the English teacher's classroom. She confirmed what Daya had told me. "I have to read out loud from the book and they can follow along in their printouts," she confided, then added, "Girl, sometimes the printer doesn't even work."

How are they not reading books in English class? This was *To Kill a Mockingbird*. It's fundamental. It's one of those books that changes you. That while holding it in your hand and turning the pages you decide to become a journalist or a writer or a public defender.

My mind was flapping with disbelief at the way they were crippling these children. This wasn't about the school needing something big, like a music program; this was a question of a few hundred dollars for books. There was always a way to scrape up a few hundred dollars. Also, I must tell you, I'd seen the principal clicking down the hallways in Louboutin heels, the red soles flashing.

I asked Daya's teacher for a list of the books she needed for the year and told her I was going to get them. She looked at me like I was crazy, but she gave me the list and I drove home wondering how I was going to pull this off. Josh and I certainly didn't have the money. I posted about the dilemma on social media to my friends and family. Everyone was outraged, but no one was surprised. I set up an online fundraiser and within a couple of hours I had the few hundred dollars I needed to buy the books. I bought every single used copy I could find. A few days later I heaved a box of books past Mr. Jackson and warned Miss Moore that I'd have to go back to my car a few more times.

Her eyes crept up her forehead as she looked from the box to my face. "Let me see if I can get someone to help you carry those."

"Thank you, Miss Moore. And I have to tell you, I love that sweater."

Daya was hovering between loving all this attention and being mortified. No one had ever been in her business like this before. She was also self-conscious about turning into one of the "good kids." There's no such thing as a bad child, but she was never the one coming home with good grades, because no one was watching. It was because grown-ups were always flitting in and out of her life. It was because she didn't go to school regularly. It was because she hadn't been fed, nurtured, and supported.

She needed to know that when I said I wasn't leaving, I truly wasn't leaving. The only time I didn't see her was when I was traveling for work, and in those moments I communicated like crazy with the girl. *Here's where I am, here's how long I'm going to be, and here's when I'll be back.* I'm not leaving.

A few months later, Daya got into my car after school and quietly said, "I got this little award thing." Her whole body shrank as she spoke, as if she could make herself invisible, as if her accomplishment didn't matter, as if she was afraid to expect any reaction to the news that her geometry teacher had given her an award for being the most improved student in class. The school didn't even have a Most Improved award. He had photocopied another award and scribbled *Most Improved* over it with a Sharpie, but he presented it to her in front of the whole school.

I started honking the horn and whooping it up.

"I still have a C in the class."

"You used to have an F!"

We arrived at my house and I put the car in park. I looked right at her as I explained, "Understand that you had to put in A-plus effort to get yourself from an F to a C. So I want you to know that means that you always could have gotten an A. The C is just where you are right now. If you were starting right now, you would have an A and it means that you would keep your A. Now, we just have to get through this semester. You're going to crush this."

Her face lit up with awareness. She hadn't realized that effort could be celebrated. That that's enough. It isn't about always being an A-plus student; it's about trying your best and seeing what a difference that can make.

I bought a cake. I took pictures of her. I made a whole event. I also told her that in the future, if this was going to happen, I needed to be there taking photos making a whole thing of it.

"Oh my God, Miss Nicole. No. No. NO." But I could tell she was pleased.

Later she admitted, "I always thought I was dumb, you know, because I'd be in school and I wouldn't understand anything."

"No, you weren't dumb—you just weren't going to school every day. That's all it was. So every time you went back, you didn't understand something else because you weren't there for the lesson before."

"Now I realize I'm really smart and actually some of this stuff is very easy."

Daya had been fighting an unwinnable war—she lived with a mom who didn't support her or advocate for her; she attended a school that didn't think she was worthy of a book, of a college education, of a future. But now she had a glimpse of what was possible.

And, I had glimpsed how much support Daya needed, how much support the whole family needed. I was cautious. That is the truth. There weren't any heroics.

It was hard to be there as much as they needed me. When I said I wasn't leaving, I became the person they turned to. Daya and Krissy would call at all hours of the day and night. They called me when there was a gap that needed to be filled: I got called to school when Daya got in a fight. I got called to parent-teacher meetings for Krissy. I got called when they needed stuff for a school project. I got called because there was no food. Or because the music was so loud that the kids couldn't sleep and wanted to come to my house.

I was just beginning to get a sense of the magnitude of their need. I could have left them. There are lots of kids who grow up in these circumstances, and some of them write stories of their own—of redemption, recovery, whatever—but they're far more likely to be lost in the system. They're far more likely to live a life of profound, unnecessary hardship—to be abandoned, abused, or raped. Would you take a chance with three lives?

Getting books for the school. Turning around Daya's educational experience. It turned out that these problems were relatively simple and easy to solve. A lot of the things I had looked at as problems or things I had treated as barriers were a lot easier to solve than I had realized. People live with stuff as unsolvable problems when actually it's a lot easier to solve them and move on. You don't have to live like that. You can change things.

I'm African, and in our culture, communal living isn't weird. It takes a village. The girls' mom had been letting people in to help for years, but no one was well resourced and everyone had their own kids and their own struggles. I could help the girls solve their problems, and if I'm telling the truth, they could help me solve mine. They gave me more than

I ever could have given them. They helped me realize how many tiny things affect our overall greatness, and how we beat ourselves up about not being able to accomplish these huge goals when there are so many tiny things we have to do first that all play a part in the larger success. We minimize the things we do well, like making sure our kids are fed and getting up every day and doing all the basic, foundational tasks for our business; we do these things automatically and don't give ourselves credit for what part they play in the bigger picture. But your ability to do those things makes you effective, and helping people is a gift and a skill, and sometimes it means you accomplish your personal goals more slowly than you'd like. It doesn't mean you'll never meet your goal; it doesn't mean you're not effective; it doesn't mean you aren't successful or aren't capable. It's just that all these little things need to happen too, one at a time.

Gather information, take small steps, and solve the problem. ROI. That's what I discovered with my blog—I gathered information, took small steps, and it grew into a business. Early on, I realized that the banner of talking about natural hair, in and of itself, wasn't the mission for me. I was passionate about feeling comfortable in myself. I believed in the functionality of that self-belief. Knowing how to handle yourself— your hair, your money, your business—is part of your empowerment as a being. That's where I heard that entrepreneurial hum. I needed to find the space where I could empower people—business was a natural transition because it created money and money is one of the greatest tools we have on an earthly level. And I knew that I could put money in people's pockets. But I also realized that even if I could show people how to make money, it wouldn't work if they didn't believe. So, slowly, I realized I was in the business of helping people understand why they are deserving.

As my blog grew, I connected not just with people interested in hair but also with other bloggers. I joined an amazing online group of Black women bloggers and would share business tips with them and people would report back, "This is gold. I just did that and it made me money." I'd see someone at a blog event doing something that didn't make sense and I would ask questions like, "Why are you doing that for free? Why don't you charge for that?" I would often find myself explaining elements of business to them—product placement and advertising, and how the financial end of the blog business worked. People would always ask, "Can you show me?"

Now, in case you don't already know, I don't do free, except for church, charity, and children. And even the church pays the plumber. In consulting you keep a calendar, and, literally, you can't get on a consultant's calendar unless you pay them.

So, when people ask for my time, I always say yes, but I have to put it on my calendar. If I'm going to put it on my calendar then I've got to take something off, and that thing on my calendar that I would have to take off was already paying me money, so if you would like to be in that thing's place, you're going to have to pay me at least as much as that thing was.

The information I shared helped. It was always really simple stuff, but I began to recognize that it wasn't just that I understood monetization, it was that I'm also a hell of a teacher. I wanted to teach people to meet problems on their own. I could help people make money, and money is a tool. People were paying me not just for a transference of knowledge but also for a transference of belief, so that they could make their own success. I wanted them to look at their business dilemmas and think, *What would Nicole do?*

Of course, you can learn tips, or single pieces of information from a lot of sources, but when you learn a whole way of thinking that allows you to believe in yourself and elevate your business, then you are changing your game.

The hum was growing to a roar. Possibility unfurled before me. It was clear this was just the beginning.

CHAPTER THIRTEEN

STAND IN THE GAP

The life Josh and I had built became interwoven with that of the girls. Every day there was something new that bound us to one another. Every day there was a choice to make about what the kids needed and if we were going to be involved. Kids need things—I bought school supplies, clothes, extra food. When I started picking Ally up, we bought a car seat, and my online community helped me get the right one and install it. We didn't have a lot of money at this point, so setting aside a couple hundred dollars every month was a conscious choice.

Each time we decided to do something more, I'd say to Josh, "If we say we're going to do this thing, there's no going back to less than this step. So if we say yes to this, we have to commit to at least this much." And I would always remind him that if this was a time that he wanted to leave, he could leave. Unfortunately, kids with trauma—and I'm one of them myself—are used to people coming in and sailing off. "These kids are used to this, and kids are resilient, so if we're going to disappear, now's the time. It'll be hard. It'll hurt. But if you want to, I understand, and it's better than going to the next step." Every time we had that conversation, Josh always said, "Yes, this is the next right thing to do."

On one of our first IHOP dates, Krissy told me she never felt like she fit in her birth family. She's a very logical, rational, sensible, smart girl and poverty defies practicality. It defies logic. So it never made sense to her. As she sat there looking so tiny on the long seat of the booth, she told me she used to pray for somebody to come pick her out of her life. She knew she was meant to live a different life. After knowing me for just a few weeks, Krissy looked up from her giant stack of cinnamon-roll pancakes dripping with icing and asked, "Can I please stay with you?"

I was gobsmacked. This girl was so nervous that she would cry if she had to order for herself, and here she was asking to live with me. I was very aware of what it took for her to say that out loud. Think about what it took for you to tell the first person you ever had a crush on that you liked them. Remember all the conversations with your friends, the practices in the mirror, all the times you passed the crush in the hall and didn't say a thing. This was just like that for Krissy—we were her family crush. We were her dream life.

We were sitting in a booth near the windows and I looked out at the parking lot. I didn't know what to say, so I settled on the truth. "What I can tell you is that I'm not going anywhere." That is the thing I've always told my kids. And I still tell them now, "I just want to let you know, I'm not going anywhere. I'm not leaving."

I didn't know exactly what our relationship would be. I called them "the girls" and they called me Middicole, which is what Ally called me because she couldn't say "Miss Nicole." Josh was Midder Josh, and those were the names all three girls adopted for us. And in the first few months, they went from "the girls" to "my girls." Immediately I loved them—wholly, fiercely, endlessly. In my heart, the minute I met Ally I knew I'd be her mother—it was the concept I'd rejected that first night in the sandwich shop, but I'd felt the truth of it right away. They were my kids in my heart long before they were on paper.

I'd met the girls in late October, and by December we had a routine. I'd pick up Krissy and Daya after school, and, when their mother would let me, we'd scoop up Ally and spend the afternoons at my house— doing homework, eating a hot meal, being together. And then I'd take them home to sleep on the new bedding we bought. On a few Fridays they all slept over in the front living room and we'd spend the weekend together. We'd do activities at home or get a loaf of bread and feed the ducks at the park. When I learned that Ally had never been on a boat, we rode the water taxi back and forth for hours. Josh loved being the silly dad; he'd dress up in tutus, make funny faces, and dance. I'd often hear his big, whole-body laugh reverberate through the house as they played. On Sunday I'd bring them back to their mom.

I struggled most with how to care for Ally. She didn't need time with a mentor or help with schoolwork; she didn't need anything but a parent. In many ways, she is the one who needed me the most, because she was the youngest and her actual physical well-being was at risk on a regular basis. The more time I spent with the girls, the more I realized they were truly lacking the essentials. Ally told me she was still pan-handling—only she called it working—with her mom, and there were scars and scabs all over her tiny body from bedbug bites, so there was a physical urgency to having her full time. But Ally was the one their mother was most resistant to letting me help with. "Ally is the one who still loves me. Ally is the one who's still good," she said.

I was afraid that if I reported their mom to Child Protective Services, they would split up the girls and I'd be locked out of their lives. Or the girls would be taken and put in a childcare system that could be worse than their home life. For now, their mom was letting us take care of them and that was enough. But we also had to live with the knowledge that she could take the girls away at any point.

A few months after I met them, Krissy texted to tell me their mother was out with Ally again. I cruised her regular spots, then went to the corner where I'd first met them and offered to take Ally back to my house for an activity and a nap. "I know you have so much to do, let me just help you out."

With Ally buckled into the car seat, I'd pepper her with questions. "Tell me about your day, cutie."

Sometimes she'd tell me that "Daddy came by." Once she told me, "The po-po came."

I had to hold my shock that this baby had encountered the police. Trying to control the flood of worry I felt, I held my voice neutral and asked, "Oh, really? What happened? Tell me more."

"They said mommy can't work there."

"Oh, okay. How'd you feel?"

"Scared. But Mommy said, 'Don't say nothing.'"

The next time I saw their mother I said, "Please don't take Ally out anymore." But she still did.

I cried all the time. I wept when I dropped them off. I cried when I was doing errands and caught a glance of Ally's empty car seat. I wanted all my babies together. I worried about what was happening to them when they weren't with me. I couldn't sleep right if they weren't together and safe.

People don't pay attention to Black girls—whether they're lost, whether they're missing, no one keeps track of them. No one sees them. One of the greatest hurts of my heart is that my girls lived down the street for almost four years and I didn't even know they were there. They could have been crossing the street as I was driving past. They were suffering and I didn't know. I imagine that I saw these girls every day, but I couldn't see them.

I'm so grateful God chose me and that I was a safe person. Because how many girls are seeking comfort in dangerous places? And no one is looking out for them. It was easier for me to start minding someone else's children than it was for me to adopt my dogs. You want to talk about something I have an issue with in America? It's that I had gone through more checks, background investigations, and inspections to adopt rescue dogs than I'd had to before popping up in these kids' lives, walking through their schools, and taking them to my home.

With all my coming and going from school, no one asked me for any proof of my relationship with Daya. I started asking more questions of the school: Can I get a copy of her report card sent to me? Can I get the test results from the standardized tests sent to me?

Miss Moore realized that I wasn't leaving, that I could do something for Daya, and she wanted to help. Until that point I'd just been slipping under the radar, but as I became more involved, I needed more access to school information, so Miss Moore let me know I was going to need to fill out a form and have it signed by Daya's mother in front of a notary. I wasn't exactly sure how that would go over, but life took a turn and suddenly the notarized paper just made sense.

A few nights later I walked the girls to the door of their apartment and smothered them in hugs, making sure they had everything—food, clothes, backpacks—when their mother came out and asked if we could talk in the car.

"Nicole, I have to tell you something." There was a playful edge to her voice, then her tone shifted. "Before I met you, you know, I made some choices and unfortunately it's looking like I'ma have to go to jail very soon." She sounded erratic. I could barely understand what she was saying.

"What's going to happen to the girls?"

"Well, I'm going to go ahead and sign over my checks to their dad and he can keep an eye on them or the state will take them."

"Well, that's a lot on their dad. And they are girls; do you want me to help?"

"Oh my gosh. Would you? It is a lot. Thank you."

My brain started firing, looking for information, organizing logistics, coming up with a plan.

"So how long are you going away?"

"Well, it is supposed to be a year, but I could get out for good behavior."

I felt like I'd been sawed in half: Normal Nicole screamed, *This is too much! Get out now. Run, Nicole, run!* Rational Nicole told me to just listen.

"Wow. That's a long time."

"Yeah, well, it's not my first time going to jail. I'll be okay, you know."

Suddenly, after having been in and out of her home with her daughters for a month, I realized I knew nothing about this woman.

"Wait, what are you going to jail for?"

"Well, you know I have a habit." I nodded, but I didn't know. I waited for her to say more. "I struggle with substances. But it's a disease, you know."

I tell you, there are parts of me that are super wise and there are other parts that are super naive and leave me wondering how I have survived in this world. This was the very first time it occurred to me that she was a drug user.

"Oh, like what?" I asked, fully expecting alcohol, or too much weed.

"Heroin," she said flatly.

How was she still alive? I gripped the steering wheel and looked out at the street until I could fix my face. *Oh my God, my kids are in a house with a heroin user.*

But still I said, "Okay, so tell me more about that." In my head I couldn't imagine these girls going through the process of a trial and sentencing when they were just starting to see progress at school.

"Tuesday. Can you give me a ride?"

"Okay . . . I can probably do that," I said as I scrolled through logistics talking to Josh, checking my calendar.

"Thank you, Nicole, you really are a blessing. My mom really did send you to me. You're like my sister."

I drove home slowly. I was going to have these kids full time, at least while their mom was in prison. How the hell was I going to tell Josh? How was I going to get him to agree? But when I talked to Josh, at minimum, he could see that this was the next right thing.

Then a whole other set of questions erupted. How could I get their school records? How could I make sure they were registered for the next school year? What if I needed to take them to the doctor? How was I supposed to figure out all these pieces? The truth was I couldn't figure them out without something that said she was the parent but that I could do a medical intervention and make decisions at school as needed. I needed something more official.

Their mom and I talked about how this document would enable me to help if something happened while she was away and her boyfriend wasn't available—if someone needed to go to school or take the kids to the doctor. I promised her it wouldn't affect her taxes—it was just a piece of paper in case something came up and they needed me. She agreed and we arranged for a notary to come to the apartment to notarize the signing of this slip of paper, which essentially said, *This person has a right to speak for my kids.*

All three girls were staying over at my house the night their mother was scheduled to report to prison. Daya wanted to come with me to drop off her mom. We were right on time. Their mother told me, "I do not want to get there a minute before I have to, but I also need to be there exactly on time."

Daya sat in front as I poured her mother into the car. She'd imbibed every substance she could and was sprawled out across the back seat like a lumpy rag doll. Her tiny body looked puffy and misshapen under the ten layers of clothes she had on—apparently those items had currency inside and that was the only way to legally bring them in.

We had a solid forty-five-minute drive ahead of us. What do you talk about while driving someone to jail? I tried to say encouraging things: *It'll be fine. We'll see you soon.* But instead of the sadness I expected, their mother told us she had lots of friends inside and that it would be good to see them again. She wondered if so-and-so would still be there. And then she mused that she'd miss her friend Jack. Then let out a gruff laugh.

"Who's Jack?" I asked.

Daya whispered, "Jack Daniel's."

Then the energy in the back seat shifted, and her mother called Daya a liar, saying she couldn't be trusted. I tried to defend Daya. Daya tried to laugh it off, but her mother didn't stop until I looked at her in the rearview mirror and told her to just go to sleep.

"That's not me talking. I've just been hanging out with my best friends Jim and Jack," she said over and over until she passed out and the car fell quiet.

When we arrived, the prison's bright lights illuminated the car. I glanced in the rearview mirror and saw her shake off sleep and realize where she was. She saw the big stretch of gate and the cold gray building and she burst into tears.

Daya's mother stood outside the car in the cold night air crying.

"Well, get out and give me a hug." Her words puffed out little clouds.

Daya's mother held her tight.

"I love you, baby. Be good." Then her mother walked up to the big gate, her white shirt bright against the night. I couldn't see any guards. I just heard a loud buzz and the gate opened and then the robotic building swallowed her.

Daya snapped the car door shut. Neither of us spoke.

"Do you want to talk about any of that?"

"Nah, I'm used to it."

"What she said isn't true, and it's not okay."

"Yeah, okay."

We rode home in silence. I could feel the sadness and relief rolling off Daya, as we made the long drive in the dark.

Half of me wondered what I had gotten myself into and the other half knew that I was exactly where I was supposed to be.

The girls stayed with me Monday through Friday, and on weekends they spent time with their dad. Once in a while, they'd pop in on a weekday, but then I'd get calls from them and from their dad asking me to come pick them up.

Krissy would call me and say, "Middicole, I need help with Ally."

"Why aren't you in school?"

"Oh, Dad said I had to stay home."

"Where is he?"

"I don't know. He's not here."

"Okay, I'm going to come pick up Ally and drop you off at school. Get dressed. Get ready. Grab her stuff."

I was like a babysitter who was on call twenty-four-seven—and I bent my schedule around their lives. The truth is, I was scared to do this. But if someone says they're hungry, you feed them.

The more they needed me, the harder it became to care for them across the two households. I'd drop off the kids to sleep and they'd call later that night to tell me their bedsheets weren't clean. But at my house there were three beds with clean sheets. Why was I taking them home only to be called hours later to come get them?

I was the auntie pinch-hitting in the middle of a family crisis. I wasn't a parent, I didn't have the tools or practice of being a parent, and yet the girls were calling on me, their mother was calling on me, and after their mother went to jail, their dad called on me.

If you have children, you know what I'm about to say, but it needs to be said: Parenting is hard. Parenting three kids between the ages of three and fourteen was hard. I gave the kids everything. I worked my day job, left once in a while for a day or two for work or to do a hair event, and then jumped right back into the roar of child-rearing.

After a few weeks, I needed a day or two off. I needed to sleep in and not have to plan activities for anyone except which shows I was going to watch by myself, so on a Friday I brought the girls to see their father.

Later that night the girls called and told me that he'd left. Then their father called and in so many words said he needed me to come get the girls, now, he was going out.

I knew that from then on, they would just stay with me. I wouldn't get frantic calls to come pick them up; they would just live with me. I wasn't an auntie, I was a parent.

We bought additional beds and transformed a room upstairs into a bedroom for the three of them.

A few months before her scheduled release, their mother called to tell me she'd be getting out early and that she wanted a welcome home party.

There was no way these girls were willingly going to go back into the unknown. With stability and routine, the girls were blooming. But

I didn't know what the new arrangement would look like. I had no idea how their mother would decide what role I would play because, frankly, it was a temporary arrangement. I knew that from the beginning. Whatever the solution looked like to make sure these girls were safe, cared for, and loved, I knew that on some level it would always include their mother. But I also knew that even though the arrangement was temporary, my presence in these girls' lives was permanent. I let each of the girls know their mom was really coming home, as we'd had a false alarm a few weeks earlier. I did whatever I could to give them some context because, if nothing else, it helped them feel like somebody was in control, which helped them feel less out of control. Still, Daya was frantic. Krissy was concerned that it would change things.

The answer to all of that was: I'm not leaving.

I acknowledged that things would be a little different, but that everything would be fine. That we would figure it out and I reminded them again and again that I wasn't leaving.

I made a promise early on to always tell the girls the truth. We tell them what's going on so they know. So I told them, "Just because your mother is being released doesn't mean I'm not going to see you anymore. It doesn't mean we're not going to keep doing things, but it does mean we are going to see your mother today."

When we got to the girls' apartment, their mother stood in the doorway calling to them, but she didn't come toward us. She couldn't—she was under house arrest, complete with an ankle bracelet. When we got inside, she was her own welcome home party, dancing and having fun, and acting like nothing had happened. That night the girls called me, saying they couldn't sleep.

The next day I called their mother. "You're probably just getting back on your feet. Do you want some time to just enjoy yourself? Let me come pick up the girls."

"Oh my God, you're so great," she gushed.

I picked up the girls, we grabbed some dinner, and went home. Krissy unloaded the dishwasher, Daya started homework, and I got Ally ready for bed. We got back to the routine.

Addiction often stems from trauma, and it is a disease. Nobody chooses to be a heroin addict. But the girls were suffering the by-products of their mother's disease. After their mother got out of jail, we had regular conversations. Their mother needed and deserved help. We'd chat on the phone, and once her ankle bracelet was off, I'd pick her up and we'd go get our nails done and talk about how she could stabilize her life. I wouldn't give her money, but I could give her space and time—to get a steady job, to get treatment, to go to meetings—to get her house in order for the girls. And she could still mother them with everything she had.

Typically, friend, I'd have some takeaway here. But the takeaway is that sometimes life is just living.

CHAPTER FOURTEEN

YOU HAVE THE RIGHT TO OPT OUT

My coworker, whom I'll call Harvey, taught me one of the greatest lessons I've ever learned. You have the right to opt out.

I had been at my corporate job for four years and helped scale that business from $2 million to $200 million. Together, Harvey and I managed a caseload of clients in one territory. We worked very closely together, until Harvey opted out of me. He decided that he didn't care about my emails or my calls. My work style was personable. I make my clients love me; I become part of their family. His style was more analytical—prove to them they'd be stupid to work with anyone else and then they'll stay with us. His method was effective; he closed sales and won clients. And so did I. However, he did not respect my way.

I filed complaints with my boss. I called a meeting about the inappropriate and disrespectful way he treated me. I brought emails to illustrate my point. She did nothing.

While we were talking to our boss, and HR was on speakerphone, he looked me in the face and said, "You're just like a hostess at Applebee's." No one said a word.

Harvey was always angry that I had stood up for myself. When I closed a big deal that he felt should have been in his territory, he accused me of trying to steal food out of his children's mouths. Then he just stopped responding to my calls and emails. At first I got worked up—he wasn't doing his job and he wasn't getting fired, wasn't even getting talked to, and there were no consequences.

Something clicked in me. Instead of feeling shut down and disempowered, I suddenly saw that I had permission to do whatever I wanted. It takes three write-ups to get fired. The worst that would happen was that I'd be notified that I had two more tries. If you are fired from a situation in which you are not able to function, who cares? So I stopped worrying about getting his buy-in and started doing what I needed to do to accomplish my goals. And then I stopped answering his calls. When Harvey caught on that I hadn't told him something, he just had to deal with it himself. Then I started crushing it at work, crushing it.

Harvey realized I was doing whatever I wanted when he got the invitation to a *big* client presentation I had set up in Florida. When our boss learned that I booked this meeting, she asked if Harvey was coming. Even though I knew full well that I hadn't told Harvey about the meeting, I smoothly told her that I didn't know because I was so focused on preparing for the meeting, and then I sent an email notifying him of the time and place—establishing a paper trail. Our boss knew we weren't speaking, so she brought it up to him. After that, Harvey had to come.

I told myself I was going to plan every moment of this meeting. I was going to do the most incredible song and dance of all time. I was going to close this deal. Harvey could just watch and learn.

When I arrived early for our nine o'clock meeting, Harvey wasn't there. He was always forty-five minutes early to our sales calls, so I was sure he wouldn't come. It didn't matter. There were all these people around the conference table to hear my presentation, and I walked in and the Nicole Show began.

I was in command of the room. Everyone was laughing and enjoying themselves. Then I opened it up for a Q&A. Just then Harvey walked in and stood in the back, his stout body tight, as if every muscle were locked.

I was firing off answers with intellect and wit, and the prospective clients had happily climbed from the conference table into the palm of my hand.

At the end of a meeting like that, usually we would do a follow-up call to lock in whatever the new client wanted. But when I said, "I will follow up with you," my point person said, "Oh, no, Nicole, we're definitely going to do this." Then he turned to the room. "Right, everyone?" It was unanimous. They took the highest packet and that was that. Then they asked me to stay for lunch. They wanted more, but my work was done.

I saw Harvey duck out of the room, and I walked after him. He hadn't said anything to me—not good morning, not congratulations, nothing. The only reason he was there was because our boss had told him to come.

"Oh, you made it," I said to him in the hall. I couldn't resist. He was surprised—I don't know if it was surprise at how well the sale had gone or if he was shocked that I'd spoken to him. All he could muster was "Yeah." I could see for the first time that I had caught him off guard.

"Are you headed to another meeting?" He told me he was, and I think he expected me to ask about it, or to ask if I could come along. He stopped walking and I said, "Oh, okay. Good luck." Then I walked away, leaving him behind.

People can just opt out of you, and although you may not like it and it might be wrong, it doesn't change the fact that it does still happen, so you need to do something for yourself. You can reserve that right too. You can opt out of relationships, people, and jobs that don't serve you. You can think bigger than the traps other people set for you.

———————

While I was holding down my corporate job and raising the girls, I was also beginning to make money through my blog and my events. At first I just made little bits of money, a hundred dollars here and there. I was ready to open my first business checking account. The problem was that most of the banks had a required minimum balance of $2,000, and I wasn't anywhere close to hitting that number. So, I opened an account with our little community bank down the street. Soon, my blog started getting traction even though, as far as blogs go, it was very midrange. People often forget that there's a lot of money in the middle. A lot of people quit their goals because they think they're not going to reach the top of their field. But let me tell you a secret: I was never a super-successful blogger, but I was still making good money consistently. Good money consistently has pride. Breathing room has pride.

I made just enough to cover my business and just enough to grow it, and whatever extra I had I was able to use for the girls, so Josh was okay with it. There were times when my blog paid for groceries. There were times when my blog paid for vacation. I knew there was potential for more. Sometimes after work Josh would say, "Your numbers have gone down. Have you done any posts today?" He watched my numbers closely—the views, the likes, the followers. He didn't understand much about the business—natural hair, social media. But it validated to him that the business made sense. And I knew better—all those factors could change. Obsessing over followers is about ego. The only number I've ever counted is the balance in my bank account. Money means options.

At Harvard Business School, they teach this concept called "going concern." In so many words, it means you never start a business with the intent to fail. Even with the highs and lows of business, the concept is critical to success, and any thriving entrepreneur understands it early and well. Josh was supportive as long as cash was coming in, but he also saw everything as potentially ending at some point. He would see a window and think, *There's no way we're going through it; we should keep running around the house looking for a door or buy another house.* Give me a window and I will crash through it and create a door.

One night, after I'd dropped the girls off with their mom for a visit and Josh and I were watching a show on the couch in the den, something gave me an idea for my business and my thoughts gathered steam. "I think I want to quit my job and go full time," I confided. I was saying it out loud for both myself and Josh to hear. I was here to work. I wanted to show up and do all the things, but as my blogging work burgeoned, I was overwhelmed by all the responsibility on my plate. I needed to choose my hard. Once I did, I could devote all of myself to doing the work and taking care of the girls.

"You can't quit. What is wrong with you? You can't make less money." He seemed worried that we wouldn't be okay.

"I think it's going to be worth it. I'd have more time to take care of the girls. I won't have to put Ally in daycare. I can clean up the house more and we won't have to get cleaners. And if it doesn't work out, I can get a part-time job."

I had to convince him that changing my life wouldn't change his life. So I did everything. I showed up every day in every capacity. I traipsed around with two laptops—my work computer for my day job and my personal computer for my business, which was taking up more and more time. I'd work my corporate job, take care of the girls, and, while Josh was sleeping, I spent long nights writing blog posts, learning coding and HTML, C++, JavaScript, connecting with people online, booking gigs, and consulting with other bloggers about their businesses.

I started booking bigger and bigger gigs, and the more the blog grew, the more my consulting business grew. I couldn't do two jobs. I knew my business paid me less, but I liked it better than my corporate job. I knew I was making enough that we could afford all our bills if I quit. And if I worked for myself full-time, I might be able to grow my business enough to at least replace my salary. How much bigger could it be?

Every time I hit a new milestone, I'd run the numbers and show them to Josh for his buy-in.

"Yeah, I see the numbers. I just don't know. I just don't know," he said, as he shook his head vigorously side to side.

We'd been in the girls' lives for a year now; even though we didn't have custody, we had complete responsibility for three kids—their education, their well-being, their childcare. And we didn't have $1,200 a month for day care.

There were so many things Ally needed to learn. When I met her she hadn't ever touched a book. She had been exposed to minimal vocabulary; she picked up language from her family and TV. She also didn't know much about how the world worked. For instance, Ally didn't realize for the longest time that adults had jobs. When I told her that Josh worked in an office and wore a tie, she squealed, "Oh, like Daddy Pig, because in *Peppa Pig* Daddy Pig goes to an office." When I took her to his office one day, she was very impressed.

I looked at all these things as problems that needed solving. Kids are not broken; they're flat imprints that you can layer stuff on. So that's what I did. I piled as much good stuff on as I could. Good habits, good manners, good food, good books.

But while I was busy establishing all these good things, I still had a job—aunties don't get maternity leave. I adjusted my schedule as best I could. I was lucky my job was so flexible, enabling me to work from home. The first thing I realized was that I needed to make more money efficiently.

The only way I knew I could do that was if I controlled some aspect of my work. I didn't know what that looked like, but I knew I could figure it out. And I knew the key was my business, not my corporate job. I made money when I put out content, but blog posts took too long. And I was never a YouTuber—to do that I felt I had to be Steven Spielberg, with the pyrotechnics and special effects, and I was not going to do that.

Twitter had just come out with Periscope, and I was an early adopter. With Periscope, all you had to do was go live. Going live meant no editing, no extra effort. I'd been doing it for years in a conference room. I could definitely do it on the Internet. I started going live and it changed my game. Two or three times a day I would share the knowledge I had gained working my corporate job. That made me money. Efficiently. Then I could pay extra attention to my kids. I'd hang out with Ally, go upstairs, go live, and come back down.

We didn't watch a whole lot of TV, but I did put a show on for Ally sometimes when I was going live, or on a call, or desperately needed an hour to concentrate on work. One day I was working up in the office and she started crying. My heart leapt into my throat and I ran downstairs.

As soon as she saw me she wailed, "The show's gone off."

I didn't give her a big reaction. I just said, "Okay. What's the problem?"

"This off," she said, pointing to the TV, tears streaming down her face. Three-year-olds are like drunk sorority girls—singing one moment and weeping the next. The trick I learned was to stay calm and not match her energy.

"Right. But why are you crying?"

"Because I can't turn it on."

"Oh, well, I thought you were hurt. Are you hurt?" I asked with a dramatic flair.

"No," she said slowly. She was really listening now, and the crying had stopped.

"Oh, well, you know, if the show goes off, or if you need help, I can show you how to fix it. There're ways you can get me and you don't have to cry about it." She kept looking at me, her eyes big. "Let me show you." Then we were playing a game where we reenacted the whole thing, only this time she called up to me, "Middicole, the TV show's over."

I came downstairs in an Oscar-worthy performance. "Thank you for calling me. Is the TV show over?"

"Yes."

"Let me help you with that."

"Okay."

"See, if you need something, you can actually just say it. You don't have to cry. And I'll help you. I'll show up and I'll help you." She just stared at me like I'd just performed magic, like I'd given her the keys to the kingdom.

The only way she would get anything from her parents would be by crying. Because they were addicts, they didn't have traditional communication. But crying was disruptive enough that it would break through their state and elicit a response every time.

After that, whenever she would cry or whine inappropriately, I'd pretend that adults didn't understand. "I'm sorry. I can't understand. I want to understand, I just can't," I'd whisper, so that she couldn't hear me over her own cries. Finally, she would stop, and I'd remind her, "Remember, adults don't understand whining."

"Oh, I forgot." And then she'd just tell me what she needed. Soon she learned that this was a house where people are responsive to her needs.

But finding pockets of time to work took a whole other level of problem-solving.

I tried taking work calls from an indoor playground where Ally could run wild, but I quickly learned that three-year-olds want you to play with them. Then we discovered IKEA. I took full advantage of their showroom warehouse. When I had an important deadline, I'd leave Ally at the supervised play center for the allotted thirty minutes, go up to the office area, find a nice desk near an outlet, and plug in. I had my computer, my phone, and a mug of coffee. Every half hour I'd go check on Ally and then I'd go back to work—the only distractions were customers asking me questions, but I'd simply explain that I didn't work there—I mean I was working there, but I didn't work there. And then at the end of it all, we'd go and get a plate of chicken tenders.

The other place I got a lot of work done was the car. Ally would nap in the car, or I'd take a call on our way to the playground or grocery store and always tried to limit them to fifteen minutes. She never interrupted. Ally was eerily good at being quiet. She learned this at her house when she was told, "Be quiet, the police are coming" or "Be quiet, there's someone knocking at the door. We have to pretend we aren't home." She was raised knowing that speaking could have dire consequences. Whenever the phone would ring, Ally knew I needed her to be quiet.

One afternoon my boss called, and I pulled into the parking lot of a grocery store so I could take notes. Fifteen minutes ticked by, but my boss kept going on and on and on. As her voice buzzed around my brain like a fly, I kept thinking, *This is not where I'm supposed to be. What am I doing right now?* When I finally got off the phone after a forty-five-minute call, I peeked at Ally in the back seat. She was quiet; I was sure she'd fallen asleep, but there she was, her big brown eyes looking back at me. What child is quiet for that long?

"Wow, you did such a good job. That was a long time, wasn't it?"

She nodded and showed me her bright, gap-toothed smile.

"Do you want to go home?" The words hitched in my throat. I was broken that day.

The idea that this three-year-old had to wait forty-five minutes for me to get off the phone, because in that moment that call mattered more, just didn't add up. It was not okay, and I promised myself I would never do it again.

I thought, *Why am I doing this?* Then I let that thought grow. Opting out of Harvey was small potatoes. I needed to opt out of my job.

———————

Opting out of something is also opting into something else. It is giving yourself permission to open a new door, to have the space to think a new thought, to follow a new pursuit and make real change.

Having to constantly fight the personification of my worst entrepreneurial fears in my own home as I pursued my greatest goals has been one of the best blessings I've ever had. I was prepared to fail. I was okay with failure. I was going to go hard, but if I failed, I needed to know Josh would still be around. I wanted him to trust what I was doing, but I was also so tired from everything else that I didn't have the energy to prove myself to him—I needed that energy to make this business work.

Although I didn't understand where I was going, I could feel I was on a path. It was hard, but it felt right.

You have to stop going to people for validation when they aren't qualified to give it. But back then I couldn't see that. I was surrounded by people who believed that anything that gives you joy had to be treated in a miserly way. Growing up, and now in my own home. That mindset is really destructive. How can something you love flourish if you don't water it? A plant might grow in the semidark with a bit of water and soil, but it will be anemic and small. Not something lush with sunlight and water, nourished and sung to. I wanted to sing to my business. I wanted to put it in the sun. I wanted to see how tall it could grow. I wanted to go all in.

CHAPTER FIFTEEN

PEOPLE ARE PARADOXES

There's a version of this story that ends after we meet the girls. There's another version that ends after I quit my job, which, you know, is what's coming next. That's the version of the story I've told most often. But I promised to tell you the truth, and the truth is a lot more complicated.

As I planned the trip to celebrate our seventh anniversary, I was filled with hope. For the last six months we had been going nonstop, between the girls, our work, and my business, which Josh finally seemed to respect. I'd even booked him a gig doing a panel discussion at an event I was doing later that summer. The kids were better than they had been. (They were spending a few days with their mom. I sent them with food, extra clothes, and all the supplies they could possibly need for school, and my sister was on call.) Our marriage was better than it had been. From the beginning, things with Josh had been a struggle, and couples therapy seemed to have helped. We were as healthy as we'd ever been, and, per my optimistic nature, I was sure we were on the cusp of something even better. I planned the trip, I packed for Josh, I told him what time he needed to get up, and what time we had to leave. My focus was the complete restoration of our marriage, and I didn't want to start a fight over packing or planning. Jamaica was going to reset the tone for our future together.

We arrived in Jamaica sleep-deprived and on the cheapest red-eye I could find. We stayed in a little guesthouse on the greatest part of Negril's Seven Mile Beach. We napped on the beach then dozed by the pool. The hotel was painted in blues the color of the sky and water. I stared at the pool with its little waterfall ensconced in a cheerful mural of a jungle paradise until I fell asleep again. Josh was reading a book he'd found in the hotel's book exchange and would sometimes burst into fits of laughter, though he couldn't explain what was so funny.

Usually I can go, go, go, but I was wiped out and wanted to turn in early. Josh, on the other hand, is very mellow, very even-keeled, very predictable. Josh, who likes his coffee at a certain hour and his dessert at a certain hour, wanted to stay out. We went to dinner on the beach. We ate and drank and stayed up too late. But Josh still woke with the sun. At breakfast he was rattling on about my blog. He was so excited about my work and interested in sales and filled with ideas, but I couldn't keep up with what he was saying. We spent the day lounging on the beach. I surrendered to the rhythmic shush of the sunlit water on the white sand, but he couldn't be still. Instead, he paced until he zeroed in on something—a crab or a shell—that would hold his attention until his restless energy erupted again and set him in motion.

Every day I walked the whole beach, passing all the fancy resorts and deluxe villas. There was one home that was hexagonal, with white stone walls, brown shingles, and a balcony that looked out on the beach. I walked past it, wondering what type of person lived there. As I walked, my mind cleared. The stress of work faded away and I thought about my business and how it was growing.

Before we left, I'd bought bathing suits on Amazon and was planning a beta test on monetizing myself. I wanted data to support my
pitches for sponsorships and collaborations. One day, I wore an orange
bathing suit with a wraparound top and Josh took pictures of me for
my blog. He'd begun to get into his role as an Instagram husband. At
first, when I was taking pictures or filming, he'd just ask if he was in my
light, but by the time we got to Jamaica, he would always think about
stopping to take pictures. When we got back to the pool, I wrote a post
that went viral. That had never happened. I had more comments than
ever before and could see the number of purchases ticking up on my
Amazon page, and soon the suit had sold out. I stayed up that night,
contacting the vendor, switching up links to make sure I could keep the
sales coming in.

That next morning I woke up and Josh was already gone. I assumed
he was on the patio reading, but he wasn't there. Or in the restaurant
for coffee, but he wasn't there either. I finally found him hovering at the
poolside bar, laughing too loudly and chattering at the bartender as the
guy set up for the day, looking like it was too early in his shift for him to
already be catering to guests.

As we walked along the beach, Josh was switching from topic to
topic. That morning, he went too fast, struck up conversations with
strangers, and talked circles around me. That afternoon I napped in our
room. Josh left to grab a water, and an hour later I found him in what
sounded like a cringeworthy conversation.

I wrangled Josh into our room. "What is going on?"

He didn't answer the question, just glided into another mono-
logue.

"Josh, you need to sleep. Something's going on, and you need to
sleep."

By this point he hadn't slept more than a few hours in days. That
night, I tried to keep myself awake so I could make sure he stayed in
bed. He would stir and I would hold him tight, hoping he felt loved, not
restrained. He would sit up and I would urge him to lie down again. He
insisted he had to go to the bathroom. He'd go and then we'd start the

whole dance again. But I couldn't keep vigil all night, and eventually I fell asleep.

I woke up in a panic. What had happened while I was sleeping? We didn't have drugs in our home, considering the girls' background; we didn't even have alcohol. Had he taken drugs? Whatever it was, it *had* to wear off. But that afternoon I had dozed off on the beach as Josh stood nearby with his feet in the water. When I woke up forty minutes later, Josh hadn't moved, but the water had risen to his knees and his shoulders and back were a blistering red. I went to his side. He was talking to the fish about healing the country with his hands.

He seemed whole worlds away from me.

Our flight was scheduled to leave twenty-four hours later. I just wanted to get him home, where I could navigate whatever he needed. I spent the last day of the trip trying to keep Josh sequestered in our room.

For our last night, the night of our anniversary, we had dinner reservations, but I didn't want to go out. Josh cajoled me into it. "It's fine. Let's just go," he said. On the way to the restaurant, Josh tried to reassure me. "I'm enlightened now, but it's okay. I'm just going to act normal. It's fine." Chills ran along my spine. What did normal mean to him? How could he act it?

Our table sat atop a cliff, overlooking the ocean. Waves crashed beneath us. Fairy lights were strung around, turning the restaurant into a little jewel box in the night. Despite the heat, our server came out in a jacket, with a napkin draped over his arm. As I ate my lobster thermidor, I tried to talk to Josh about all the normal things—work, the girls, my business. But talk of my business seemed to rev him up. I didn't recognize the man before me. And sitting there with him, I couldn't taste the sweetness of the life that was all around us.

Back in our room, I packed everything up and lay in bed to keep vigil. I'd doze off into a gauzy unconsciousness and then startle awake every time Josh moved.

Eventually exhaustion won, and when I woke, I found him by the pool talking to an expat lady who lived up on the hillside. He told me he was thinking about going with her up to her farm. My heart fluttered. My blood went hot and then cold. He could have just walked off and I wouldn't have known how to find him.

We took the group shuttle to the airport and Josh talked the whole way. At the airport I kept him next to me and worried that if he did anything out of the ordinary, we wouldn't be able to get on our flight. We made it past security and sat near a fake palm tree in Margaritaville, which was a little island in the airport, a remnant of paradise. The warm sunlight poured through the windows, the sky stretched blue and far, but my world felt small and scary. I bit into a Cheeseburger in Paradise. Josh didn't eat. He hadn't stopped talking all morning; the words came fast and he jumped from topic to topic, his voice loud and insistent. I couldn't make sense of anything he was saying. When I told him I couldn't understand, he said, "Everything's fine. Everything's going to be fine, Nicole. We're going to lead the world together."

I thought about getting home; I thought about the girls and the reality of our jobs and responsibilities and all the things we were returning to. Then, for the first time, I allowed myself to consider the fact that Josh might be having a medical issue. I needed to get him back to America, where I had more options, where I could navigate medical care, where I could get him help. As the plane left Jamaica, Josh ran his hands along the window like a blind person reading braille.

"What are you doing?"

"I'm blessing the land."

I was too afraid to even go to the bathroom on the flight, but by the time we stepped into the Miami airport, I realized leaving him there was an even scarier prospect, only it was too late. I desperately had to pee.

I found a seat as close as possible to the ladies' room. Then, like a mother delivering life-preserving directions to a toddler, I took his hand and looked him right in the eye and said, "Josh, I know that you're feeling a lot of feelings right now. But no matter what you think you need to do, don't move from this seat. Promise me you won't move. I'll be right back."

"Of course, of course, that's fine," he said.

Before I rounded the corner, I turned back and mouthed, "Do not move."

Coming out of the bathroom, my feet flew between walking and running, and everyone else disappeared from view until I turned the corner and there he was, just as I had left him. I exhaled hard. The world filled with noise and people and oxygen.

I was delirious. I was tired and confused. In Miami I had phone access once again, but I wasn't sure whom to call. I needed to get to a place where I had quiet. I needed time to start plotting my ROI. On the plane to Maryland I collapsed into a sleep so deep it was one beat away from death.

Once we were inside our home, every single muscle in my body relaxed. I could take it from here. I could figure it out. But I needed time. Over email, I explained to both our bosses that Josh was injured during our trip and put in for more days off from our jobs. Then I took him to urgent care.

As I drove to urgent care, Josh told me, "Listen, Nicole, they're not going to understand me, and they're not going to understand who I am, and I can't let them know. So I'm going to be normal in there and they're not going to know."

I was overwhelmed by fear that we wouldn't be able to get him the help he needed. Was he going to pretend he was okay?

"Well, we should find out what's going on, you know."

"Everything's fine. I'm just ascended."

We parked in the shopping center. While other people were picking up their Chinese food, or spooning up their frozen yogurt, we sat in the urgent care waiting room, between a coughing kid and a guy with an ice pack over his eye. Finally, a nurse led us down a hallway and brought us into a room barely big enough for the exam table. I stood beside Josh as the doctor talked to us. No matter what I said, they couldn't see the signs of illness. They gave him something for his sunburn—the skin on his shoulders was angry and blistering. But Josh didn't seem bothered by it.

I led Josh out of the office, holding his hand in the parking lot to keep him close. Nothing was better. I had brought him to the wrong place.

At least, I thought, we were home in our room, in our own bed, and he could sleep. We would figure out the next step in the morning. We lay down and I held him, wanting to keep him in bed. He kept starting awake, his whole body jolting straight. I touched him gently on his shoulder and he swung an arm out.

"Get off me!" he screamed as I held his wrist away from me, my heart thudding in my ears. I didn't know what this was, but I knew it wasn't normal, and I knew I wasn't going to get hit.

He looked right through me, and I felt that he was all the way gone. Inside, fight and flight rose up in me at the same time. I wanted to fight this thing, whatever it was, *and* I wanted to run far away. But I was the only person who could help him fight whatever was happening.

"We're going to the ER."

When I told Josh to get dressed, he didn't argue. And when I asked him to promise that he would do what I asked, he agreed.

As soon as I'd turned the key in the ignition, the sky thundered open. Rain pelted the car as I slowly drove through the night streets to the hospital across town—I was afraid of the one in our neighborhood. Josh just kept talking, leaping from one thought to the next. We'd gone just a few blocks when I realized I needed gas. As I stood at the pump with Josh in the car, it was quiet except for the rain. I breathed deep, the smell of gas bright in my nostrils, and willed myself to keep it together.

My knuckles were tight on the wheel and the windshield wipers were ticking manically, as if they were keeping time with my heart.

We arrived at the ER just before midnight. They took his vitals and we filled out the intake form. There was nothing obviously wrong with him, but I was insistent that he wasn't okay. Every bone in my body was telling the nurse admitting us that I was not leaving unless they physically removed me.

The waiting room was quiet but crackling with frantic energy. The gift shop was dark for the night. I sat in the hard chair beside Josh and leaned my head back. My stomach churned; I couldn't remember eating since we'd left Jamaica. I hadn't showered either. My basic human functions had been suspended. I didn't know what we were waiting for, but I knew we weren't leaving without seeing a doctor.

Josh was talking incessantly, insistently. The doctors didn't know what was happening to him, but it was clear something was going on. It was a relief to hear someone say that. Up until that moment I'd been all alone.

We sat in that room and waited. I sat in fear. I could hear other people moaning and ranting. Josh kept talking and asking for apple juice. At last, on our second day, they gave him something to help him sleep. The nurses said I could go home for a little while. When I got into the car I was so tired that I was worried about making the drive, which was only two exits down the highway.

I made it home, but I couldn't even make it upstairs. I passed out on the couch, and when I woke up, I had a message that Josh was being transferred to another hospital. I showered. The water was ice-cold, and I couldn't figure out what was wrong. That was a problem I didn't have the energy to solve. Then I fell asleep in the guest room, where I slept the whole time he was gone.

I didn't immediately tell anyone what was going on. I didn't want to spend more time managing other people's emotions than managing my husband's care. Josh needed all of me. The only time I wasn't by his side was when I visited the girls. They were really scared. It was so unlike me not to come get them right away and I knew they were worried that this would be where I would leave them. But I wasn't going anywhere; I just needed a little time to stabilize everything. I needed time to ROI. I took groceries to them at their mom's house and took them out to eat and explained that Midder Josh had been hurt while we were away.

"It doesn't mean I'm going anywhere. I'm not leaving, just like I said I was never leaving, but it means that I'm going to have to check on you instead of you coming home with me. But I'll have you back as soon as I can."

"How soon is that?" Daya asked, anger bubbling.

"Maybe another week or two."

Krissy's big doe eyes widened as she held back tears. Ally looked at her sisters, trying to gauge how she was supposed to react. I knew how I was supposed to act—like a mom, managing my reaction so they were allowed to have their feelings. I had to show them that we'd all be fine. There were lots of hugs, lots of kisses.

I wanted to reassure Krissy and Ally, but it was Daya I was most worried about. The more time you spend away from certain spaces, the harder it is to go back—it becomes deeply, profoundly hard. How much longer could she stay at her mother's without some disaster erupting? I knew my time was ticking; I needed to get the girls back. I was just hoping nothing went wrong before I could.

I didn't know how long Josh would be in the hospital, and I was terrified. My life flashed before my eyes. My biggest fear was that Josh would never come home.

When I wasn't by my husband's side, I was doing something for him or I was sleeping and eating. My life was happening between moments of visitation. I was always waiting for three o'clock, when I could see him. All I wanted was a glimpse of him still there, somewhere deep inside.

I was trying to be as strong as I could, but I was utterly broken. My depression stayed in the house. Sometimes I left it in the car. I'd cry for hours on end, then I would scrape myself off the couch and pick out bright clothes—sunshine yellow, fuchsia—outward projections of happiness. Then I'd go visit Josh or see the girls. When I got home, my depression was waiting.

If I wanted to talk to a doctor, I had to wait till the doctor was on call. My husband was going through hell, and the only barrier to better care and communication was money.

I'd see him in a big room where the other patients were also visiting with their loved ones. Every day I asked him what he wanted to eat. I'd drive all over Baltimore to find whatever kind of food he wanted and he always said that he'd get the drinks. I'd bring a bag of food and he'd bring two little plastic cups of apple juice with foil tops.

I had to figure out how to navigate letting people know my husband was not well. I needed to figure out our log-ins to pay our bills. I had to figure out the systems. I had to figure out how to raise my babies. In my car, my body collapsed into the seat and I wept a salty mess of tears and snot. I tried to take deep breaths, but I wasn't breathing; I was drowning.

I sat in the car and lost time. I felt like I had blinked and it was dark. Maybe I had fallen asleep. All I knew is that it was much later and I was still sitting in the parking lot, dazed. I knew I needed food, but I couldn't even think of what to eat. I picked up a sandwich at a gas station deli. As I headed back to my car, I noticed something on the ground. It was a white slip of paper from a fortune cookie. I'm not sure why, but I picked it up: YOUR SMILE ALWAYS BRIGHTENS THE CLOUDIEST DAYS.

This was one good thing, and it carried me forward.

I burned through all my vacation time, and then HR told me I had to go on unpaid leave. I did.

We were both virtually unemployed. One residual payment from a client I'd already finished working with came in, but that was it.

Everything was moving so fast that I wasn't paying bills or invoices yet. I was preparing myself to get slammed with a bill that was $50,000. (It ended up being closer to $10,000.) It was still money we just didn't have.

Josh's recovery would be ten times harder if he came out faced with more debt. We already had $30,000 in debt, a mortgage on an old house where things broke, and now, because of me, we had these three kids.

Over and over I asked myself, *How am I going to do this?* I wouldn't let this thing I couldn't control break our family. I had already been the principal breadwinner; I could take on more responsibility. I would make this money. I would make sure that when he came out he had a fighting shot at just focusing on being well. I would make sure that the girls didn't have to suffer, because it wasn't their fault that they stepped into something else crazy.

We're not supposed to have worry. That's biblical. It's like shame; it is an unproductive feeling. You can worry, but the problem still exists. But it can be hard to remember that worry is unproductive. That is why people do Bible study, therapy, or meditation—to remember not to reside in worry or shame; they are distractions. I knew that for however long I stayed in worry, I was being extremely disobedient to God. I had prayed to God repeatedly, and my business was flourishing. Not listening to what He was showing me was an act of disobedience. I was more scared about being obedient to God than I was about what would happen if I continued to not listen.

Each day I sat in my house by myself. I was determined to make money. I had no one to shuttle around, feed, or tend to. I could sit weaving webs of worry or I could work. I could build my business. My business could save us. Slowly, I started singing to it.

There was a surge of interest in the blog and in me, and I needed to keep creating content and building the business with my entrepreneur clients. I kept booking consulting calls with clients, and the hardest part was acting like everything was okay, but somehow, I turned on my energy and lent people my expertise and my belief.

You can really do more than you think, especially when you are inspired by something that is greater than yourself.

I had an event in Philadelphia and wasn't talking about hair; I was talking about business. I was enveloped by the enthusiasm and support of everyone there. I got dolled up. I looked my best. I smiled. I learned a lot about what I was able to do while I waited.

In life, the waiting window is the worst part. If you can be good during the waiting window, you can be good through everything else— waiting for the money, the diagnosis, the change, the opportunity. The greater the hardship, the more difficult the wait.

After the event, I returned home to the other fork of my bifurcated life. I had been training to operate in two worlds my whole life.

At home, I never knew if the electricity would be on or how much food would be in the fridge, but I went to school with the children of some of the wealthiest, most powerful families in the world. I was a Black woman in corporate America. I was African and American. I was a child-free woman with three children. I was contradiction heaped upon itself. I was always many things that would normally exclude one another. So now, as the wife of a sick husband, I was simultaneously scraped hollow and soaring at my highest level—making more money than I had ever hoped for, laying the foundation for a business that would make millions for my family, and coming into my own in an entirely new way.

Everyday life was hard. If I wasn't on a work call, if I wasn't trying to sleep, I was in a stupor. I'd sit on the couch and blink and it would be an hour later.

I started congratulating myself for doing small tasks. *Oh, you ate today Nicole, you did a good job. Oh Nicole, you got up off the couch, good job.*

I took a cold shower every day for the first week Josh was in the hospital. I didn't have the energy to solve that problem. Then one afternoon I mentioned it during visiting hours. "Everything is fine, just the water in our shower isn't getting hot."

He looked at me, really looked at me, and said, "Oh, yeah, I put it in vacation mode before we left. So the water heater needs to be turned back on." Time stopped and I stared at Josh, at his scraggly beard and haggard face. I saw my husband there.

When I got home, I crept down to the basement and switched the water heater back on. I turned on the water and puffs of steam filled the bathroom. Taking a hot shower for the first time, I wept. I couldn't tell my hot tears from the hot water.

———————

The whole time, I kept the weight of this struggle to myself. Then one day Maame showed up at my house. She had grown into an over-functioning adult. It was comforting to know that I had one person who could step in and shoulder some of the weight. My sister and I are constantly in touch, and when I hadn't responded to any of her calls or texts she drove over on her lunch break and let herself into our house.

I was sitting at the kitchen island when Maame appeared and demanded to know what was going on. I tried to sidestep her questions, but she's a social worker and is trained to ask questions and address distress. But as much as I wanted to handle it all by myself, seeing my sister cracked something open in me. I had been so alone, and here was this raft holding the person I trusted most. I started crying and told her everything that had happened since we'd arrived in Jamaica.

Saying everything out loud to someone who loved me helped. We talked about Josh's treatment, the prognosis, the girls and what was best for them. She gave me her regular matter-of-fact support that kept me tethered to the ground, putting one foot in front of the other.

After talking to my sister, I also told my mother. I spared her the details but told her that Josh didn't seem well and was in the hospital.

She asked two questions: "How long will he be there?" and "Do you need me to come?"

I'm not good at asking for help, so I often simply tell people that I'm not okay and hope that if something happens, they know how to help me. In some ways the call was my first line of defense, so that if things got worse I could call and she wouldn't be surprised.

"No. It's okay," I said, my voice hitching in my throat. I didn't even know what I needed. "I just don't know what this is, you know?"

"We'll pray for him. Just give it time. He will be okay."

While Josh was in the hospital, I started operating on two planes: I was near catatonic at home, barely able to scrape myself off the couch, and my business was taking off.

———

I promised to tell you the truth, and that's the truth. It is a little messy, and very gray. But I'm learning that grace exists in the gray. I'm more than one thing. I'm many things. And so are you. People are just a lot of things; we all are. We are all people of paradoxes. A paradox is essentially the fact that we are both things side by side. That's what human is. We are a bunch of different ideas, feelings, and beliefs all smashed together. We're not one or the other, and that's what makes us incredible.

Paradox has a negative connotation, like you aren't being true or straightforward, but it's not that; it's just that we are both. Grace lives in the acknowledgment of paradoxes. It's how God sees us. I am both a hot mess and excellent; I have traditional perspectives and liberal ideals; I'm a great mother and a terrible mother, and none of those labels dictate what tomorrow brings. I am both. So many of us believe that our lives have to be one thing or another—a mess or a success, on hold or in progress, someone is unkind or caring—and it can be challenging to see that both can be true.

We're not all one thing. We're not red or blue or purple. There's no pride in being fiercely one thing, which is the messaging that's most prevalent right now. Where do you stand on America? Where do you stand on gun control? On climate change? Everyone wants you to take a firm stand on every issue. Society is fostering polarization, as if there is pride in polarization, but there is not. Polarization creates fear, and through fear, people are easily manipulated. But when you start acknowledging that everybody has gray inside, then maybe you can see a little bit of yourself in me, and it is a lot harder to be enemies when there is connection.

This grace can be applied to our politics, ourselves, and our relationships.

CHAPTER SIXTEEN

PROMOTE YOURSELF TO YOUR PURPOSE

I lost everything in the span of a month—my husband, my girls, my peace of mind. How could I go back to work and sit behind a desk? I had this fear that the financial pressure would mean I'd have to quit my blog, not my job. If I didn't make money, I was going to have to give up this thing I loved.

I was always sitting with my two phones and my two laptops side by side on my desk and at the kitchen table in my parents' apartment. If I was waiting in Josh's hospital room while he had an appointment, I'd be answering calls. I would answer work emails and while I was waiting for a response, I'd work on a blog post.

I worked at all hours of the day and night, churning out my future.

After the event in Philadelphia, things happened rapid-fire. When I came back, I was invited to more events and I had a raft of new private consulting clients. Other bloggers saw me going to these events and getting booked and they saw my numbers—the engagement and the sales. They knew I didn't have the popularity or the "look," and they wanted to know how I was getting the kind of numbers I was hitting.

My secret was that I had learned that the money was in the how. This was actually something I'd learned as a kid sitting in my dad's cab as he dropped off a fare. We pulled up to the man's house in a posh neighborhood and I noticed his Rolls-Royce. I'd never seen a car like that, so I asked him how he got it. He explained that he was a boxing manager. I was very confused—the boxer was the one taking the blows and doing the work, but this guy had a Rolls-Royce. The smart guy is the one who doesn't take any punches but still gets paid. The manager can work with a whole list of boxers, never take any blows, and get paid exponentially more than the boxers themselves. The boxing was the "what," what the manager did was the "how." I'd seen this as a kid, but I hadn't learned how to apply it myself. But now I saw that I could work every day to make money and get rich—I could do this with my corporate job, or I could do this with my blog. Or I could sell my knowledge, which is an infinite resource with low overhead, and I could become wealthy. The money is in the how. Consulting is a game changer. That was the turning point. When I was doing the "what," I made no more than a few thousand dollars a month, but once I started focusing on the "how," I started making $10,000 a week. If I could just build up a nest egg, then I'd be able to quit my job and at least try this thing for a year.

Just as I'd needed to know what my own hair looked like and how to manage it, without anything extra, I needed to know how to make money in some way that wasn't reliant on a corporate job or someone else cutting me a check. And, just as I'd given myself permission to wear wigs after I'd gone natural, I had to tell myself that I could always go back to a corporate job if I quit this one. I was terrified. I was challenging the notion that traditional work was what I was supposed to be doing. I was thinking of leaving the thing that my family, through time immemorial, had told me my worth was wrapped up in. My corporate job was the one thing that would keep me stable, the one thing that defined who I was, the one thing that meant I'd be successful for my whole life. But every part of me was itching to quit.

In some of your biggest moments, you're going to be by yourself. We're often afraid to leave the bad job, the bad relationship, the wrong church because we think the bad thing is better than being alone, better than nothing. You need to get okay with aloneness.

In my struggle with aloneness, rather than trusting my gut, I went on a what-would-people-think-of-me tour. Even though I lived only forty-five minutes from my parents, I didn't get to see them often. Between the girls and Josh and work, I was on a relentless hamster wheel. But my dad's Parkinson's was progressing. He now walked with a shuffle. His hands would tremble when he ate, so he couldn't eat his Ghanaian food correctly. He could no longer form his perfect cursive or shave, so his cheeks, which had always been clean-shaven, were now covered in gray stubble. Whenever I could steal the time, I'd go visit my parents, deliver money to them, or just make sure they were okay. But this time, while I may have been checking on them, I let my mom cluck over me. She worried that I was working when she went to bed and when she got up in the morning. She worried that I hadn't eaten. She made me bowls of stew and jollof rice in the pot with the broken lid.

My mom was doing the dishes after lunch one day. (The dishwasher beside her was used only to store paper towels. "We don't have enough dishes; it feels so wasteful," she would say.) I was staring at her hands, all covered in suds, and suddenly the words were bubbling up out of my throat.

"Mom, I think I'm going to quit my job."

She looked at me and then she turned off the faucet, wiped her sudsy hands, and said, "You know you have to."

I was floored.

I turned behind me to look toward my parents' bedroom to make sure my dad couldn't hear her.

My mom had her own paradoxes. My dad's illness radically shifted her perspective, but still she hadn't completely broken out from under him. If my dad had been sitting with us, she would have said, "Well, maybe you can take more time." But here she was, encouraging me to run for it, to go get everything. It was the first time in my whole life that my mom was telling me to do something outside the lines, something that would anger my dad.

"Well, you know you can do it."

"I'm making money; I just don't know if it's a thing yet. I feel like I know what I'm doing, but it's not clear. I'm going to try to make more money. I'll quit once I have more money. I'll probably quit by November. I just need a few more months to make more money."

She looked at me and said, "I know it'll even be before then." I must have looked confused because she continued, "God has already told me: August."

I thought she was crazy. I needed a whole lot more money before I'd feel like it was reasonable to quit, but her faith gave her certainty.

"You work hard. It'll be okay. God has you. Everything I was supposed to have in my lifetime will pass to you."

Next, I called Maame. She is very practical. She's anxiety driven, and that manifests in her being very rational and not at all interested in niceties.

"I think I'm going to quit my job."

"Why'd you call me?"

I can talk to Maame more plainly than I can talk to anyone else. There aren't as many filters between us, so I simply told her the truth: "I'm really scared."

"You can do it."

"Really?"

"Yes. And if it doesn't work out you can always get another job."

The first time I ever quit a job I was sixteen years old.

I was desperately trying to find a summer gig. I applied to sweep floors at a hair salon, to wash dishes at restaurants; I would do anything at all, but no one called me back. I couldn't help but wonder if it had something to do with my distinctly Ghanaian name—Nana Abena Kobi Forson. One night I changed the name on my résumé from Nana to Nicole.

My dad always wanted a traditional Ghanaian name for me and my sister, but he went by the name John Elvis Forson for forty years. He was baptized as John (a relic from British colonization) and chose the names Elvis and Forson when he moved from the village to the big city and got a nine-to-five. I guess that is something we have in common.

I printed off a fresh stack of résumés and got five callbacks within a week.

With my new name, my white phone voice, and my cheerful disposition I set up five interviews. Every time I showed up and said, "Hi, I'm Nicole," there would be a long pause and they'd stammer out something like, "Oh, you sound different on the phone." I knew what that meant. But I also knew that if they had called me, it meant that I was fine on paper and all I had to do was get them to like me in person.

I got a job working the register at a sandwich shop. I hated doing service work. One day my boss asked me to move the refrigerator and clean behind it. It seemed like an odd request.

I asked one of my coworkers, "Have you ever done this before?"

"No, girl," she said, and shook her head so I would know that she thought our boss thought I was young and dumb and could take advantage of me. That twisted hot in my chest.

I marched into my manager's office and told her, "I'm not cleaning behind the fridge. You clean it. I quit."

That was how I felt now. The pressure started in my toes and pushed up into my chest. I was going to scream if I didn't quit. Work felt stupid, it felt oppressive. It felt like I was crazy for still being there. But even with my instincts screaming loud and clear, even with my mother's belief, my sister's practicality, I forged ahead with my what-would-people-think-of-me tour. I still had to talk to Josh.

———

After several weeks it was time for Josh to come home.

A few days after that, I picked up the girls. When I pulled into our parking pad with them, our dogs pressed their noses against the sliding glass door with a view of the car. We had awful hanging blinds, and they were shifting wildly as the dogs wagged and wiggled, excited we were home. Inside, Josh was sitting on a kitchen stool exactly where I'd left him twenty minutes before, just staring off.

The commotion of the girls, the dogs, and me snapped him out of his reverie. He smiled and the kids ran to him. Before he got sick, I don't think there was ever a time when Ally had run to Josh and he hadn't swooped her up into the air, thrown her over his shoulder, or swung her around the room. But today he just stood there and let the girls hug him. Daya and Krissy threw their arms around him and Ally hugged his thigh, because that's what she could reach. I ushered the girls into their routine—wash hands, help with dinner, and together we found our family rhythm.

The very idea of the girls seemed to help Josh. He eased back into work and slipped into a groove.

With everyone home I was getting derailed by all the cooking, cleaning, and caring that came with a husband who was healing and three kids. I told Josh I was going to a hotel to work—to film more content, to make my business more formalized, to start building out this course on entrepreneurship I had begun to imagine. I thought I needed to build something more tangible before I could quit. I told myself I just needed three solid days of hard work. But the truth was it wasn't even about me preparing my work; it was about me preparing myself.

It was August, and I told Josh I wanted to quit by November. Surprisingly, he didn't try to talk me out of it. I practically ran out the door before he could utter a word of doubt.

There was a brand-new hotel in Baltimore. When I told them I was going to be there for three days but needed to work and wasn't going to leave the room, they put me in a suite I could never have afforded. The room was C-shaped, with the desk in the middle, as if all the energy in the space was pushing me to work. I set up my computer and went over my aggressive punch list of work to finish while I was there. The throw pillows on the bed were a bright orange. The pop of color called to me, and after I'd reviewed my list, I lay down on the pillow-top bed for a catnap and slept through the entire first day.

I woke up feeling guilty. I'd stolen a day away from my future.

I spent the second day worrying. I'd pace and sit and pace some more, like a caged lion. I'd have a brilliant idea. Then I'd toss it away. I kept thinking, *I need more time.* I still needed to put in vacation to take off for my live event with a big national brand in Tampa later that week. When I looked at my work calendar, I saw that my performance review was scheduled for the next day. I'd been waiting for this review since January. I knew I should update my notes, but I wanted to be working on my business.

I was anxious about my performance review. I didn't know what my new boss would say. He'd probably have feedback about how I could have worked on this or that, that I should smooth out my relationship with Harvey, or maybe he'd say great things, but I didn't care. My thoughts whipped spirals in my brain. Then I was struck with a fierce clarity.

That was the moment I quit. I told myself I had already quit and that the next day was just me telling my boss it was over. I called my husband and braced for impact. "Hey, Josh, I think I'm quitting tomorrow."

God works in mysterious ways. All Josh said was, "Are you sure? Tomorrow?"

"Yes."

"Okay."

"Are you mad?"

"No. Are you going to get another job?"

"Well, I want to try this thing out for a little bit."

"Are you sure?"

"No, but there's money in the bank right now. I can at least try it for a couple months, and I'll keep applying to jobs in the meantime."

Josh dove into practicalities. "Well, the credit card has some room on it. All the bills are paid up. And with the money you've made so far we can take care of the medical bills, and we can pay down the card some more. So that should give us some room as long as the money keeps coming in. But you're going to have to take on a lot of clients."

"Okay."

"Okay." Then we hung up.

A part of me wanted to call my mom and Maame. But I decided not to say anything to anyone else. I already had everything I needed.

I woke up nervous. Light poured into the tall windows as I put on my wig and makeup. I went live and told everyone I was about to quit my job. Immediately, a chorus of responses bloomed on my screen. I got off my live to call my boss. He didn't answer.

I didn't want anyone to feel like I'd left them hanging, so I went live again and explained that I was waiting for my boss to call me back. All my Internet friends were asking me not to end the live session; they wanted to watch.

I didn't even know if I could do that, so using my work phone, I called Josh, who did some quick research and told me that without my boss's consent I could record only my half of the call.

While I was livestreaming, he called.

I forged ahead.

"Hey, Nicole," my boss said.

I had no idea how to do this. I was trying not to look at my personal phone, alive with pyrotechnics. Comment bubbles and hearts streamed up my screen. Then my phone started buzzing with text messages. I had to stay focused and block out all the commentary.

"I actually need to talk to you about a couple of things. The first thing being, effective immediately, I am resigning from the company."

My boss asked me why.

"The reason is that I don't love it anymore." Emotion fluttered in my throat. I took a deep breath and continued, "I'm looking for more. I think the day my heart died was when I said to you, 'What's next? You know, like for someone in my role, what's the next role?' And you said, 'Well, this is kind of what you do for a while.' And I know that that may have been just a quick answer, a quick cavalier thing, but I've gotten that impression for a while. Maybe I'm just doing the wrong job or maybe it's just not the right fit. It's not just about money for me. I have more motivation behind me, and in the meantime, I've established a business for myself outside of this. And I'm super successful and have great opportunities and I just don't feel like I'm being fed in this company. And I don't feel valued. And I learned a lot though. I learned so much in this role and I love the company. That's the part that's hard. I'm just not sure there's an alignment of future trajectory. So, I'm going to work for myself. I'm promoting myself to work for myself."

My boss was surprised, telling me he thought I was a natural salesperson.

We spoke for a few minutes about my passion for my business, about the success I was having, and my desire to do more than simply make money. To my surprise, he told me that if I was making enough money doing what I loved that I should pursue it. As he spoke, all the pressure and worry, the need and stress, the months of sleeplessness, the anxiety over Josh and whether I could take care of the girls the way I needed to—all of it bubbled to the surface. My throat tightened, and my eyes stung.

"I wish I had the guts to just pursue what I wanted to do."

That was one more confirmation. If your goal is to be the boss someday and you can tell that your boss hates their job, then why are you still at that company?

"So what exactly are you doing?"

"I don't know."

"Well, I don't doubt that I'll see you on TV someday."

"Maybe I'll have a company I can hire you for, if you really want to live in your purpose."

He chuckled and we said goodbye.

All my doubt, my equivocation, all the noise in my head went quiet.

I looked at the camera and said, "I guess I just hired myself. I promoted myself to my purpose."

CHAPTER SEVENTEEN

NICE THINGS ARE ONLY FOR WHITE PEOPLE

After I hung up with my boss, everything went quiet. For a moment I sat in the muted tones of the hotel room and just breathed. But then the world rushed in. My phone was vibrating and pinging, messages flooding the screen. My head spun and I was so dizzy I had to sit down. It wasn't the quitting that had upset me. I had already hired myself. It was the tsunami of interest that I hadn't anticipated. I wasn't creating chaos for attention. All the attention created chaos within me. I'd made a radical change in my life, for myself and my family. I had told the people watching I was going to do something and I did it. I didn't realize how many people are talkers and how few are doers, or that actually just doing the thing I said I would might create such buzz.

The blood rushed from my head and limbs; my body felt light and untethered. I could see the momentum building and I stood up and thought, *Am I supposed to do something with this? Am I ready? Am I peaking? What has happened? Oh shit! Oh shit! Oh shit!* Dizzy, I sat down again.

Panic made me stand. Anxiety made me sit. I circled the room like a warped game of musical chairs: sitting in the desk chair, sinking into the tufted velvet armchair, perching on the edge of the bed. It was a good thing they'd given me a suite. The relief I'd felt when I was talking to my boss had been replaced by fear.

I was riddled with doubt. I wasn't sure I could run it by myself. I thought I needed someone to save me. As an entrepreneur coming into my own, I was always looking to someone else to help. The first person I leaned on is the extraordinary woman I'm going to call Gayle—as in she is the Gayle to my Oprah. Gayle and I met through our blog work.

Months before quit day, I had been part of a campaign of some of the top natural-hair bloggers who were dedicating our blogs for a week to talking about racial injustice. Our group had a couple of project planning calls, and I was just happy to be in the room. Everyone was buzzing with ideas and talk of color and design, but very few of the bloggers had a corporate background and the skills to build out a schedule, develop a marketing plan. This is just one of the many little pieces that made me begin to see how I could make consulting for entrepreneurs my full-time business.

I noticed that Gayle would often drive the group's conversation forward, getting us to work strategically. She and I started talking and then developing the plan for everyone else to sign off on. I would get off these calls and look at Josh and say, "If God could just send me someone like that, I feel like I could really quit my job and do this thing." If God could just send me someone like Gayle, then I would have someone who could fill in the gaps and hold me accountable.

Gayle and I spoke the same language, so I wanted her with me in this new phase of my business. She was my entrepreneurial sister. She was also Ghanaian—we share culture, and we share blood. Almost immediately we began conspiring to catapult our businesses and undermine the man. But on my quit day, I wasn't at a place where I felt like I could hire anyone. I felt all alone.

In the hotel room, in the chaos of my quit day, I was panicking. In the bathroom, I splashed some cold water on my face and told myself to breathe.

The phone rang. It was Gayle.

In her very high, clear voice she said, "Hey, Nicole. I've been watching your content for the past couple months and it's pretty inspiring, and I just want you to know that I feel called to help you. I'm here to help you make this whatever this is."

I held the phone away from me for a moment.

"Listen, Gayle, I can't pay you." My whole business and brand are built on the concept of charging what you're worth—don't do free. But at that point, even though I'd made about $50,000, I didn't know what the next six months would look like. Plus, I'd promised Josh I would get another job if I couldn't make enough money. I didn't want to do that, so I was afraid to spend anything. I was going to launch my $1K1Day course, but I didn't know all the pieces. I'd already reached out to other people in my life for help with the technical aspect, and even offered them half the profits in perpetuity, but everyone had said no.

There was a little pause and then she said, "That's okay. I think we'll work it out somehow."

"I don't feel like I can ask you to do that. I don't even know what I need at this point. But what I will tell you is that you will never want. I will never eat before you eat. I will always make sure you are okay, whatever that means and whatever that looks like. I am a hard worker and as long as there is something here to work from, I will do it so that we can get ahead. I will show up."

"Okay," she said simply. I didn't know anything—what the business would look like, whether it would work, how much I would make, but Gayle was there and that felt right.

The other person I leaned on was Chalene Johnson. Chalene is a motivational speaker and online personality, and she came in the package of a person I never dreamed might support me. She dismantled one of my first internal barriers. She was the physical representation of what I thought I should not, could not, attain. Chalene is this petite, bouncy, perpetually positive, ponytailed, tan, fit, blue-eyed human. She loved to work out. She roller-skated. You could mistake her for Malibu Barbie, but that would be your mistake. She is smart, direct, generous, savvy, capable, cool. And that is what we had in common. People could look at me and assume, "Oh, there's a chubby Black woman who doesn't know anything and little did they know, *I'm coming for ya.*" I was capable and confident and able to help people improve their lives.

Chalene and I both recognize what we have and how people view us, but we are not letting that be who we are. It would have been so easy for her to have just played into being pretty and smart and cute. Just like I could have leaned into being an entertainer. But both of us knew we had more to offer.

Chalene had seen me on Periscope. She liked my content and reached out. I had never heard of her, but it turned out she was famous and had built a powerful brand. She encouraged me to use social media to amplify my business (not to be the business itself), and she told me I could really make money in the motivational space, which was an answer to my prayer about being onstage. But Chalene was so casual about it, so California laid-back. I wanted to scream, *I need you to understand that if this thing doesn't work, I'm screwed. There are a lot of factors here that I don't know if you're aware of—I have these three babies and a recently ill husband. I live in my two-hundred-year-old house in Baltimore where I can hear gunshots and helicopters overhead. I appreciate that for you this seems straightforward and that you've worked with other people before, but I am not other people because my life is dear to me. This is not a hobby.*

She offered to mentor me and encouraged me to run my business full-time. So, even though cash was tight, three days after I quit I spent the money to get myself out to California. She had one of the nicest homes I'd ever been inside. My shoes clicked on the marble. Chalene was chatting to me, but the only sound I could hear was my steps reverberating in her foyer. That was a sound I'd only ever heard in museums.

Everything in her orbit had been chosen for beauty and ease. Her house was on a hill—rich people live on hills; it's impractical, but everything they need can be brought to them. The infinity pool overlooked her tennis courts and the whole city. There were three living rooms, stairwells I couldn't even find, and a glitter wall she had specially painted. When I first walked in I saw what she had, and over the coming days I saw how she lived.

I couldn't afford a hotel room, not for that extended period of time, and Chalene had invited me to stay at her house. I saw what her days looked like, how the toilet paper in her bathrooms was as plush and soft as a washcloth, the way her refrigerator was organized with all the fresh fruit and vegetables washed and prepared so she could throw a salad together in a moment. She even fed her dogs fresh food, and I noticed the way her staff cleared out in the afternoon so she could focus on her kids when they came home from school. I saw how Charlene used her money as a tool for creating the life she wanted, a life designed to support her priorities and goals.

Seeing her success imprinted on every inch of her life, I was daunted and confused. Her life was so distant from mine. Until I'd seen this, I couldn't imagine this level of success. It wasn't that I couldn't see it for myself; I had just never seen it. Period. I didn't know what it looked like.

Just like when I'd thought I had a great corporate job and Laura Lerner came along and showed me there were other places that could challenge me, Chalene was here showing me what success could look like and affirming that I could achieve it.

One night we were standing outside chatting. I was looking up at the expanse of stars hovering over the city and asking Chalene business questions. But as I stared at the ocean, I got quiet. I grew up in DC around old wealth, slave money, hedge-fund money, bootlegger money, but I'd never seen self-made money. I was astonished by what she'd built and before I realized it, an inside thought had become an outside statement: "This is a lot. I've never seen anything like this."

"Oh, you'll have this and so much more. You'll make a million within your first year," she said casually. Chalene was telling me *Here's how I did it*. She pointed out that she'd started her business when she had been twenty years older than I was. I just needed to figure it out. Silently, I thought she was crazy. But standing in her home, which she had acquired by being herself and helping people, overlooking Laguna Hills, who was I to say that she didn't know what she was talking about?

The gift Charlene gave me was the transference of belief. I'd walked into her home unable to imagine how big it could be, because I'd never seen anything like it. What I took away was that *I could do it*. I thought I was going to her home for social media tips and strategies for the marketing of products. I walked into her house ready to write everything she said down. I had an old notebook in my hand. She took one look at my old employer's logo printed on it and said, "You have to get rid of that." The next day I ran out and got a new notebook. I had thought this trip was about learning the ropes and that I would see how she made her business successful. But it turns out, I was really there so I could learn what success could look like. I already understood my business, but Chalene transformed my vision of what was possible.

She was the definition of the kind of success I'd been told my whole life I could never expect. And here she was saying to me, No. That's a lie. Yes, you can. By operating in your purpose, you can attain the type of success I had believed could only be inherited.

I didn't want what Chalene had—everything she had was designed by her for her. But seeing her life, I saw that I had been living in someone else's design. I knew I wanted to live a life that I designed.

———

Witnessing what self-made wealth and a self-designed life could look like helped me rewrite the internal narratives I'd learned growing up.

My parents had always expected me to be successful, but they also expected there to be a limit to my success. When I was growing up, I'd ride around DC with my dad and he would point to the big, fancy homes and tell me, "Only white people live there." In a thousand ways, he told me that nice things were only for white people. That nice things weren't for me. When I was younger, that thought was in my head, and it became something I internalized and allowed to limit me. Being an entrepreneur, my taking initiative, my saying, "There's a problem and I'm empowered to fix it," has always been who I am. And the only thing that's ever stood in my way is when I allowed other people's negativity, their projections, their doubt, to cloud my instincts.

I began looking at the things I had been told were obstacles or limitations and realizing that it simply wasn't true. Whether it was my dad telling me that nice things are only for white people, or that I couldn't be a broadcast journalist, or that I needed a particular degree to avoid poverty, or that I shouldn't expect to ever attain a certain level of success because there's no way—people who are poor like us don't ascend that far.

It's so important to interrogate where our thoughts come from. When my kids have thoughts and concepts that don't serve them, I always ask: Who told you that? If you can't come up with an answer, that means it wasn't an original thought and that you don't have to receive it.

My therapist told me that one of the biggest issues we have is that we hear things in our heads in our own voices. We all start off as this blank piece of paper. Everything is put into our heads by someone else. But, because you don't hear it in their voice, you absorb it into your own thought loop, and if you aren't aware, you can end up living your life based on some foolishness you didn't even need to own.

Until age twenty-one I was just hearing everyone else's thoughts in my own voice. Change only really began to take place when I began rejecting those thoughts and said, "That's not me. That doesn't apply. I want to do things differently." Breaking away from those external thoughts is a gradual and ongoing process; it is what led me to start my own business. It's important to reassess—to question not just what you heard but also how you heard it and how it was intended.

Recently I began to rethink what it meant that my dad would say things like "Nice things are for white people." Those thoughts weren't original to him either. He was passing on generational trauma. Originally, it must have been uttered to protect our people. To keep them safe—a warning to stay away from things that look too wealthy, away from things that look too nice, because they probably belong to a white person, and getting too close to them will be to your detriment. But now that phrase lands differently.

Some thoughts you can, and must, rewrite. Nice things are for Black people, white people, purple people. Nice things are for people. We are all deserving. When you buy a small luxury, make sure it's something that leads to your future. An elegant wallet that reminds you to weigh the significance of each purchase and helps you remember what you are saving for, or a computer that enables you to open your own business. You have to lean toward the bigger life you imagine.

But some thoughts must be accepted: You can use the evidence of your life to help tell the truth. There's no rewriting racism. I had to rewrite the idea that there are certain things I'm not allowed to have just because of the way I was born. But the idea that it would be hard to get them and that I have to do specific work is just true. It's a balancing act.

My dad used "white" to indicate something that wasn't attainable because I wasn't born to it. He used "white" as an example of something I would never be, something I couldn't transform into; it was aspirational. When I changed my name he said, "You can call yourself Nicole, but you'll never be white." When I got married he said, "You can marry a white man but you will never be white."

I have literally never wanted to be white. What I wanted was all the options.

It had never even occurred to me to want to be white because I never had a problem with my Blackness. I grew up with immense pride in being African; I was proud of my Blackness. I didn't see my Blackness as something that would limit me. Naturally, I was aware of all the things I would have to fight past and the risks that come with being Black in America. And I understood my lot as a Black woman in this world—that I would be hated, despised, challenged, disrespected, and questioned. All that stuff is true. Racism is real. If you are Black in this country, you're going to have to fight the oppression while you fight for your own freedom, however you define that. That is something I have been aware of since I was very young. I'm going to fight injustice in every way I possibly can, including earning all the money and putting it where it needs to go. However, while I'm carrying my burden, I *am* going to succeed.

So, when my dad said *This is for white people*, what I heard was *Oh, but there's a chance*. What I heard was that for me to acquire it, I was going to have to deal with the challenge of being Black, being a woman, being questioned, abused, and disrespected, but that I could still do it.

Now I believe that my dad telling me that nice things were for white people wasn't him telling me: Don't fly too high. He wasn't trying to keep me away from those things; he was trying to explain that if you want those nice things that white people have, you're going to have to do things beyond what's normal. "Nice things are for white people" is my dad's way of explaining that white people start with a host of advantages, so they have room to fail. For them, there's a backup plan. There's someone who's going to help them. I wouldn't have space to get anything wrong. That's what his experience was. Whereas if you're Black, you can get pulled over at any time, and you can be shot jogging through a neighborhood. There's just no room for you, and that means you can't speak out too much in class, you can't be the person who gets the B. You must aim for perfection. There's no space for flaws. There's no grace. That is what my dad was telling me—you are a Black person, and thus you get no grace. And that's why I am in therapy. I stopped giving grace to myself. I didn't understand how important it was to give grace to others. How critically important grace is to the foundation of life.

No one's coming to save you, so grant yourself some grace as you save yourself.

CHAPTER EIGHTEEN

YOU ARE DESERVING

By Christmas, we had known the girls for a little over a year. Josh had been back at work for a few months, and I had quit my job four months earlier. I wanted the holiday to be special. Up to this point, Christmas for the girls had always been a parade of charity. Presents came from a local toy drive or someone their mom knew dropping off sweaters. The girls struggled to come up with Christmas lists. They didn't know what they wanted. They didn't really have hobbies. More than anything, I wanted to give them the joy of Christmas. As a kid, I'd tried to do the same thing for Maame. I gave my sister everything I could.

My family never celebrated Christmas and we never had a tree. In Ghana there are no pine trees, there's often no electricity, and Christmas meant church. The commercialization of Christmas was something I had to introduce into our home, even in childhood. One Christmas I saved up all my money. When Dad got a fare that took us close to

Woolworths, I persuaded him to take me inside. I moved quickly, before he could change his mind, gathering up a tiny, threadbare two-and-a-half-foot tree and the cheapest ornaments I could find—the Styrofoam balls wrapped in string and the plastic ones with the sharp edges. I carefully chose a few gifts: nail polish, a little stuffed animal, a deck of cards. I wanted to get Maame an Easy-Bake Oven, but I only had enough for an EZ 2 Make! Mrs. Fields Cookie Maker Play Set. When the total popped up in green numerals I saw that I had just enough money. Then the cashier added tax and I was a few dollars short. Dad paid the tax for me.

At home, I happily pushed the little fake boughs through the metal loops of the ornaments and wrapped an old bedsheet around the foot of the tree. A few days later my mother moved the tree and completely redecorated it. I had to admit, it did look better. I wrapped everything up and after Maame went to bed on Christmas Eve I slipped the presents under the tree. I decided to sleep with the lights on so that everything would look perfect when Maame came out. In the morning, she raced out and carefully unwrapped each present. When she saw the cookie maker, her smile lit up the room.

We never even got it to work; I didn't know that it required a light bulb. But it didn't really matter. My mother doesn't like clutter, so before it was time to go back to school, she gathered all the gifts and supervised from our front door as Maame and I carried our toys down the hall to the trash room with the smelly chute that shot down into the bowels of the building. We never sent the toys down the chute; instead, we set them neatly against the wall for some other family to discover.

That Christmas, Josh agreed to a tree, and we all decorated it together, tying an extravagant silver and white bow on top. I stayed up late wrapping presents, imagining the morning—a stampede, the mad tearing of paper, maybe some squealing. On Christmas morning, everyone was wearing the fun pajamas I'd bought, and the girls came down the stairs very quietly. They walked into the living room and sat down like they didn't know what they were doing. The truth was, they didn't.

Ally squatted beside a gift and tapped on it—she had just learned to read her name. "Middicole, this one says Ally." She knew they were for her, but she just kept tapping the packages, not picking them up.

"Guys, let's just open gifts," I said with a clap, and piled their presents in front of them. "Come on guys, go crazy!" They began to open their gifts gently, like people who didn't know they were deserving.

Afterward, Ally curled up on Josh's lap and we all cuddled onto the couch and watched *A Christmas Story* until it was time to drive the girls to their mother.

––––––––––

We weren't parents, but we were parenting and had to start making decisions like parents. Their mother said she was letting us "rich people" help her. Whatever she wanted to call it was fine as long as the girls were getting what they needed.

The girls were coming to a lot of transitions. Should we move to the suburbs where the schools are better and there's more space? Should we stay in the city and consider private school? We'd already struck out with boarding school. Come the following September, Ally would be old enough for pre-K and Krissy would be starting high school, and Daya needed better educational opportunities as soon as possible.

Parenting wasn't easy. One day, I saw a picture of Daya on social media wearing what looked an awful lot like my wig Rebecca (all my wigs have names), and I'd recognize her anywhere.

Let's just be serious about this: if you've been reading this book, you know I believe in grace. I had enjoyed being Daya's auntie, and I wanted her to be able to function in this world. Had I failed as a parent? Accurate. What I needed to teach her was that there were boundaries and limits. She had to learn that you don't play with people's wigs.

When I asked her if she'd been playing with my wigs, she said no. This was a huge deal. There are three rules in our house: no drugs, no babies, and no lying. Josh and I gave each other a look that said, *Oh, now we have to parent. Why is she making us do this? This is so unpleasant.*

"Lying can't be a thing in this house," I reminded her. "If indeed you were playing with my wigs, I need to know. Because what I don't want is a situation where we're not telling each other the truth."

Daya doubled down, swearing on her grandmother's grave that she would never, ever do that. I let it go for another day, then asked her again. Again she denied it. I gave it another two days, but she still wouldn't change her story. Finally, I told her that I knew she was playing with my wigs and that I'd seen a picture.

"Daya, listen, I just want you to understand that the wig was never the issue. It is the fact that you are holding on to the lie and that must have sucked for you."

"Yeah."

"What was that about?" She just looked down at her feet. "Girl. Look. Life lesson: If anyone asks you something more than once, then they already know, so just own it. Don't double down."

The edges of her lips twitched into the faintest smile as she realized I wasn't going to chew her out.

"I want you to understand that I'm here for you and my stuff is here for you, but you have to ask me so that we can make sure we're on the same page."

She nodded, and I reminded her, "And you know I'm not leaving. I'm not going anywhere. But understand that now you're going to get a parent. It's my responsibility to come up with some consequences, which probably would have been small if you had just owned it to begin with. And just so you know, I'm not enjoying this even a little bit. Can you understand that?"

"Yeah, I get it."

For the next few years, she warmed up, she leaned in, she trusted. She was willing to let me come in and take care of her. I was always aware when she did something wrong but most of the time it wasn't worth saying anything, because it was just normal stuff; other times we'd work through problems together. She was a great kid and when we moved to the suburbs, she had top grades and graduated with a 4.0.

I think all Daya ever wanted was a chance to be a kid and figure things out as she went along, developing without worrying about bigger pieces—food, shelter, her sisters, safety. I was focused on the bullet points: love them, let them know they are worthy and wanted, and get them to the milestone marks. And within that we all need rules, parameters, structure in order to do all the things, including loving them. We try to help them hit their marks by giving them tools, but random things happen, and sometimes they miss milestones or they change, and while you as the parent might start to worry about what that means about the rest of the milestones, your kid is over there wondering, *Did I screw up my whole life?* And we have to calmly and truthfully tell them that everything is not over but that we don't have the answers so we're going to solve it together. The core of parenting is always giving them just enough to carry. But figuring out how much is enough is so hard.

I needed each of my girls to know they were deserving. That they were worthy of being loved and celebrated. That they were worthy of good things and nice things, and of joy.

So many of us settle. We settle because we don't really think we are worthy. I'm going to say it again: You were worthy when you woke up this morning, and so were these girls, and so was Josh, and so was I, though that was a lesson I was still struggling to learn.

So many of us are unable to recognize and celebrate our self-worth, even when proof of it is staring us right in the face. Some people don't start their own businesses or chase their dreams because they worry it won't look like what they believe. Spoiler alert: If the reason you aren't doing it is because it won't look the way you imagined it, it never will. It won't look like that when you start, it won't look like that when you are doing it, and it definitely won't look like that when you get there. It will never be what you think. But it can be better than you hoped.

A lot of us won't even try because we are so worried about what other people will think and say. If you think you're going to have this perfectly greased, crystal-clear path to success, where no one's going to have something negative to say, get that idea out of your head. People only talk about folks who are doing something. I have never in my life heard anyone talk about the person who's sitting at home. But they go on and on and on about the person who's on TV, cashing those checks, losing the weight, getting married, getting the house, going on vacation—that's who they talk about. Please let me be *that* person. *You* want to be that person.

I don't subscribe to the "women don't support women" nonsense. It's just not true. I found some of my earliest and most ardent supporters in the group of Black bloggers in which Gayle and I met. They were the first ones to come to my webinars; they promoted everything I did. But as my business took off, a few women complained that our group threads focused too much on monetization, which was one of my buzzwords. The whole point of the group was to support the success of all of us Black women entrepreneurs—and my work specifically was about educating entrepreneurs so they could grow their businesses. And my particular way of doing that was by teaching people how to monetize their passion. Nevertheless, there was resentment as well as doubt that my little blog was making the type of money I was making.

One woman, a really big hair blogger whom I had considered a friend and who had asked me for business advice, called and said, "You're a fake. You're a fraud. One of these days people will catch you." I hung up the phone devastated. Your enemy will use the exact things you fear to try to keep you from your greatness. If someone tells me, "Nicole. all you care about is money," it doesn't affect me—it couldn't be further from the truth. In fact, when I hear that, I recognize it as a calling card of the enemy. But being called an imposter spoke to one of my greatest fears at the time.

I suffered from imposter syndrome. In the very beginning I was shocked by the way money was flowing into my business; I didn't feel like I deserved everything that was coming to me. My life was changing at a pace I couldn't comprehend, and that flew in the face of everything I'd experienced up to that point. I kept asking myself, "Do I deserve all of this?"

And yet, I maintained a conviction that I was living in my purpose. I loved what I was doing and was making money at it. But I hadn't shored up my self-belief. My issues were around self-worth, not around the money itself. I realize how fraught and tension filled people's relationships with money are. But the way I see it, money is an earthly tool for me to be able to do heavenly things.

———————

I talk to God in big and small prayers. For instance, there are tiny prayers in my heart that I never articulate out loud because I feel they're too small for Him to care about. But what's great about my relationship with God is that not only does He know those things but He also delivers them. One of the tiny things I prayed for was a house with a red door and one of those archways connecting the house to the garage.

Oftentimes I don't feel like I'm in a position to be picky with God. I've been given so much already. And I've survived so much that I should just be grateful for what I have. But what I've learned is that it's healthy to have expectations of someone who loves you and it is okay to ask for what you want, and God is not drawing boundaries with me around that.

I wanted the good schools and I'd wanted to get the girls out of their environment in Baltimore, and instead of their feeling like they had to fit into our lives, I wanted us to build a life together.

I settled on two different houses—one that was a very small version of what I wanted, and one that was the God-sized version. I showed them to Josh. The small version was the house I thought I deserved. The neighborhood was a little rougher, the house a little more outdated. Everything was a little cheaper, and some things didn't make sense, like the fact that the refrigerator was smaller and positioned awkwardly, and there weren't enough bedrooms. The house represented inconvenience and discomfort around simple things, but I was used to that and it was still a slight improvement from where we were. The house reflected my planning for where I was then, not where God wanted me to be.

The other house represented a version of comfort I was afraid to get comfortable with. It lent itself to creating and making memories and living with ease—only, I had always thought living was, by nature, a struggle.

When we opened the door for the first time I thought, *Thank you so much, God. This is more than I ever thought I would deserve.* The God-sized house had a red door, an archway that connected the garage to the house, and a room for every kid with walls that were miraculously already painted the color each of them wanted. It had a bathroom the whole family could fit in and chat with me while I was doing my makeup. It was the first home that we'd moved into intentionally— together as a family—and it was exactly what I'd dreamed of.

After we moved in, we'd sometimes spend an afternoon on a long drive through the country. Krissy and Ally would be sitting in the back seat. The girls would ask questions. We'd tell stories. We didn't listen to music. After all the years we hadn't been together, we had too much catching up to do.

One time I pulled over to get gas. Ally watched me through the window and when I sat down to wait for the tank to fill Ally asked, "Middicole, do you think if I call Midder Josh something, he'll laugh at me?"

"Well, I don't know. What do you want to call him?" I asked and waited for whatever she wanted to say.

"Daddy."

I inhaled sharply and bit my lip to hold back my tears. "I think he'd be okay with that."

After that Ally started calling us Mom and Dad, and soon after Krissy and Daya did too.

———

In September, the girls were going to attend some of the top schools in Maryland. Before Ally started pre-K, we had to make sure she was properly immunized. This was the first time I'd taken her to a regular checkup, but this checkup was anything but regular.

After the routine of taking her vitals and administering the immunizations, which I thought was the worst of it, the pediatrician asked the nurse to remain in the room with Ally while he talked to me in the hall. He asked me several questions: So how exactly did they come into your life? Ally is a little on the smaller side; has she always been this way? I also noticed there are some scars on her lower back; do you know what they're from? They had to file a report with Child Protective Services (CPS) because she was too small. I knew Ally was tiny, but she had a healthy appetite and ate well. I didn't know that she was severely underweight, because I wasn't the one taking her to the doctor and I'd never had a five-year-old before. CPS came to interview us and inspect our home, and their investigation determined that the only way that the kids were safe was if they stayed with us instead of their mother. The way CPS saw it, we had worked out an arrangement that was working for everybody. As long as the arrangement was intact, they weren't going to strip the mother's parental rights. Their mother and father came to a meeting with CPS and me and we all agreed on what was best for the girls. CPS didn't give us permanent custody, but they did give us an official document that granted court-authorized custody, which had to be renewed every year. It was more than the little piece of paper we'd been working off for two and a half years.

The girls were thriving. They were building a structure. They were getting great habits. They were like plants in a garden with premium poop. We were a hot mess, but somehow the mess was coming together beautifully, and the girls were soaking up the nutrients and actually growing.

While the girls were flourishing, I was panicking. My life had become a double-edged sword. After sleeping on the couch as a kid, I was in this magnificent mansion, with these gorgeous kids that I'd spent years caring for, and the first day I had a panic attack. I couldn't even give myself twenty-four hours to rest. The new house had more than doubled our mortgage payments and everything that made our new home special reminded me that the bar had been recalibrated. I worried about how I would keep it up. I worried about how I was going to get us to our next thing. I worried that I would let the girls down.

I said to them, "I'm an entrepreneur—it's an up-and-down thing. You can trust that I'm saving, and I'm not taking big jumps without being prepared, but I'm doing this new thing and I don't know how it'll work. I'm hoping people keep showing up, that I keep doing a great job, and I will work day and night to make the money. But things can happen, you know? If I can't afford to keep our awesome new life going, would you guys be okay if we had to go back to something smaller?" I imagined us all huddled in a car.

The girls looked at me.

Then Krissy asked, "Would you still be there?"

I looked at her confused. Then I realized and said, "I'm not going anywhere."

"Okay."

But even with their blessing, for our first few months in the suburbs I felt like I didn't belong. I was in someone else's dream and at any moment it would all be taken away. This life was for white people. (I know this because everyone in my neighborhood was white. But . . . I was there. There's always got to be a first and I'm okay being first.) This feeling was confirmed when I got a notice from the homeowners association that the weeds in our garden were too high. I put on some old clothes, got down on my hands and knees, and began weeding.

"Oh, no, no, no. Don't do that. People are going to see." It was my neighbor, whom I'll call Cathy. She was a dream neighbor. My family and I were different from everyone else in the neighborhood, and she was open to us—generous, gracious, and kind. She often helped with Ally—picking her up from the school bus, inviting her over to make cookies or play.

"Well, who's going to do it? I've got to get the weeds out of here."

"Stroke that check, girl. Get that done."

I didn't care who saw me weeding, but Cathy was telling me a lot more than about hiring a gardener. She was explaining to me that I needed to use my money to give me time. Time to invest in my business. Time to spend with my family.

With those words, Cathy became my "how to think rich" coach. I learned by observation. Money is a great tool to access the things you want. Shocker: Rich people do everything differently. Everyday people pick the cheapest flights; rich people select the flights that are most convenient for them. When non-rich people move, they get a new lease and move in twenty-four hours—packing and schlepping in a frantic mess of U-Haul rentals, parking tickets, friends volunteering. But if you're rich, you hire someone to do it for you. You take your time, and you walk into your new home with everything unpacked, organized, furnished, and your refrigerator stocked. It was another lesson that money is about having choices, about having room to breathe.

But as Cathy was teaching me how to be rich, I just kept worrying about how to keep what I'd gotten—not just for myself but also for my family. Rather than putting all my energy toward envisioning how to grow it, I was afraid of losing it. My fear threatened to turn me into an enemy of my own progress.

———————

For a long time I carried the trauma of poverty into every decision I made. Trauma is the emotional response to a terrible experience—whether that's poverty, abuse, loss, or an accident. Trauma affects your decision-making; it rewires you to disbelieve your own worthiness. People often talk about the trauma of poverty in the context of crime or substance abuse, but it doesn't have to be only that—trauma can also affect your joy. When something good happens, you immediately wonder if the rug is going to be pulled out from under you. You know how you got there. You know the work it took to get there. You just don't believe the good thing will stay or that the opportunities will keep coming. You can't be happy in the moment if you are always worried about the next thing and that's often a direct result of trauma. Because I was so used to being without, I didn't allow myself to experience hope in its complete form. I always felt like I had to reserve something for when I would have to fight back again. I still carry that, but because I can see it now, I have started making decisions to fight against that tendency.

We are all automatically hardwired for greatness. You are good enough to be in the room. You are good enough to be loved. And when you have success, you deserve to enjoy it.

CHAPTER NINETEEN

NO ONE IS COMING TO SAVE YOU

I was on the cusp of something big. Chalene had invited me to her large annual marketing training event. All the speakers go to teach, network, and offer their services to thousands of attendees who come for information and inspiration. The year before, I'd spoken onstage and had so much fun. It was easy. I wasn't selling a product; I was there to entertain. But this time I would be speaking in front of my biggest audience yet—fifteen hundred people—and this was an opportunity to offer my $1K1Day product and reach a whole new audience. ($1K1Day is a program I created to help my students develop a business through sustainable, legitimate corporate strategies.)

I started to prepare. I picked out the perfect outfit. I went over everything with my first employee. At home, I cooked meals for all the days I'd be gone—pasta sauce, a curry, a big container of rice. I stacked everything in the refrigerator in the order it should be eaten so nothing would go to waste, and then I typed out a menu of what they should eat each day, so Josh had to do as little as possible. For our entire marriage, I had plated his food every night—I didn't want any disruption while I was away.

Everything was packed, but I still hadn't finalized my speech. I'd been dancing around writing the keynote, finding every positive distraction* under the sun. There were a whole host of things holding me back. One of them was that I wanted to share my daughters' story for the first time. People knew I had my girls—I called them "the tinies"— but I hadn't really talked about them. I never wanted it to seem like I was using them, but I also knew that, as somebody who was going through parenting, to not talk about them was not authentic to who I was; parenting my girls was a big part of how I was growing. Finally, at the last minute, I pulled a speech together, hugged my family goodbye, and left for California.

As our plane was readying for takeoff, my phone rang. It was my employee, my head of operations, the person who handled the day-to-day workings of my business—my new number two. "Hey, Nicole, I wanted to let you know I'll be terminating, effective immediately."

"I'm sorry?"

I was headed to my biggest event ever and I had no one to manage the business. As I hung up, my heart sank and my head spun. Frantically, as the flight attendants were telling us to put our electronics away, I called Gayle.

———

Since she had joined me in building the business, Gayle was the person who was with me. Gayle had a rare suite of abilities that allowed me to ramp up the business the way I needed to. And she was willing to show up to an opportunity and share some of the risk even though she didn't have to. Gayle was willing to chase my dream as if it were her own. We

---

*   Positive distractions are doing things that are valid—like spending time with your kids, working out, even working on other business things except the task you most need to do, the one that actually propels you forward.

had long conversations about our goals—for the business and for our lives. We were sisters.

We're very well-balanced. She is as introverted as I am extroverted and she is the marketing strategist, whereas my strengths are financial and business consulting. She helped me with her marketing genius; I coached her in how to develop her business. I hired her as a consultant, and although she was still working on building her own firm, she really was my head of operations and she kept me on task. She'd say, "Nicole, we have to get this done," "Nicole, I need this for a turnaround," "Nicole, we have to get this material finalized." Sometimes I'd be exhausted or annoyed, but I'd remember what I'd promised her—I would show up.

Gayle showed up too. She found events and I pitched them. She was the assist to my jump, the Pippen to my Jordan. She's very good at keeping her eye out for opportunities and I'm very good at slaying them. She was always looking for the big gig that would catapult me to the next level. She wanted me in bigger and bigger rooms.

It's important to have the right people around you. We are hardwired to feel fear when we come up to the ledge, even if we're about to jump into the pool that we brought ourselves to. That's why having someone who's cheering you on from the other side of the pool, rather than someone who's saying "That's dangerous, don't go," is so important.

The people we surround ourselves with can lend us belief, or they can lend us fear.

I don't know about you, friend, but I have enough of my own fear. I don't need someone else's. I can't have someone who has their own money fears speaking to me when I'm doing entrepreneurship; I'm scared enough. It's even better if you can find someone to help you release your fears. That's the beauty of mentorship. Sometimes it's not just about finding someone who's able to show you the way, to point out the missteps; it's about just finding someone to lend you their belief until you can build your own.

Gayle and I were an amazing team. We also fought a lot. We fought when I didn't understand how important a deadline was. We fought when there was a product she didn't want to spend money on even though my business could afford it. We fought because we loved each other and the work we were doing. We were fighting to stay together, not break apart.

We were both growing. She had a vision about how her work and life would be shaped, and I am *a lot*. And Gayle was working on how to draw boundaries with her clients. She is a very dedicated business partner, but she is also a very private person, and for a long time I knew very little about her personal life. I did know that Gayle spent every Friday with her mother. And while I appreciated the time she spent with her mom, as a new business owner things came up, and I'd occasionally call with something I needed to wrap up right away. She always gave me that time.

Then one day, about three months before my flight to Chalene's event, Gayle told me things had shifted in her life and that she was terminating our contract; she wanted to focus on building her own business. I heard everything she said. Professionally, I knew she had every right to focus on her own business. But personally, I was devastated. How could she leave me? We were friends. She had lent me her belief. I didn't know for sure if I could run the business without her.

Not wanting to leave me in the lurch, she offered to stay on long enough for me to hire and train some staff support. I dragged my feet hoping she would change her mind, but eventually we hired and spent three months training a bright young woman. This was the woman who had just called to tell me I was on my own.

Back on the plane, I explained the situation, panic creeping into my voice. "You can't leave now," I pleaded with Gayle. "I know you were scheduled to leave, but you can't. I'm calling in a favor as a friend. I'm about to get onstage. I've already committed to doing this speech. We're at an inflection point. . . . I can't. I can't. I need one more week. This is crazy."

And then Gayle taught me a powerful lesson on boundaries. "I'm sorry that this is happening to you. Unfortunately, the contract is done. It just is what it is."

I didn't even have time to call Josh—the airplane wheels retracted and I lost service. I was in the air.

For the next six hours I sat with my anxiety. My hands were sweating. My heart was racing.

By the time the plane landed, I had decided my keynote wasn't good enough. Though really, I thought I wasn't good enough.

I carried all my doubt into the sound check, which is supposed to give you ease that you're ready. All the speakers were there, and they sailed through their talks and managed their slides effortlessly. My deck wasn't even done. When I felt how solid that stage was, I knew that I wasn't. The stage was vast. There were lots of screens. I fumbled the remote for my slides, I fumbled my talk. I hadn't left myself enough time to practice my speech and it wasn't flowing. I felt like a rookie. I was sure I was going to fail and embarrass myself. I thought I had to change the whole thing, that it wasn't good enough. That the audience would hate it. That it was too salesy. I stared out at the thousands of empty seats and my stomach became a pit.

Speaking from stage is not an easy thing to do. You have forty-five minutes to transfer belief. You have to tell a story that takes people on a journey. You have to be vulnerable so that people can see themselves in you. You have to get the audience to believe that your system works so they can believe in themselves. But you cannot transfer belief if you don't have any.

I was terrified to ask people to join my journey. I didn't feel like I had a right to do that. I was acting like I was holding the audience hostage, rather than that they were willing participants. How was I going to deliver something that was really going to serve? How could I go onstage and tell these people how to build a business when right then I was running this all by myself? I thought to myself, *I'm a fraud. I'm not good at any of this.*

How many times are we in the room, questioning our seat at the table even though we are already at the table? Some of us even built the damn table! But we're still sitting there saying that we don't deserve it. What a waste of time, what a waste of brain space.

I was afraid and I made the mistake of thinking that my fear meant something; that there must be truth behind it. That is never the case. I still get scared. But now I recognize that the fear doesn't define me.

By the time I was supposed to go onstage, I had criticized myself to pieces—my speech, my outfit, my whole business. It's like when you're getting ready to go out and your shoes, your hair, your lipstick, none of it is right, so that after the fourth outfit change you don't want to go out anymore. Only I still had to show up.

Chalene gave me a warm introduction; the audience was beautiful. Then I stepped out into the bright lights and everything was wrong. I was awash in fear, but I couldn't leave the stage, or the room. And whether my performance was bad or good or someplace harmlessly in the middle, inside I was falling apart.

I could feel the sweat dripping down the small of my back. My Spanx were boa-constrictor tight. I kept talking but the audience felt so far away. I was suffocating onstage, in front of over a thousand people.

When I got offstage, Chalene handed me a margarita.

I looked at her and said, "I'm sorry."

"No." She smiled wide and gave me a publicist's spiel about how everyone loves me. That Chalene wouldn't tell me the truth—I was terrible—only made it worse. What I needed was balanced context. Like, *Hey, this was good and this bit you need to work on. But remember, what you did was more than good enough because you did it. There are fifteen hundred people who are still sitting out there who didn't do it, and one person who did—and you're sitting here beating yourself up. What the heck is wrong with you? You did it! Whatever happened happened; now move forward.* That's what Gayle would have done, just laid it out practically so we could learn from it.

Someone put a stack of order forms in my hand.

My whole body was hot. My clothes felt too tight. I wanted to rip my wig off and cut my Spanx with shears. I set the margarita down and fled. I willed the elevator doors shut before anyone else got on, jabbing my finger into the button. The small box felt close and airless. I was on mile twenty-five of an emotional marathon. I was spent and sucking in air but not getting any oxygen. In my hotel room I stripped off my clothes and wig and collapsed on the bed sobbing. I just needed to breathe. But I couldn't.

This is it. This is how I fail. This is the end of the business. The dream.

My phone was ringing and buzzing and pinging. I was sure it was alerts from the apocalypse—my bank telling me my account was empty or my husband telling me that the house had been repossessed. When I finally looked at my phone, I realized they were orders.

Then I remembered I had no one to manage them. The idea of getting them all into the system was overwhelming. Rather than proof of success, this was simply another thing I would fail to deliver on. Downstairs, onstage, I had just told over a thousand people how to build a business. I was offering a course on entrepreneurship, and I was sitting there in my hotel room, a business of one.

There was a knock on my door. I threw on a bathrobe and peered through the peephole. There was a woman in a black pencil skirt and bright blouse. "Nicole," she said through the door. She introduced herself as Dr. Mcayla. I recognized her; Chalene had introduced her earlier. She was a psychotherapist who was also speaking at the event. Tentatively I opened the door. She was calm and clear, and her energy pulsed out into the chaos of my room. I was hopeless at that point. Nicole Walters had left the room. In my place was nine-year-old Nana doing her best to navigate this big world. Dr. Mcayla was trying to talk about my feelings, but I was having a full-blown panic attack. What I needed were logistics. Instructions on how to put one foot in front of the other.

I slumped on my bed while she sat in the armchair. She didn't look at my Spanx rolled up on the floor or the rumpled sheets or the way my bathrobe gaped open—she looked me right in the eye and explained that I was having a panic attack. We didn't talk about the high-level things that had brought me to this point. We didn't talk about my keynote. In her soothing voice she had me break down what I could do at that moment, how I could take immediate problem-solving steps. On the hotel notepad she began making little drawings. With a few strokes of the pen she broke down the state of affairs.

Dr. Mcayla told me, "You need a session; you need several sessions. You need to come to therapy and unpack all of this. No matter what, life is still here. There are still problems. You still need to solve them." What I heard was: *You're crazy. We're all crazy. No one's coming to fix it for us and you still have stuff to do today. So, what are you going to do? Sit here and worry about being crazy? Or are you going to do the stuff you need to do knowing that you're going to have to keep working on your crazy, because these are your options. That's it.* She said it all in a Dr. Mcayla-clinical-professional way, which was very nice.

She helped me realize that I can only do what I can do, which is the next right thing. And that whatever I chose had to be something I could actually do.

"So, right now, because this isn't going to be a quick process, I need you to understand that we need to look at these problems"—she gestured to her drawings—"and figure out what we can do. What can you do here, in the hotel room?"

"I can input the orders. I can eat. I can sleep."

"Very good. Which ones are you going to do?"

I pointed to the list I'd made.

"Very good."

Her words were a lifeline; her calm a preserver. If I could just figure out what I could do in that moment, I would do that until I could get to the next thing.

Chalene had brought me there so that I could transfer my belief to the audience members, and here Dr. Mcayla was transferring her belief to me. She believed I could save myself. One step at a time, she guided me out of my panic attack. I stopped crying. Oxygen eased back into my lungs. She wrote her number down on the pad, encouraged me to make an appointment, and then left.

Well, if these were my last sales ever, I could process them. I could serve them well. The simple thought *What can I do? I can be a person who will do what I say I will do* has been something that has held true in my whole business. I looked in the system and realized I didn't even know what to do with the first order. So, I figured it out, step-by-step. Then I processed tens of thousands of dollars' worth of orders that had come through since my talk—the talk to end all talks, the talk that had me hyperventilating about my failure because of my disappointing performance.

By the time I was done I felt spent, but the tension in my back and the lump in my throat had dissipated. It was as if my body realized that the marathon I'd been running was actually over.

———————

Confidence is actually saying that you're afraid out loud. I start a lot of my speeches with an admission. If I stutter while I'm onstage, instead of my being embarrassed, I just say, "I'm sorry, I recognize that I just stuttered there." Just get it out of the way. Stand in the truth with them. People aren't looking for perfection. They are looking for honesty. When I say my Spanx are really tight I know everyone's thinking, *Girl, me too.* We're all going through it.

Life gets hard. Problems will occur. No one's coming to save you, and no one's coming to do all the work for you. You won't be rescued and whisked off someplace safe. However, saving yourself doesn't mean you're on your own. You're not an island, having to figure it out by yourself, and you're not a superhero having to do more than is humanly possible. At every turn there are life preservers, but it's up to you to reach out and use them. People can drown surrounded by life pre-servers—because they don't think they're big enough or because they don't believe they will hold their weight. Things are always happen-ing to help you save yourself; however, you still have to receive the help.

God sent Dr. Mcayla to my door and I opened it.

When you go into rehab and say, "I have a problem," you are saving yourself. When you ask for help, you are saving yourself. When Krissy, the girl who would cry when we asked her to order what she wanted because she was too nervous, said out loud that she wanted something different from her life—she helped save herself.

No one was coming to save me. Gayle wasn't coming. My first employee wasn't coming. Josh wasn't coming. Once I accepted that no one was coming to save me, and that I was able to save myself, then everything was different.

CHAPTER TWENTY

YOU ARE THE ONLY YOU

When I got home from the gig, there was nothing more sobering than the knowledge that I had to run this thing myself. I left with a team and came back without one. The business was already too big for me not to have a person.

I confided my fears to Josh. "I have a business I've never run by myself."

Josh looked at me and said, "You've always been by yourself. Chalene wasn't there when you started your business. Gayle wasn't at the table when you decided to quit your job. You were already doing it by yourself."

I wasn't convinced, but unless I wanted to give up and go back to corporate, I didn't have a choice. So, decision by decision, I ran my business.

I missed Gayle every day. I was mad that I had to do my business by myself, but mostly, I just missed her. I was hurt, scared, and worried about her. I didn't like the boundary she had drawn, but I respected it. I knew calling and texting would feel like too much pressure, so, instead, I'd write her emails telling her I was still there for her and that I loved her and cared about her. I didn't care about her coming back, but I wanted to know that she was okay.

If you want to be seen, you have to tell people where you are. People can't pay you if they can't find you. So, it is important to go places you may not typically go, and Gayle was always really good about looking for new places for me to go. We both knew that if she could get me in the door that I'd close the deal.

The motivational-speaking world is still fairly segregated. While Black entrepreneurs will follow and pay white motivational speakers, a lot of white entrepreneurs don't even know about the Black speakers, which makes it harder to break into the higher echelons. The average Black woman is becoming an entrepreneur at a rate of nine times that of the average American. We are jumping into entrepreneurship, but we are lacking in visibility, which affects our access to investors and venture capital. Because I'd had a platform in a white space at Chalene's event, I was strategically positioned.

I pitched myself to a personal-finance expert I'll call Jim, host of a popular show, a devout Christian, and an exciting entrepreneur who'd built a big business helping people with their finances. He was starting a new brand geared toward women. If I could speak there, I would reach a whole new audience.

Jim's team said no. They didn't know who I was, and they were very careful about who they brought into the fold. Before anyone spoke on Jim's stages, they had to do a series of calls with his team. These aren't regular work interviews. They are deep assessments of character. They want to know about your personal life, your belief system, your moral code, even your financial standing.

But when the person they had booked dropped out, they called to get to know me. I loved it. The team was made up of warm, good people who genuinely wanted to help and serve the world. I was thrilled I'd booked the gig, even though it was just a talk on a small stage and a panel discussion.

I approached it with the same intention I had approached *Wheel of Fortune*—I would give it my all, and make sure that I left a sprinkling of Nicole on that stage and in every room. If you are given an opportunity to use the mic, be prepared to use it well. The world is going to respond to what you give—so give good.

I gave a talk on business-building strategy, and the audience responded. I talked to everyone from the janitor to the camera guy to the person running the event. I learned their names, their work, if their work made them happy. I got on that small stage and performed as if it were a stadium. I found out that the team always surveys their audience members. My ratings were so high that they asked me to stay an extra day and come speak to the entire team.

The building was a small brick one. I saw one of the personalities who is part of Jim's brand walk through the lobby; the air shifted around them. People come from all over to commemorate getting out of debt. That day a couple was telling their story. I clapped and hollered along with everyone else in the lobby and felt a pulse of energy zing through the room. Jim drew people in and changed their lives.

It's important to see where people start. Whenever I drive by businesses with my kids, I remind them that every single business was started by one person—it doesn't matter how big or how many of them there are now—and that one person was just like them.

When I saw Jim's building, the studio, the audiences, I thought, *Oh, this is what I want to build.* I was able to see how someone had turned the work I was doing into more. Jim had leveraged his name to hire hundreds of people. I stood there taking it all in. Just as seeing Chalene's life and work had opened up my vision for what self-made success could look like, seeing Jim's empire taught me about scale. I had never imagined anything like this. Looking around, I could see how much bigger my business could become. I had been thinking too small.

We can only dream as big as the world we've seen. We'll never be able to dream as big as God has for us. If you want to go to the next level, you need to see new things.

Sometimes you have to go places that are really uncomfortable for you. Sometimes we think that if we don't have anything to offer, or if we don't think we can attain a particular outcome, that we don't need to go. But the reality is that sometimes you need to stand in the room so God can do whatever He needs to do for you. So you can receive whatever it is you're meant to receive. Sometimes it isn't about going somewhere with some magical intention, it's about stepping into the room to receive whatever the heck is going to be sprinkled on you.

I had gone out there to reach new people, and I left with a whole new vision around how big my business—and maybe even my whole life—could be. For me, this was a season of learning. Over the next year, I was booking gigs. I was building the foundation. I brought my membership group up to over $1 million in revenue. I hired a team. Although managing people was not where I wanted to spend my time, it was a skill that served me well. I knew I could do it but I didn't want to. I was doing everything my business needed and I could see what I knew to be true—God kept showing up for me.

And I kept showing up to do the work. No matter my performance, I showed up at the marketing event, I showed up for my business when I returned, and I showed up when I'd gone to Tampa and given them my best self.

Sometimes people ask me how they can stand out. I always tell them there is only one you. You can't fall behind other people if you aren't running the same race as they are. If you want an edge, be personal where everyone else is technical. Automate your systems and not your relationships so that you can be more of yourself. You are the only you. The flip side of that is that there is only one you. You must care for yourself, replenish, and nourish. You are your most precious resource, and you are finite.

———

During this season I was caring for Josh, I was caring for the girls, I was caring for my business, but I wasn't caring for myself. When I'd come

back from the marketing event, I did an intensive session with a therapist, but I treated it like my way out of "real" therapy—I wanted her to
quickly put me back together so I could get back in the game. I didn't
have time to be an emotional wreck. For a long time I didn't do therapy,
because I felt like it wasn't a financial priority and because I thought I
couldn't take the time to do it when there were so many other things
that needed to be done. Things always need to be done. Caring for yourself has to happen—no matter what else is going on. That is nonnego-
tiable. But that's not what I'd learned as a kid.

I grew up believing that caring for myself is frivolous. My mom wore
her selflessness like a badge. She chronically puts herself last. She dedicated her whole life to caring for my dad and she does not know how to
prioritize herself. She's the person who goes to a party and spends the
whole time cleaning up rather than sitting down and then complains
that her feet hurt.

A lot of people think that trauma is informing only the negative
things in your life, but it can also inform your perception of the positive
things.

I share a Slack channel with some of my top clients. At one point
they were all chiming in about how stressed they were—"I have to
go to this pitch," "I just had a breakdown," "I'm crying." Eventually,
I gave them an ultimatum: I'd close the group if they didn't all start
working on finding a therapist. By three o'clock that day, I wanted
to know that all of them were interviewing therapists or that they'd
already booked a session. If I had said to get an accountant, they'd
do it, because that's quantifiable. It is harder for many of us to justify
therapy, and yet a therapist is as essential to your business and your
life as an accountant, a lawyer, a doctor—you need one. Every single
one of them did it.

Then my clients and I were able to get back to focusing on business.
Some of them decided they needed to switch their overall business
ideas, which helped them really step into their work. Some ended
up working ten times harder because they stopped wasting time on
narratives that didn't serve them. But those are not things that happen

through more work in your business; all that stuff is actual inside work. But that deep emotional work serves you in every aspect of your life. One client started therapy, lost sixty pounds, competed in an Ironman, and then crossed the multimillion-dollar mark.

Whenever I can detect that a client is feeling unfulfilled in one way or another, I send them to figure out what that is. I'm not going to let them stand around and expect me to tell them it's their business. Without therapy, either you'll never make the money or you'll make it and you won't enjoy it.

What if I told you that you could enjoy life more? What if I told you that your cake today would actually taste even better if you weren't thinking about your ninth birthday when it was destroyed? We all carry so much and yet so many of us are afraid to do therapy. Therapy is essential.

Your brain's internal narratives can be dangerous because they put a rule system around problem-solving that doesn't necessarily integrate who you are, what you're facing, and what your best abilities are. That's a huge problem, because if your internal narratives aren't aligned with who you are, you will constantly be at odds with yourself.

Imagine the voice of somebody like a six-foot-four man telling you the rules of lifting a boulder. Of course you're going to feel like you can't do it, because it's being driven by this narrative that doesn't belong to you. That doesn't mean you don't have the problem to face, but you can alter your approach to the problem based on what you believe you're capable of doing, which includes tapping into your resources and asking for help. But you can't get there if you keep thinking you're supposed to perform like the person who put that narrative in your head. Imagine how much more you could achieve if all your energy and strengths were in alignment.

CHAPTER TWENTY-ONE

SEASONS OF STILLNESS

I'd made enough of an impression that Jim's team wanted to continue our conversation, and we began a business dance. Over the next few months, I came down a couple of times to meet with the team. I did events with them. I went on tour with them. I met with Jim. After about four months they told me that Jim loves to find new talent to support his mission. "We would love for you to come on board."

They told me I would do very, very well and be very impactful, but that I had to understand that I was coming on as talent—the role of CEO was already filled. They were offering a lot of what I thought I needed: access, a team, direction. My family and my business wouldn't want for anything, but I had to be sure I'd be there forever. I headed to Tampa for a final meeting with the Krouse team.

When I sat down with Jim, I was up-front: "The only reason I think I may want to work with you is because I'm not sure if I can do this myself and ultimately, the only thing standing in the way of my coming on board is that I'm worried that if I don't say yes to this that I'll never be able to get where I'm supposed to be in life, like I won't get to what God has for me." I didn't want to make this decision based on doubt. I wanted to make it based on belief.

Jim said to me, "No matter what, you're going to get there. Because you and I are the same. The only difference is will you get there as fast without me?"

Fortunately, God being so good, what I took from what he said was that I could do it. It may not be as "fast," but as long as I was okay with doing it in God's time and not my own, it would be good.

During this season, I was in internal turmoil. Running my business was hard—I loved it and hated it. I felt like I wasn't being a good enough mom because I was working all the time.

I was also working on my faith, which was being challenged. After parting with Gayle, I asked God, *Why did you put me in this position? Everything was coming along nicely. What are you trying to prove? Is this what I prayed for?* Because basically if I joined Jim's team I would get everything and almost right away. I would get the platform. I would be able to do the thing I said I wanted to do, which is go in every day and reach people with podcasts, books, and talks onstage everywhere. (Jim can make one phone call and put me in whatever room.) I could have all of that instantly. And I could go home every day by five, because it's all built in.

I kept saying to myself, *This is exactly what I'm trying to build, and here it is prepackaged; why wouldn't I take it?* I couldn't find a rational reason to say no. And yet, when I thought about saying yes, I felt this weight.

I spent a lot of time up late at night sitting outside by myself. I wrote in my journal, listened to the crickets, watched for shooting stars, talked to God, and waited for him to talk to me.

I started looking at homes to move my family—a prerequisite to signing on with the team. But I was still cycling through these conversations with myself about whether God was asking me to humble my-self.

I wished I had a mentor I could go to for guidance. And the very lack of that figure was further emphasizing that maybe I needed to do this.

Josh and I talked through all the pros and cons of moving. He's so even, which is his best trait and his worst. Sometimes I want to scream, *Can you please meet me at my level of anxiety?* Always, very evenly, he responds with calm, as if to say, *No, I'm not joining you. This isn't an event, and we don't need to make it one.* "We'll do whatever you want to. It'll be fine one way or another," Josh assured me.

I was trying to will myself into a decision. I wrote in my journal:

> June 7, 2017: I will work for Jim.
>
> June 12: Working on my faith and my religion. I'm going to be on Jim's team because I'm capable and I'm good enough to do so.
>
> June 13: The reason why I didn't want to do this was I felt like I wasn't worthy of the opportunity.
>
> June 15: I'm grateful for the opportunity. I just want some structure and consistency. I'm grateful for choices, because there are so many people that don't have them or feel like they don't, and that sucks.

My brain turned circles until I thought I might go insane. And then I talked to my friend, the daughter of a pastor. She was the Bible App before Bible App—she could give you a verse for anything. When I told her my struggle, she said, "Have you asked Him?"

"I don't know how to ask Him."

She texted me a piece of scripture. Amos 9:13–15:

Things are going to happen so fast your head will swim, one thing fast on the heels of the other. You won't be

able to keep up. Everything will be happening at once— and everywhere you look, blessings! Blessings like wine pouring off the mountains and hills. I'll make everything right again for my people Israel.

I sat with these words for days. Every time my anxiety bubbled up, I prayed. I recited the scripture and talked to God. After I prayed, I had the impulse to say no to the offer. I was confused. My head was already swimming. But instead of the lightness of blessings, I felt chaotic. I wasn't sleeping properly, I was short-tempered, I was anxious. Knowing that God is not the author of confusion, I decided that what I needed right then was to focus on my family.

I took a few weeks off to be with the girls, to be still with myself, to be quiet. I didn't take on new gigs, but I kept the gigs I'd already committed to. In the stillness I thought about the three things that appealed to me most about joining Jim's team. One of the things my heart ached for most was community. The idea of being in an office full of people instead of living in suburban Maryland was hugely appealing. I also needed mentorship. I wanted to know where I was going and not feel so alone on the journey. I also wanted freedom from my responsibility as CEO.

Sometimes as a business owner, or a mom, we burn out. Not because we're not good at what we do, not because we don't love it, but because we're exhausted. But when you're burned out it's hard to tell what you really want, and my burnout had me thinking I didn't want to run my business anymore.

When you're exhausted, you want to burn everything down. Anytime someone who loves what they are doing tells me they don't want to do that thing anymore, even though there's not something fundamentally broken in their business, I know they are burned out. If you feel like that, take time off. And not just a personal day but an intentional and substantial amount of time. If you keep going, that feeling you have of wanting to quit is going to permeate everything until the thing you've created quits itself. Take time off, because if you don't, it really doesn't matter what's there when you get back.

You can't stand still as an excuse not to do, but sometimes instead of trying to push, you need to flow. This was the first time in my life that I allowed myself to realize that *not* doing is also a choice. That not-doing could also be a way of saving myself. Saving yourself isn't always a forward-moving action. Sometimes it's standing still.

CHAPTER TWENTY-TWO

GUARD YOUR GREATNESS

In the middle of my break, I was scheduled to speak in Boise, Idaho, at the Craft + Commerce Conference. I flew first class. First class as an entrepreneur is a business investment. It means I'm sitting next to either my clients or my partners. I am an extrovert, so for me to not put myself in the room when they are being held hostage for two and a half hours is crazy.

I was on a crack-of-dawn flight to Atlanta. A man sat down beside me and I issued my standard caveat: "Hi, my name is Nicole. I'm sitting next to you. I'm an extrovert. I recognize it is early. You don't have to talk to me but if you are a talker, I am a talker."

He exhaled an awkward little laugh and then I peppered him with questions about his security company, his passion, his journey. We landed in Atlanta and I boarded my flight to Boise. I was seated beside this standard-bro entrepreneur who was typing away on his laptop trying to squeeze every second out of the minutes before takeoff. Classic entrepreneur.

So instead of doing my intro, I said, "Oh, I'm an entrepreneur too. I'm actually heading to Boise for a conference."

We chatted about the conference, and I told him I was one of the speakers. He told me he ran a software company. But he didn't say much else until the plane started to take off and he had to put away his computer and surrender to our conversation. His company was called SamCart, and then I realized that he was Brian Moran, one of the pioneers in Facebook ads.

I told him about my business and he grinned at me. "I knew you were an entrepreneur when you got on this plane at five a.m. talking about what your purpose is. I heard your conversation on the last flight and thought, 'Please don't let that be who I'll be sitting next to.'"

I loved his playfulness; it matched my own wit. It turned out that he lived twenty minutes from my house in middle-of-nowhere Maryland and we went to the same church. He showed me pictures of his new baby, a boy. I told him I'd subscribe to his software. And then we both got on our computers. I ordered a piggy bank in the shape of a baseball from Tiffany and sent it to his house and then I subscribed to SamCart.

His laptop dinged. He looked over at me. "You just signed up for SamCart?"

I hadn't expected him to know that I'd enrolled. There was an awkward moment. "I get a notification when any business over a million dollars signs up." We laughed. By the time we got off the plane, he'd invited me to come work in his space anytime I felt like being around other people. Community!

The first thing on my list had been community, and I found it on my flight to Boise.

That evening the conference was hosting a speakers' dinner. People don't know this about me, but I get a lot of social anxiety. It's not prohibitive, but I worry about what I'll say, what I'll wear. I'll worry that I'm going to be around cool people and that I'll be awkward. So I dither about wanting to go, and wait until the last minute to get ready, and then feel anxious that I'm late. I just need to remind myself that I will have a great time, that I like people, and that I actually get even better when I'm around people.

When I stepped onto the elevator, I was running late to meet the van to the speakers' dinner, and I was sure I'd be the last person in the lobby and the whole evening would start off weirdly. Finally, I looked up and noticed a bald guy in the elevator with me. He was wearing brightly colored glasses and smiled as we made small talk.

"I'm a speaker at the conference," I told him. "But in case you can't make it to my talk, I'll give you a freebie: Always exfoliate." Then I eyed his head and suggested, "In fact, you could go all the way back and exfoliate your whole head."

He laughed hard. Since my humor had won him over, I suggested he take a picture with me, so we stood together in the elevator and snapped one. Then the doors slid open and I realized by the fawning that happened in the lobby that he was Seth Godin, the headliner of the whole event. We spent the evening in conversation.

I woke up with gratitude. I thought about delivering my keynote. *I'll leave it all on the stage. I'm going to do the best I've ever done. I'm going to create change and action in other people's lives. I'm going to serve.* And that is exactly what I did. I was on fire—every point was crystalline, every joke landed, and every ounce of my belief was transferred to the audience.

Afterward, Seth found me. "You're a fifty-thousand-dollar speaker." That sounded like an astronomical figure to me then—I didn't think people like me made that much speaking. I must have scrunched up my face in shock because he asked me how much I charged. I told him my ballpark and confessed that sometimes I spoke for free if I felt like I could leverage visibility. Seth told me my raw talent was unbelievable but that I also needed a lot of work. No one had ever said that to me before. I knew I spoke well, but it wasn't a core part of my business; it was a part of my marketing, not a revenue source. He asked me about agents and speakers bureaus, and I had no idea what he was talking about. But as I listened to him talk about how much bigger it could be, something in me shifted. Before I could stop myself, I told him about the Krouse offer.

He looked me in the face and said, "Why are you scared to be your own CEO?" I hadn't thought of it that way but it was true.

Seth invited me to New York to continue working through how to develop my business. By this point I'd had this offer many times in my life, so I knew what to do. I always get on the damn plane. But this time I knew he wouldn't be giving me the cheat codes. Instead, if I was lucky, I would receive a new piece of the puzzle, one that would help me reevaluate and imagine the next level. I had mentorship.

And then Seth looked right at me and said, "Every few years I meet one or two people who become great friends. This is that moment." The weight I had been carrying lifted.

I wrote in my journal:

June 25: Three amazing things that happened today:

1. **Seth**
2. **I chose me and my mission**
3. **I deepened my faith**

How could I have made today even better? It surpassed my wildest dreams.

Only you can decide who you allow to influence your mindset. Don't give that power to anyone who doesn't deserve it. Surround yourself with people who will be there to support you, challenge you, and speak the truth you need to hear when you need to hear it.

———————

Jim's office building was empty and quiet when I walked in, and all the magic of the place swept over me. I wasn't nervous. I wasn't scared. I felt clear. I sat down with the team and they excitedly started discussing our next strategy session to map out what my transition into the company would look like. I needed to rip off the Band-Aid.

"This is really hard to say." My stomach fluttered. "This isn't going to work for me. I don't think this is what I'm going to do. It's not going to work."

At first no one said anything. Then there was a clamor of talk about not losing me, about terms and numbers. I told them we didn't need to do that; that I was sure I wasn't going to accept the offer. They had me wait until they got the contract for me to look at—until that point I hadn't actually seen the offer in writing.

The contract was just a few meager pages, and to be honest, it didn't matter what it said. I didn't want to sell my business.

Friend, if people are coming after you trying to buy your business, then it isn't the time to sell; it's the time to hold (unless you were already planning on selling). I'd spent all this time wondering if they would want to take me and they were wondering if they could get me.

Jim's team would not accept no for an answer; they suggested I go to lunch. As if maybe I was hungry and a meal would change my mind. I know the power of a good hot meal, having grown up poor, but as I ate my fried grouper sandwich, I was annoyed that I hadn't finished the conversation. Was I really doubling back on this, again? I knew what I wanted to do. And yet there was still a small scrap of doubt.

I went back to my belief that God is not the author of confusion. That this shouldn't be that hard. I was trying so hard to make the whole thing work. I had already been CEO of my own company, and although I didn't like it, it wasn't confusing to me. So why was I trying to enter confusion?

If the path is literally foggy, don't go there. It will become clear.

I called Seth.

"I just said no to them, and now I'm having second thoughts. Am I crazy? Am I just afraid that I'm not worth this opportunity?" Was I just too much of a sucker to own up to the fact that this would be the best thing for me? Did I think that I didn't deserve it?

Mentors usually offer guidance. They talk you through both sides of something, help you think your way through it, and then give you tactical strategy. But this was Seth Godin—thought leader, industry guru, wise author, and my actual friend. He very matter-of-factly said, "You're good enough to say yes, and you're good enough to say no."

It took some more therapy to really get the full wisdom of what he said—that your worth is not defined by the opportunity. You're not validated by the offer. So, if you say yes to it, it doesn't say anything about you. If you say no, it doesn't say anything about you. I didn't understand that at the time, but what I did take away was that I could say no and I'd be just fine.

When I went back, the lobby was filled with people, and the air was charged with joy and anticipation. I told the team that I had decided to do it myself. Even better, I decided to do it with God.

When I left, the lobby was quiet again. I knew that this was the last time I'd ever be there. I touched the cool metal of the front door and felt relief and a rush of wonder at what I had just done. I took a deep breath. I'd gotten halfway down the stairs when I heard a woman say, "Excuse me." I kept on walking, assuming the words weren't meant for me.

"Excuse me," a blond woman said again, her voice firm and confident.

I thought, *God, not this again.* People often stopped me—either because they recognized me from social or because they had something to tell me. I searched her face to see if she was someone I knew, and then I thought I'd have to tell her that I'm not going to be with the company. But when I asked her who she was, she was vague. "Oh, I just work here." Then she told me she'd noticed my light and energy. Had she been watching me? I'd been outside all of two seconds. I wondered if she needed something.

"I just wanted you to know that God called you to do great things," she said, and then told me I would be just fine and asked if she could pray over me. Florida is a weird place.

"Thank you, God, for using Nicole." I didn't remember telling her my name, but I must have. She said I was doing great and asked God to ease my heart.

It was scary and wonderful at the same time. Goose bumps spread over my arms. Tears pricked my eyes. After we said goodbye, I got in my car in a daze. A feeling of comfort and readiness flowed through me. I'm so grateful to God, not just for the quiet messages He sends but also for the way He can use anybody to speak His word and will into my life. God bless that woman for pouring life into me. I'm so thankful.

PART THREE

PART THREE

CHAPTER TWENTY-THREE

LIFE IS WHAT YOU ARE DOING

Almost two years after my quit day, I had vendors and agencies working for me and I hired six full-time employees. I even hired someone whom I was paying six figures. My name was trademarked, I had reached the multimillion-dollar mark, and what mattered even more was that I was hitting the marks God had promised me. I was in a season of relative calm. Anyone who has multiple kids will tell you that at any given time one of them is running wild, but this was a rare season where all my kids were good. It was peaceful, which meant I was able to focus on growing the business.

Our lives were changing. We were moving to Atlanta. This was a move the five of us had talked about and were looking forward to. Atlanta was a vibrant city with lots of opportunities for the girls. It was a travel hub that would make it easier for me to get to and from my gigs so

I had more time with my family, and we had found a beautiful, spacious home where we could begin our new, better life.

So much was changing at once.

By Daya's senior year of high school, she was earning straight As and was beginning to settle into herself, but when it was time to go to college she behaved as if she didn't want to go. When she turned sixteen, she refused to get her license. She told me she was comfortable being a passenger. She was telling me in the only way she could: I'm not ready. But I thought this was my first teenager "teenagering." I was just a teenager myself not too long before and had a rebellious season of my own. I told her that if she went to college and used her tools she would be fine. What I didn't understand was that she was just scared and didn't yet have the belief. We needed to hold her tighter.

She struggled in college. Her grades plummeted. When she came home for Christmas break, she was on academic probation. Standing in the kitchen, we talked about what had happened and why.

"What are you doing at school that might be keeping you from your success?" She shrugged but didn't speak. "You don't know?" So, leaning against the island, we broke down all the things. Some of it felt like normal kid stuff, but stacked together it was overwhelming proof that Daya was acting as an enemy to her own progress.

"Are you eating well?"

"No, I eat pizza." Normal kid stuff.

"Are you using your agenda book?"

"No." Normal kid stuff (and some adults too).

"Are you going to class on time?"

"No."

"Are you sleeping well?"

"No."

"We can help you with that," I said. And then I drilled down into what we could do. We talked about accountability checks, about using her agenda book, about school resources. I gave her a lot of the information I learned when I had struggled at Hopkins and a lot of the things I had learned helping Maame through college.

Then I asked if she was staying out too late, and she nodded yes.

"Are you going to parties and drinking?"

She didn't say anything, and I gave her a version of the warning I'd been issuing to her and Krissy. "I need to let you know, with the world you come from, this is not something to play around with. It can get out of hand really quickly." She rolled her eyes at me. "You are wired differently. Addiction is hereditary and a disease."

I know what it feels like to be floundering in college, so at the end of our conversation I also told her, "Know that if this isn't working, you can come home. You can go to community college, or you can live at home and commute. Let's talk about what this looks like so we can figure out what we need to do."

She said, "I want to go back." But what I think she was actually saying was "I don't want to live at home."

Months later, when she came back for summer, I discovered that she had been put on academic probation again. All of this was familiar to me; I knew exactly how she felt, having carried both trauma and financial burden while trying to succeed in college many years ago. What I realized for the first time was that even though I was here to help with the financial weight and security of home for Daya, trauma alone was the barrier preventing her from thriving in school. And there was no way to fix that overnight. Though she could still go back, there would have to be a real change first. Once again, we were leaning against our kitchen island discussing her future.

"We're moving to Atlanta. If we're going to leave you here to go to school, we've got to figure out what's going on, or you need to come with us because this is not working."

She said we were forcing her to be a nurse when that's not what she wanted to do. "The reason I'm not going to class is because I don't like these classes. I'm too stupid to go to class." I had heard that kind of talk from her years before when I'd first met her. The demons from her past were bubbling up; I could see that much. But I couldn't see the full picture and all she could see was that she was failing. She thought college was life, so the data she had was that she couldn't do life.

There are so many things that you can do, I told her, but she had stopped believing me. I'd told her, "Go to college and use your tools and it'll work out." Well, it wasn't working out. It was hard. It was scary. She was alone. She wasn't using her tools, but people don't realize when they're not using everything they have.

"You don't have to do those classes. Let's figure out what we can do so that you're successful."

Come to Atlanta became my refrain. I thought she should take the year off and come move with us. But we also had rules. "When you come to Atlanta, know that you aren't going to be in our home just hanging out. You'll work. Also, know that a lot of things that were happening last summer and were happening in school need to stop. Drinking and staying out late are going to stop. I get that you feel like you are old enough and that you've spent a year doing this stuff, but it's illegal. It could get you arrested and it's not going to happen in my home. So you can come but you'll live at home until we figure out what you want to do next."

"I don't want to do that. I want to go back to school."

This wasn't an option because we were not going to pay for it. I asked her what she wanted to do, and she breezily answered, "Well, I just want to go off and do my own thing. I'm moving out."

"The way you're saying that it seems like it's not that serious, but it's very serious."

"Well, it feels right in my head," she said as she stared at the black granite, avoiding catching my eye.

"Do you understand what I'm saying to be logical?"

"Yes, I do. I hear what you're saying. I can tell that it's right, but I just want to try it my way."

Daya had a lot of clarity around what she didn't want to do, but she didn't have clarity around what her responsibility was to get and make a life for herself. That was part of the conflict within her. I grappled with how to mother Daya—how to show her unconditional love while trying to keep her safe.

That summer was a nightmare. She was home with us, but she'd stay with her mother on the weekends and run around Baltimore with her old friends. She was coming in late, sneaking out, neglecting her responsibilities. These were things we'd never dealt with before. It was as if she were saying, "I want to be a kid forever."

I knew she came to me with a preexisting life and will. She felt like she could go out on her own because she'd been on her own for so long before I'd met her. I couldn't argue with that. I wanted to scream, *BUT YOU DON'T LIVE THAT LIFE ANYMORE.* But she didn't believe that. There was trauma, so much trauma. And it was all coming up at once.

Daya knew only certain worlds, and she wasn't open to discovering new ones because trauma makes us fearful. And the two worlds she knew were radically different—her first life, abject poverty with addiction, and her second, living with what she believed to be a ridiculous motivational-speaker millionaire. Her experience of the world was that it was exactly the polarized place my dad had presented to me—either your name is on the building or you're scrubbing the floors.

We were sitting in my Tesla, with creamy white leather seats, having another conversation about college and career when she looked at me and under her breath muttered, "You know, Mom, not everyone wants to be a millionaire."

I glanced at her out of the corner of my eye and thought, *You're lying. Everybody wants to be a millionaire. It's just a question of what you want to do to have that money.* But I held my tongue.

"I just want to have a house and a husband," she said. But I think that what she was saying was, "I want stability and I don't want to work as hard as you." She wanted to be in the middle, but she'd only ever seen the extremes. So, she was afraid that if she listened to me she might end up with my life. And the other way she knew was what she was most familiar with.

Before we moved, I invited Daya to come to Atlanta with me for the weekend. I wanted her to have all the data. I wanted to show her the unknown of where we were going. Maybe if she saw the home. Maybe if she saw her room. Maybe if she saw the city she would know there was another way. I was trying to do what Chalene had done for me.

In high school, Daya had complained about her social life. She resisted our rules about going out. They were pretty simple: If you want to go out, I need to know in advance where you're going, who's going to be there, when you're leaving, and when you're coming home. She would complain that her friends didn't plan like that. I would always answer, "I care about you. You belong to somebody. I can't just act like you don't matter."

But even if she had made plans and communicated them, the reality was we lived in a rural place and you needed to drive forty minutes to get anywhere and she never got a license. In Atlanta, however, we'd be in a city, close to places to meet friends, work, and go to school, if she decided to do that. I pointed all the possibilities out to her. I was hoping our trip would show her that there's so much more to life. Since she'd first gone to college, she was trying to play the adult the best way she knew how, but she was very quickly learning that her version of being an adult wasn't matching the world's. She had formed her version of adulthood when she was eleven—when being a grown-up meant buying clothes, getting her hair done, and looking out for her baby sisters. She didn't know it meant showing up on time, doing your work, being responsible. She didn't have any context for that kind of adulting. But in Atlanta, maybe she could reimagine herself in the world.

On that trip, I glimpsed a version of Daya I had never seen before. We were in Atlanta the summer after her first year to set up the home for our family, and all she wanted to do was go to the mall. She had always been someone who thought of family, of her sisters, of the greater picture. But in that year she was away, for the first time in her life, she had to worry only about herself and she didn't want to give that up. I understood that she had tasted freedom, but it was freedom that was leased from me, because I was paying for her life.

When we did go to the mall, I saw a girl who was insecure, and that insecurity was manifested in meanness. She trashed other people's outfits and had a running commentary of snide remarks. She spent all her time wanting to text her friends on campus. The house didn't have Wi-Fi, and she was sitting outside on the ground so she could use the neighbor's network. She wanted to be as far away from reality as possible.

In one of our conversations over the weekend, she said, "You told me if I went to college I'd be fine. I don't know what I want to do anymore. I don't want to go to school. I don't want to plan."

She'd been running her whole life and she was exhausted. I understood that. She didn't want to do any of the hard work of adulting. But she didn't have a choice. Whether it was in college or on her own, adulting was going to find her.

"I understand, but do you recognize that you're going to run into other problems?" I asked if there was a different goal she had. "Because if there's a different goal, you can come up with a different plan, but no matter what you have to plan." I explained that she could be part of the process, but that we had to figure something out. Operating without a plan is not an option. Planning is a real thing—not because any of us like it but because it's necessary to keep us structured and functional.

I told her, "If you at least agree that you don't know what you want to do, and that you need time to figure it out, then let's take that time. Just come to Atlanta."

I was trying to be a good mom by giving her a choice. I should have been a firm mom and said no. I think she would have received that better, but I was scared that she would have run. What she needed then was to be held tighter. But I didn't know. I had never had to do that before.

At the same time, I could also see she was responding to Atlanta. Together we sat above the garage in the room that would become my office and hashed out what the rules of life in Atlanta, with us, could look like. We wrote everything on my whiteboard. She would suggest something and we'd talk through it. I would suggest something and ask if she was comfortable with it. Together we came up with a set of rules that she could live with. I glimpsed a future where she could thrive.

As we were leaving Atlanta, she agreed to come with us.

When we landed in Baltimore, sitting on the airplane waiting for the seat-belt sign to ding off, I looked over and she had tears rolling down her face. I put my arm around her shoulders and asked, "What's the matter?"

"I'm so confused."

When people say they are confused it usually means they're struggling with an internal paradox. Life in and of itself is not very confusing; it's rather matter-of-fact. I'd shown her a beautiful life filled with possibility. I'd broken down the ways we could make that life a reality. Yet here my daughter was, crying and confused. She didn't feel like she deserved to go. She worried that because she'd messed up before, if she came with us, she would mess that up too. She had held together her brokenness for five years, and now her brokenness was showing, and if she came back into our home and showed us her brokenness, she would lose us too. She had a narrative that she had to leave our home and be on her own, and our trip had given her data that maybe that didn't make sense. That maybe there was another way, and yet she still felt so strongly that she had to leave. I'm sure that part of her didn't want to, and that she was scared. But she didn't have the words for all that.

Part of her fiercely wanted to be on her own, and part of her was drawn to the life I was showing her. I could see the confusion in her. I understood it because I felt that kind of paralyzing confusion when I'd thought about selling my business. Back then I'd had to ask myself, *Are you too afraid to own your own life right now? Or are you willing to accept it?* But Daya was too young and too immature to know how to do the necessary internal work to answer those questions.

"I still want to be on my own. I don't want rules."

"Look, I understand that, but you need to understand that some of that stuff is because your brain isn't developed all the way. You can't listen to all of it."

"I want to believe you, and part of me knows you're telling the truth, but somehow I don't. For some reason I just want to trust myself."

I had nothing.

As soon as we got back to the house, things started to spiral out of control.

We had a rule in our house: No using your phone late at night. I had rules around cell phones in general. Since I worked on social media, I knew *exactly* the type of stuff I didn't want my girls getting into—so all phones stayed downstairs while they got their much-needed sleep. No one in our house got a phone until they turned sixteen—and even then it was just for emergency purposes. I needed the girls to have a sense of self that wasn't developed or affirmed by whatever the Internet says. It's crazy how it messes with your brain. Because I worked on the Internet, you'd better believe I understood how it functioned. We all abided by the late-night-no-phone rule. But Daya kept breaking it, to talk to boys and to friends, so I changed the Wi-Fi password.

She came into the TV room where Josh and I were sitting with Krissy. It was ten thirty and Daya was asking for the Wi-Fi password. I played it off quietly. "Oh, no, no. Go to bed."

Her whole face contorted. "I'm not playing these fucking games anymore."

She had never spoken to us that way. I was shell-shocked. I just stared at her thinking, *Who is this?* It was like someone else had taken over her body. This was the Daya I'd heard about from her mother, or from her teachers way back, but I had never met that girl. Finally, I managed to say, "I'm sorry. What?"

"What is all this? You're trying to control me."

I'm a defuser. Whenever I walk into a room and there is a heightened feeling, I'm great at lowering the temperature and just letting the issue be the issue, so it just sits, impersonally, in the middle of the room. This is a skill I learned growing up with my unpredictable and combustible father.

"Nope, I assure you, I really don't want to control you. That's not what this is. You just need to go to bed."

"No I don't. I don't have to deal with your shit."

"Listen, I'm not going to force you to do anything. Whatever it is you want to do you can do it, but this is ridiculous and you're not going to be in this house acting like this."

"Fine, I'll leave."

Mothers of teens may recognize that this is par for the course. But up till then, none of us thought we would ever choose not to be there. We all chose to be one another's family. We all looked at one another, stunned. Daya was glazed over with rage. I thought about wrapping her in my arms as I would Ally. Could I physically keep her there with me?

Through tears, Krissy yelled, "Why are you acting like this?"

Hearing Krissy's voice shocked me back to reality. My girls didn't argue, and Krissy never raised her voice.

"Just go to bed, Daya. We'll talk about this in the morning," I said in my firm mom voice that has a lot of bass and is crystal clear.

"I don't have to do this shit."

She went up to her room. I heard a ruckus and walked upstairs. She had started to pack.

I couldn't keep up with the moment, but I knew I didn't want her to go. Standing in the breezeway that connected her private apartment to the rest of the house, I watched her furiously throw things in garbage bags. I said, "You cannot go. You don't have anything."

Finally, when it was clear that she wasn't listening, I said, "You can't take anything you didn't buy."

She dropped her bag and walked out.

I went outside to find her, and when I didn't see her, I thought she was walking to blow off steam. It was three miles to get to the top of the subdivision. The biggest threat to her out there was a rogue fox, and I was sure she'd be spooked by some deer and come back. Still, worry pooled inside me and I got in my car and slowly patrolled the neighborhood.

Do I report this? I didn't know what to do. Is this the type of kid I have? A kid who just leaves? She was treating us like we were a temporary solution, but we were a family.

I texted her and saw that it was "read" so I knew she was alive and had probably had a friend pick her up. I left the door unlocked in case she came home. Josh said she'd be fine, but I wasn't sure and I cried myself to sleep.

In the morning I expected Daya to be in her room, but she wasn't, and it was in the tornado-struck state she'd left it in. I thought I'd find her fixing herself a bowl of cereal, but she wasn't in the kitchen. Around midday she showed up to get some things with a friend, as if she needed a bouncer. Her friend was standing awkwardly in the kitchen. I still thought she needed to blow off steam.

I didn't understand what was happening; it was like someone had taken over her body. She was in survival mode when there was no threat.

"Oh, we are not doing this," I said.

Maybe she didn't care about her existence, because then she said, "Okay, Nicole," pointedly using my first name. I almost snatched her into next week.

"You can be as mad as you want to, but I'm Miss Nicole to you, or Mom."

She didn't say anything else.

She left, and I fell apart.

The next morning I woke up feeling like someone had died and I was grieving. But the hardest part of any type of loss is not the loss—though that part is hard—and it's not the living itself but having to live and grieve at the same time. I still had two kids; I still had to move our life forward. But I was bereft, and Josh didn't understand. Sitting in my bathroom I called my therapist and caught her up on everything and told her that I was afraid Daya wouldn't survive. She told me, "You're worried about her, about whether she will be okay. But remember that she still has everything you've ever taught her. She knows how to survive. She'll use those things. When she needs them she'll know what to tap into."

"I haven't given her enough."

"She has enough. That's how humans work. She would not have walked out if she didn't feel like she had some degree of what she needed. It'll be enough for now and we'll see what happens. She's going on her journey."

But how could she go on this journey without me? I wanted to keep her safe; I wanted to help. Instead, I was sure I had done something wrong. Then my therapist told me, "With a kid with this level of trauma, given what she has seen and experienced, this was going to happen no matter what. As a matter of fact, I'm surprised she's lasted this long."

I didn't *really* know what she meant when she said that. I was plagued by the feeling that I had done something wrong, that I had missed something, that if I had done something differently Daya would be with me, that she would be okay.

We'd been a family for almost five years—through Josh's illness, through the birth of my business, and through this recent run of success—and the girls had always been by my side. Daya was in every way, shape, and form my firstborn. She was the first one I mentored; she was the first one in our home. When she decided to stay in Baltimore, it didn't almost break me. It broke me.

A few days after Daya left, I went to the community bank, where I'd deposited the first earnings from my business, to close my account before our move to Atlanta. I had become the bank's biggest client and they always pulled out all the stops for me and going there was a pleasure, but in the aftermath of Daya leaving, the thought of pulling up anchor left me feeling nauseated and dizzy. How could I move and leave my baby behind? It was one of the first times in my life I'd ever felt ill about money.

We were choosing a home and we were choosing a city. This was the freshest of fresh starts. It was this beautiful thing we'd all talked about, the security of knowing that we chose to be together, but now Daya wasn't there. Could we even move to Atlanta?

When I got back in my car, my hands were trembling, the air was close, and the car felt small. I felt lost. I didn't want to live. I had disappointed the people I love, which left me confused about my existence. Even though my therapist had told me this wasn't my fault, what I heard was, *It's not my fault, but I'm their mother; how did I not see this?*

I called Josh. I could barely breathe. "I'm not okay. I just want to keep driving. I don't want to come home. Maybe it's better for the girls if I'm not there. I don't know how I hurt her. I don't know why she left. I thought I was doing things right. I don't know what went wrong and that scares me more. I love her so much I'd rather take myself away from the girls than risk making whatever mistake it is that might make them leave and put themselves at risk. I wouldn't want to do that again. I would never want to hurt them, so maybe I just shouldn't be around them. I would rather just go."

Josh said, "You're in a dark place right now. Just come home."

When I hung up, I knew I needed something Josh didn't believe in: an interventionist God. I called my friend, the pastor's daughter. When I tried to lean on other people, she always reminded me, "You're leaning the wrong way, sis. You should be leaning into God. God can take better care of her than you can," which was humbling. I couldn't help but acknowledge that God had taken care of the girls until I got there. So, if I was just turning it back over to the being who was in charge the whole time, everything was fine. The girls had got to me, and I could trust that they would get to wherever they needed to go next. I was in partnership with God. That meant I could petition Him to watch over my girls. That gave me ease. I realized that whatever was happening here, God already knew. The same way I hadn't known that I would get my girls, this was all by design, even the pain. In that moment, when I was feeling so dark, I thought of the sheer light I had never expected these girls to bring into my life. The God that does that can do everything else.

I believe in an interventionist God. He wasn't going to show me a bright light or send Daya walking across the parking lot, but He was there with me. He helped me sit up, take a deep breath, and start again.

Just at my breaking point, a woman I knew a little bit from the marketing world invited me on a business trip with two of her girlfriends to Hawaii, the place my father had always dangled as a carrot if I could be perfect enough. They were going for a marketing event and had gotten a house together. Even though I didn't know this woman particularly well (I knew her Internet persona well), and Hawaii was an eleven-hour flight away—fourteen if you included the mini layover in Los Angeles— and we were getting ready to move to Atlanta, and it didn't make any sense for me to go, I went to Hawaii for four days. I still felt like I had to get far away.

I cried at the airport. I cried on the plane.

When I arrived, Jen, Nikki, and Jadah greeted me warmly. I looked the way I felt. They asked if everything was okay. I said I was just tired and then I went right to my room and crashed into sleep. When I woke, I asked if there was food, and from that moment they handled me delicately. They didn't push; they didn't pry. They brought me food. They brought me blankets. They built fires—outside in the firepit, inside in the fireplace. They didn't even know me, but they kept me warm and held space for me to share.

I confessed that I thought I was messing up being a mom. My daughter had left our home. I was embarrassed. I was worried. I was scared I might be screwing up Ally and Krissy. Maybe I shouldn't even have my kids anymore.

This was a level of vulnerability I hadn't gotten to with Josh, that I hadn't gotten to with anybody. I was aware that they could use everything I was saying to ruin me. But I was learning that if you don't tell people what is really going on, they can't help you.

The whole time, these incredible women held me up. They became my lifeline. They all had children of different ages. Jen reassured me that this chaos was part of raising teenagers. Then she said, "But I feel bad because you would have never had this issue if she was yours from the beginning."

This is when my therapist's words made sense. I wanted to neatly put away the things from the past, and that was impossible. All this stuff happened because Daya had a whole life before I met her at fourteen. I'd ignored her preexisting trauma, but what my therapist and Jen were saying was that this was always coming.

"So, who's going to help her?" I asked.

"No one. Daya's got it," Jen told me.

"I never thought we'd be a family of four."

Without missing a beat, Nikki gave me her firm mom voice: "You are not. You are always a family of five. And always say that."

I kept saying that Daya was gone, and Nikki made sure I saw that she wasn't gone—she was just someplace else.

They looked me in the face and convinced me somehow that it was okay, that this was normal, that this was parenting a teen, that kids come back around, that it was just different for me because the girls and I had other complexities. In four days they stitched me back up so that I could heal.

We all went to the Four Seasons for our final meal. Overlooking the ocean, we committed to doing life together. We were choosing our friendship. We promised not to break up. In the gift shop we bought a postcard and wrote out our friendship contract, which we all signed.

> Rule Number 1: Be regular
> Rule Number 2: Be extra
> Rule Number 3: If you're not sure how to friend, do Rule Number 1 and Rule Number 2 over again

I'd always thought friendship was an extravagance I couldn't afford. Jadah, Jen, and Nikki taught me it was something I couldn't afford to live without. I went into the trip believing I was the problem. I got back on the plane understanding that this was life. Life is occurring; if I'm going to live, I'm going to experience it.

A few days later, Josh, Krissy, Ally, and I left for Atlanta with our two dogs. Daya came to say goodbye.

As soon as I hugged her I erupted in tears, and then Daya did the same.

"What are we doing?" I asked.

"I don't know. I don't know," she said.

"What is it? What can we do?"

But all she could say was, "I don't know. I don't know."

I told her I loved her so much and she should take care of herself, whether she was crashing on a friend's couch, staying with family friends, or in her own place. But no matter how hard it got, she could always come home. "Wherever I am, you always have space." The last thing I said to her was, "We will always be a family of five."

———

Parenting is helping inform kids so they can make their own choices. In order for them to know what choices are right they have to experience the outcomes of their choices—the right ones and the wrong ones. If they don't experience the negative outcomes, they will always, always, always, always, without fail, come back to the headache. That's true of kids and that's true of spouses and that's true of anyone you find your-self rescuing again and again.

Each of us is responsible for our own choices—understanding that is an act of empowerment. We don't realize how often people tell us the life we're living is insufficient. Society is always telling us that our lives are not enough—that we need more of something, or less of something. That in one way or another our lives, and by extension ourselves, are not enough. That's not true. Life is what you're doing right now. It is always valid. It is always meaningful.

Remember how I told you that I am a fixer, that I like to find ways to make things better? Maybe you've already noticed that this is almost an obsession of mine. I call this "fixing." My therapist uses the word *rescuing*.

Being a fixer is at once my best and most profitable asset and the one that's to my total detriment. My fixing habit has made me a mom and a multimillionaire. I take a lot of pride in fixing, particu-larly when I get paid to do so. But, because we are celebrated for fix-ing in our professional lives, before we know it, we may be putting our fixing where it doesn't belong—on our friends, our children, our spouses.

My husband was used to my being a fixer, and yet none of the things I had done seemed to have brought him deep happiness. I wanted to leave all the tension Josh and I had in Maryland. I wanted to cross our new threshold as the people we'd always said we wanted to be. I wanted us to be the people who show up, together. The power couple.

But the truth was we were already the people and the couple we were. We showed ourselves in the things we did (or didn't do) each day.

Up until this point it seemed there'd always been a "reason" Josh couldn't enjoy our life, couldn't be positive, have joy, or work hard. But now I couldn't see more reasons. We had the money, we had the dream jobs, we had the house, the family, and each other. By the time we moved to Atlanta, we had absolutely everything we needed, more than we'd ever dreamed of. I believed we were doing better. I didn't realize I had no context for what "better" was. I saw bad marriages growing up. I'd been in bad relationships before my marriage. I didn't understand what a good relationship was. But on some cellular level I must have known things weren't right because I was trying to make change. I'd tried to change all these other aspects of my life—every woman does that. We cut our hair, we start businesses, we go shopping. I dropped a million dollars on a house in a new state.

I kept looking to Josh for the reasons he couldn't enjoy our life, but I wasn't focusing on my own. When I had gotten married at twenty-two, my goals had to do with survival. Now that we had all these things, far beyond what we needed for mere survival, I had to know what the goals were going to be for the next chapter, and we couldn't agree on them.

The Bible talks about couples being equally yoked—both oxen can be strong, but if they are not equal they will not be well matched. With Josh and me, our strengths and our steps were not in sync. For me to get to where I was being called to go by the Lord, I could not be yoked to someone with different strengths and a different sense of direction.

We argued a lot about charity, children, and the church—and those are the only things I do for free, which is how you know I care about them. I wanted to honor my marriage, but I was sacrificing honoring myself. This was becoming a recurring theme. Still, in the name of fresh starts, I wanted to make sure I had tried everything.

Before we left for Atlanta, I told Josh I did not want to carry our old problems with us. In preparation for our new, better life, Josh and I went back to couples therapy for a few sessions. We had gone to therapy before, but back then, I hadn't done my own. Now that I'd been working on my trauma, I could see more of our dynamics, but I still couldn't see our relationship clearly. Friend, you may have predicted that this was inevitable, but I never, in a million years, would have thought it could end badly. When it came to Josh, I hadn't fixed anything, and what I was beginning to suspect was that it wasn't mine to fix. I've had to learn that sometimes the way to help is to *not* do, and that has been the hardest lesson.

It's not your job to raise yourself a good assistant. It's not your job to raise yourself a good husband. It's not your job to raise yourself anything but great children. There's a big difference between parenting and raising.

Our family was in the middle of tectonic change and Daya was terrified—and I was powerless. It was all hers to carry—and I had to trust that she had everything she needed.

CHAPTER TWENTY-FOUR

EVERYTHING IS DIFFERENT NOW

At home in Atlanta, I found new life in discovering that I still had places to serve. At bath time, Ally's shrieks of joy and her gentle splashes reminded me of where I was. Pulled into the present, I realized I wasn't causing harm; I was doing important work that matters. And I'm blessed to get to do it.

Some days Krissy would randomly tell me, "Oh, you're good at this," or "You're the best mom." One day I dropped her off at school, and in this easy voice she sang out, "Thanks, Mom." I sat there for a minute and reveled in the sound of that word in her mouth. Somehow, I was managing to build even more trust with my babies.

Another point of light was Gayle, who had just moved to Atlanta. When she'd called to tell me the news I burst into tears. We'd known each other for six years but always lived on opposite ends of the country, and now we were twenty minutes away from each other.

It had been ages since we'd last spoken, and I missed her terribly. Once in a while I wrote her an email telling her I was thinking of her, that I loved and cared about her. I let her know that I didn't expect her to respond, but that I was there if she ever wanted to talk. That fall she wrote me back: "I wasn't ready before, but I am now. Let's talk."

As soon as I read that, I was dialing Gayle, and when I heard her high, girlish voice on the other end, my eyes filled with tears and I wanted to laugh. We talked and talked.

Just before Gayle ended our contract, her mother had been ill. She had been winding down her business so she could spend time with her—she'd always had a close relationship with her mother—but, being such a private person, she didn't want to tell me the details at the time. I remembered all those Fridays Gayle had given me when she could've been spending time with her mother. Back then, neither of us knew her mom was sick, or that she would pass in a little more than a year. Still, I felt like I owed her a lifetime for giving me all those afternoons.

When we reconnected, Gayle was spending as much time as possible with her mother. I could hear in her voice she was tired yet joyful. I knew the impact of too-much-tired. Gayle isn't a receiver. Her instinct is to say, *I can do it myself.* Her heart is wired to give. I missed her. I flew out and did whatever I could to just stand in the room, the way she always did for me. In this moment, she could have all my Fridays.

Even then, when I was there, Gayle and her mom were teaching me. There were two things her mom shared that I'll remember for the rest of my life. She told me, "You two need to stay together and you need to take care of each other." She also told me that anytime Gayle had to be up late doing her homework, she would always stay awake with her and lend Gayle, who was sitting in some other room with her head bent over a book, all her energy. That's what moms do. You can't really do anything except give all your energy and hope that's enough.

I don't know who taught Gayle's mom about lending belief, but she passed it down to Gayle, who used it with me, and she taught it to me and I used it with my girls. And as our lives changed, this was a lesson I was going to need more and more.

A few years earlier, a production team had reached out about a reality show. I shrugged my shoulders, thinking this was some pie-in-the-sky Hollywood thing, and I wasn't eager to do reality TV. For two and a half years they pitched, then the USA Network finally showed interest and I began to get excited that I'd be able to reach more people, but the network kept us in limbo for months.

At the end of March 2019, while we were still waiting on news about the show, I was supposed to do a launch, but at every turn, doors were being closed, and the final straw was the venue's canceling on me. There happened to be a dentists' convention in town and every hotel I tried was booked. I thought I'd have to call off the event. Then, I was driving through Decatur, Illinois, and I noticed a hotel. They happened to have that weekend open. It was the most successful event I'd had to that point.

A few weeks later, almost a year since we'd gone to Hawaii, I was in Sedona with the girl squad. The whole trip, I worried over the fact that the show didn't seem like it was going to happen, and I allowed that to spiral into questions about what I was doing and how I was going to grow my work. Again, the girl squad tethered me.

We were at a resort carved into the center of Red Rock. We were in the center of mountains that rose around us like flames. At sunrise it looks like the world is on fire. But this wasn't my kind of resort. This was a place where rather than well-lit paths they give you a flashlight to navigate the unspoiled darkness. My suite had a Murphy bed—there's nothing luxurious about my having to set up my own bed every day. (Childhood trauma!) But every morning having breakfast on a terrace overlooking Red Rock was magical.

The four of us went to get massages. When I lay down on the table, the massage therapist told me, "Before we get started, I want you to take however you're feeling and put it in a box and put it under the table." Then she proceeded to run a feather over my back.

"I don't know what type of massage this is, but if you don't touch me, I'm not paying for this." I was very clear.

"Oh no, I'm channeling your energy, but I can feel maybe you have more to put in that box."

Afterward, all four of us emerged in the hallway in our robes and busted out laughing. We had a spa lunch—you know the kind I'm talking about: a lettuce leaf and some slices of cucumber—and then it was time for the hot tub. Jadah is obsessed with hot tubs. I don't believe in them.

As I sat on the edge of the tub, dangling my feet in the water, I explained to the girls, and the other stranger in the tub with them, why I don't do hot tubs, especially public ones. Why would I share boiling with another person? I told them they were all disgusting.

They laughed at me and coaxed me in. I decided to be a good sport. The lady who had been observing our conversation was very nice. "Maybe you need an ice pack?" She leaned over and handed me a cold pack. We boiled together for a few minutes and then the lady proceeded to get out as we chatted on. As she walked away, I saw a stream of blood coming down her leg. A look of horror crossed my face and the girls all asked "What?" Wordlessly, I pointed.

By the time they had turned back around I'd leapt out and was scurrying away from the tub. Jadah swung her legs over the edge. Nikki, who'd only ever had her feet in, pulled them up. And Jen was sitting in the tub laughing. After that, they promised to never ask me to get into a hot tub again.

The day we left, we stopped at the Chapel of the Holy Cross. The building shoots straight up out of red rock cliffs. When I stepped inside, I was staring out at an expanse of sky and desert. I lit a candle, made a donation, and prayed, *Oh God, I'm going to let this one go. I'm trying to handle this one, and whatever this ends up being is fine. Just help me be okay with that.*

On the ride back from the church, I got a phone call.

"It's the network," I half whispered to my friends.

I listened to the voice on the other end. I thanked them and then hung up. Tears were streaming down my face. I looked at my girls. "I got a show."

I was building myself up to learn to listen and pay attention to all the ways He communicated with me, and to do it in a daily way. My friend's husband was a pastor, and in that season, we talked a lot about how our relationship with Christ is personal, intimate, and constantly interactive. The pastor would often ask me, "Did you ask Him? Did you put that in front of Him?" Sure, I don't feel like if I want to get a sandwich I have to ask but knowing that I can is important. Knowing that He is always with me and always listening is important.

I decided I was ready to be baptized. I'd dunked in the mikvah when I converted to Judaism, but since then my faith had evolved. I'd been walking with Jesus and wanted to formalize our relationship. Baptism for me was an outward display of an inner commitment. I wanted people to see that I am fully committed—the way a wedding marks a marriage within a community. Although, it didn't feel so much like I was starting something; rather, it was a conclusion. It was ending an old way of life to step into something forever.

A few weeks after my trip to Sedona, I was in Cancún to get baptized. The idea of being baptized in the ocean made me feel connected to the world and to Him. I liked to imagine that through the water cycle, a single drop of the water that would wash over me had touched countless shores and could be the same water that Jesus had been baptized in.

The night before I was so nervous; it felt like a wedding day. He had already chosen me, but now I was choosing Him back. I hadn't felt this way before visiting the mikvah. I didn't just have butterflies in my stomach; my whole body was aflutter. But when I awoke, I felt very calm.

I was baptized at sunrise. The beginning of a new day.

I woke up in the dark and went to the rooftop to talk to God. All I could think was how good God was. He's so good to me. God did all these things: He had created this gorgeous world; He had carried me to this moment and brought me more joy than I ever could have imagined for myself. I was overwhelmed by gratitude. I wanted to scream from a mountaintop. It felt like love. I wanted to be baptized. I wanted to do this for God because He had done so much for me. I was so grateful that I was alive, that I had made it to this moment. My every nerve was tingling. That's what commitment feels like for me; when I became married to entrepreneurship I had nerves. When the girls became part of my life, I had nerves. When I committed to Christ, I had nerves.

I put on a simple white sundress I'd bought years earlier in the hotel gift shop in Jamaica after my first launch. It was beautiful, but I'd never worn it. I slipped into a bathrobe. The morning was cool. It was early and we were the only ones on the beach—the pastor, his wife, and me. The wind was pushing off the water, waking up every cell of my being. The sand was cool beneath my feet, and as I walked toward the water I was overwhelmed with gratitude. There was no fear. No apprehension. No worry that I was about to lose something. Christianity isn't about loss. It's about gain. What I felt was abundance.

A few feet from the water, the pastor spoke to me and took my hands. All I felt was God.

The clouds were heavy in the sky, but beneath them the sun had begun to glow orange on the horizon, turning the sky pink as day arrived.

I waded into the water, the waves choppy against my ankles and catching up the hem of the dress. When the water was at my hips, I turned to face the shore and the pastor guided me under water.

Once I'd pushed under the waves, I felt like a celebration.

I felt different. I felt the way you feel when someone you love puts that ring on your finger, and you know it's never coming off again. I had dedicated my life to Christ, and I was never going back.

The wind at my back, I wrapped the robe around me. My skin was cold in the ocean breeze, but there was a warm stream of tears running down my cheeks, and I couldn't stop smiling.

God really was everywhere in that moment with me.

Friend, I hope you get to feel something like this. And whatever it is, wherever you find it and feel it—this type of commitment, this certainty, this clarity—you deserve to feel that about something in your life, whether it is motherhood, marriage, work, or your purpose. Now that I have love, now that I know how it can be, I can't flee from it.

In that moment, you could not have told me I didn't make the right decision. And I still feel that way to this day.

"Everything's different now" is a phrase I often use in my business. Whenever you dawn upon a new business idea, whenever you accept a new truth about yourself, whenever you rewrite an internal narrative, whenever you quit a job, whenever you build a new relationship, you can say "Everything is different now," and approach it differently. Occasionally in life everything will be different, and you won't have anything to say about it.

CHAPTER TWENTY-FIVE

MAKE A DOOR

At that time there was so much to celebrate—our life in Atlanta, my business, Ally was thriving, and Krissy was about to turn seventeen and graduate from high school in another year. This was going to be her summer of fun, and it was going to start with her birthday present—a trip to New Jersey to see BTS, the world-famous Korean boy band. She was obsessed with them; she didn't speak a lick of the language but could sing all the words. We were going to stay in a swanky hotel and eat in fabulous restaurants. We'd been planning the trip for months. But everything went awry.

I may not know a lot about parenting, but I ask a lot of questions. Every single day I ask my kids: How are you feeling? How's your self-esteem? What do you think about yourself? How do you feel about yourself? Do you think you're pretty? Do you think you're smart? Do you feel safe in this world? I never accept "good" or "fine" as answers. They know that we're really going to talk about it. I am interested in how they're doing. And these questions are better than just asking how they are because it makes them reflect and tell me things that, as a mom, I can analyze. But, more than anything, I want them to get into the habit of checking in with themselves when I'm not around. Having kids really taught me the power of language and our capacity to describe how we feel and what we're going through.

I've always been particularly attuned to this with my girls because their communication around being sick is really poor. They had been in a home where if you were sick, you handled it yourself and there was no medicine, and no nurturing. So, we came up with systems to work around that. One of the things we use is a number scale. What I discovered was that if I asked "How do you feel?" their answer was always "I'm fine." So I learned to break it down. If yesterday you were feeling a level-three tummy ache, and level five is "I'm going to need to go to the hospital, it's the worst thing ever" and level one is "I don't feel anything at all," where are you now? They could say two or four or five. Otherwise, they couldn't articulate pain, because they just didn't think their pain mattered.

Krissy was a dancer and tiny to begin with and has always been a picky eater, and I noticed that she was looking too thin. The kids always had to walk to the school bus, and she was a teenager, so complaints were normal. She said she felt tired all the time: teenager. That her book bag felt heavy: teenager. Then she got a cold and it lingered. I asked her using our number system, "How do you feel?" She rated her discomfort and told me her chest felt full. Being the mom that I am, I checked her temperature. She would spike a fever, but then it would break. I kept her home and she'd feel better, but it kept going in cycles. After a few weeks, I noticed that her leggings were baggy. She already wore a size XS. I called her pediatrician.

There's something really nice about a pediatric office because they're usually not dealing with sick, sick kids. You sit in the waiting room and you might see a kid sneeze, or someone sitting with a frown, but mostly it is all routine—newborns there for their checkups, families needing last-minute summer camp forms filled out. That's what they do at our pediatrician's office.

So we went in and they did the usual. They listened to her lungs and told me it sounded like a cold, maybe a mild case of pneumonia, but the doctor wasn't worried. Her breathing was a little rattled, but otherwise her numbers were good—her temperature, her blood pressure. The last thing they could do to be sure was a blood draw. Quick answers for a routine nothing. She was going to do a quick blood draw, a finger prick, just in case. It could be something like mono.

All along the journey of being a mother—I know that I came to it unconventionally—you have little signs that let you know that you're in it, that this relationship is different. Suddenly you find yourself in a grocery store and you see a little kid reaching for something that's a little too high up and you know it might fall on them and you find yourself lunging, even if you're too far away to reach them. That is what it is to be a mom. That tickle of knowing. It was in that way that I felt a quick draw was not enough. I wanted a full panel. Run it for everything. Let's get this thing locked up and know all the answers.

The doctor looked at me quizzically, as if I was questioning her expertise, because there was nothing wrong here, just routine teenager stuff. But, if I wanted to pay extra for the full labs, I'd get the results the next day.

We stopped at Chick-fil-A on the way home.

The next day was Saturday and I slept in. Lord knows I love a sleep-in. My miracle morning is when no one bothers me before eleven o'clock. When I finally woke up, I did the thing we all do and picked up my phone. There was a voice mail from the doctor's office. Usually they leave a message saying everything's fine, so I wasn't going to listen to it right away. But then I thought, *Let me just knock this out before I get out of bed and the day whisks me off.*

"I have Krissy's results. Please call the office at this number when you get the message. I'm going to call you on your other line as well. And whenever you call, make sure I get to talk to you. Even if I'm with a patient. If I have to leave the room I will, because I need to talk to you."

Even if I'm with a patient. When I heard that, I sat up. I dialed right away and stared at my bedroom wall as the receptionist pulled the doctor out of an examination room. She came on the line: "Ms. Walters. Thanks for calling back. I'm really sorry to have to tell you this. I think Krissy might have cancer."

I felt like I was listening to someone else's life. This is not something that fit in our story.

"Okay. What makes you think that?"

She told me she'd looked at the labs and that the numbers were not looking great. She'd conferred with a couple of her peers and showed them the labs.

"So what do I need to do?"

"You need to take her to the ER right now. I've already called ahead and they're expecting you." Then she told me which hospital to go to.

Before she hung up I asked, "Hey, you have kids, right?"

"Yes."

"I'm a new mom. Would you tell your kid?"

She stopped for a moment. The line was quiet, and then she said, "You know, as a mom, I'd say wait till you know more."

"Okay. Thank you very much for calling. I appreciate this. I'll take care of it." The words felt weird on my tongue. The woman had just given me the worst news of my life.

"Okay. Good luck. Please keep us posted. We're hoping for the best."

I heard the gravity of the situation in the tone of her voice. Doctors don't give diagnoses over the phone like that, so whatever she saw in the labs alarmed her. I knew Krissy definitely had cancer; I just didn't know how bad it was.

My feet felt uncertain beneath me. I took baby steps until I'd edged around the almost insurmountable perimeter of our king-size bed. By the time I made it to the other side I had formed the thought, *Her life is never going to be the same again.*

I didn't know what to do with myself physically. My brain was starting to piece it together, to find order, but my body wanted to pass out or lie down. I stumbled into my closet. I needed to put on clothes but what was I supposed to put on for this? Everything seemed like it didn't have an answer; every single thing was stupid and trite. I couldn't organize my muscles to do this simple task. My brain was going in list form because I didn't really know what the next steps were: take her to the hospital, call Gayle to come watch Ally, call Josh. Still standing in my closet, I told myself to call my husband. I needed to tell him. I needed him to help with the logistics.

Josh had been up for hours and when I called him he was in the drive-through ordering his coffee. "You need to come home right now," I said, my voice shaky.

"Okay. I'm on line at the drive-through—"

I cut him off. "Josh. Understand. You. Need. To. Come. Home. Right. Now."

"Okay, I'll be there."

A few minutes later, Josh called. "Hey, I'm pulling up now."

"Stay outside. I'm coming to you."

Somehow, I put on clothes and shuffled out of the closet, out of the bedroom, to the TV room where the girls were curled up on the couch watching a show. I looked at Krissy's face. It was the last time she would ever have the face of someone who did not have cancer.

"Hey." My voice came out calm and even. "Okay, Krissy, I need you to get dressed right now and meet me down here. We're going to run to the doctor." I chose my words carefully, balancing my desire to not lie to her and to get her out the door without scaring her or Ally. She said okay and hopped off the couch to change. I told Ally we had to go out and that I was calling Auntie Gayle.

Josh parked in the driveway and was already walking around the car when I came outside. I got a step away from him and my legs gave out, but I knew he wouldn't catch me and I managed to find myself again.

I looked at him. "They said Krissy has cancer. I can't lose her. I just got her."

"What?"

Then I bumbled through the little information I had.

"Nicole. We don't know anything yet. The most important thing we need to do is find out the answers."

I kept saying okay, okay, okay. Then I asked, "What do I say to her? How am I going to . . ."

"Let's just get to the hospital."

Then I called Gayle. We have this thing where whenever we need each other to answer, we whisper "I need you to answer," and it always works. As the phone rang, I whispered, "I need you to answer. I need you to answer." She picked up.

"I'm so glad you answered." I spoke very carefully. "I really need your help right now. I have to handle some stuff with Krissy. Can you come here, please, and stay with Ally?"

I'd never asked her to do anything like that before. But she didn't miss a beat. "I'll be there in fifteen minutes."

"Thank you very much," I said robotically.

Gayle walked into my bathroom and I told her everything we knew. "Gayle, she can't die."

She looked me right in the face and said, "Nicole, Krissy is not going to die from this. It's going to be hard. This is going to be unpredictable. Some days are going to be really good. And some days are going to be really bad. And it's going to look, on the days that it's really bad, like it's not going to be okay, and that's just what it looks like. That's just what cancer looks like."

Gayle lent me her belief when I didn't have my own. Most of the time I have plenty of belief—in me, in God, in the next right thing. But at that moment I didn't have enough, and Gayle handed me hers and I slipped it in my pocket.

Then Josh, Krissy, and I drove to the hospital.

The prayer I was praying then was, *God, just give me a chance. Just give me a window.* I didn't ask Him to make it go away. I just got into logistics, like I always do, even with God. *Just give me a window, whatever it is, Lord. Give me a tiny way and we will make it work. I will run with it.*

I was scared. I didn't know what Krissy had. I didn't know how severe it was, and I wasn't sure if we would get a chance. But, still, I had to believe there was a window, because I'm Nicole Walters—if you give me a window, I'll make a door.

CHAPTER TWENTY-SIX

DO ALL THE THINGS

When you grow up in trauma, you need a lot of data, because trauma usually means you're getting incorrect data or lacking it. "Incorrect," meaning that you're experiencing something accurately but somebody's putting it in a context that suits them rather than you, or you've been put in situations you should not have been in, and you're just not getting things the right way. Since we'd gotten in the car, the need to tell Krissy had become a steady drumbeat in the back of my brain. I am Krissy's mom, and I knew it was cancer. And I wanted to make sure she wasn't hearing it for the first time from a doctor. I wanted her to know that her mom told her the truth, because what I needed her to do, all during this treatment time, was trust me. It felt wrong to know that this could be on the table and not prepare her. Because the worst that could happen was that it wasn't true. But I also did not want her to stand in fear.

We checked in at the emergency room and they didn't ask us to take a seat in the waiting area; they brought Krissy right to a room where a team of doctors started running all these tests because cancer usually isn't what kills you—it's the depleted immune system and all the infections and your body's inability to fight them.

The doctors talked to Josh and me in the hall. They told us Krissy had pneumonia and started her on broad-spectrum antibiotics, because time was of the essence until they could pinpoint what we were actually dealing with.

I needed to tell Krissy what was going on. She was getting poked. She was getting prodded. I needed to tell her the truth. But Josh felt that we should wait until we had more concrete information. At this point, we still only had the pediatrician's hunch.

I told Krissy, "You're here because the doctors are pretty certain there's pneumonia going on. And they're also concerned about the weight issue, and why that's happening. Obviously, it's pretty bad; you don't feel good. So we've got to figure that out." She took that all in. Then I explained that they were going to do blood draws, that there would be needles and lots of tests while they figured it out. I didn't tell her about the possibility of cancer. But as my daughter watched the nurses and doctors darting in and out like fish through coral, I was overwhelmed by the need to tell her the truth.

In our family, we always tell the truth. My rule had been that if the kid is old enough to ask, you have to tell them the answer. If it's something that affects the whole family, we decide as a family. Even if it's a bad thing, like someone's going to die, we tell them the truth. Our kids have been through too much. They know when people are lying to them, and it matters far more for our relationship that they know that we are people who will tell them the truth.

Every so often I pulled Josh out into the hall. "I need to tell her. This is how we are. I have to tell her." And he would say, "Let's wait until we know more." After four hours at the hospital, Josh relented.

I went back in the room, Josh by my side. Krissy seemed so fragile. Her small brown hand was a mess of needles and wires. I wanted to hold her hand but was afraid to hurt her. I got as close as I could navigating the IVs and machines and tried to be as normal as possible.

"Hey, Krissy." She nodded. I took a breath. "Krissy, I just want you to know that this could be mono, or it could be an involuntary form of anorexia. It could be a tapeworm. But it could be everything up to and including cancer."

"Cancer?" She drew the word out so that it filled the entire room.

"Yes. That is a very real possibility."

Neither of us spoke for a very long moment. Then, she looked at me with a spark of surprise and said, "Well, if it is cancer, I know that I'm not going to die from it. I don't feel like I'm going to die."

"Okay. You're not going to die."

I had my marching orders. My kid had told me she wasn't going to die. Everything was different.

"I do want you to also understand that God being so good, Mom has a lot of money. Like, we will do everything."

"I know, Mom."

"No, but I need you to not just know here"—I pointed to my head—"but to know here," and I pointed to my heart. "If there is an answer on this planet, we will find it. We will do all the things."

"I know. Okay, Mom." I was certain she believed me.

From that moment, this was no longer a thing that was happening to us; it was something we were taking on together.

Later that day, they moved Krissy from her ER room to a slightly longer-term room. It had a couch with a tidy stack of pillows and blankets, evidence that this was a place where people stayed. Although it was clear we weren't leaving, I had no idea how bad the situation really was.

The signs were everywhere—the fact that our pediatrician insisted that I talk to her no matter where she was, the fact that they didn't send us home, the pillows on the couch—but I didn't know how to read them. I'm a person who grew up learning to read signs. Growing up with a father who would rage, I used signs to figure out what was safe and what wasn't. In my marriage, I used signs to figure out what level of helpful husband I was going to get on any given day. Professionally, I am good at reading signs and using data to see what's working and what's not. Entering this new scenario, I had no idea how to read the signs—and that was a good thing. I didn't know that every day Krissy was in the hospital was a bad sign. I didn't know that people don't usually do cancer in the hospital. More often, you go to chemo and then you go back to your life. But Krissy had so many infections rolling around her body that she had to stay. I didn't realize it was so much worse than I thought, which is one of the ways God shields us.

God doesn't let you see the whole circumstance, because if you did, you wouldn't attack it, you'd run screaming from the room. There's a reason why God didn't tell me my kids had a heroin-addict mom who was going to jail when I met them, because if I knew that, my logic would have had to override the impulse to bring my babies into my home. I never would have done it. With Krissy's cancer, if I had known what this fight was really going to look like, I still would have done it, of course, but I wouldn't have had the level of hope required.

Three days later, the doctors talked to us in Krissy's room and told us she had cancer. But they didn't know what kind. The typing of the cancer could take another week or two. That was the worst part of the entire process. I was sure the cancer was stage 4, but it could have been either Hodgkin's or non-Hodgkin's. If it was Hodgkin's, she'd have a 70 to 100 percent survival rate. If it was non-Hodgkin's, it was a different type of fight.

We had to wait for ALL the information. We had to wait before we could do all the things. The weight of that sat on me. All we could do right then was fight the infections and keep her comfortable. And that, at least, seemed to be working. Her pneumonia was clearing up and she already felt better. But what were the next steps and when could we take them?

Nicole Walters, the queen of planning and business strategy, couldn't do a damn thing. I had lost control. It was humbling. I couldn't move at the pace I wanted to, which was breakneck speed. I had to go at the pace that was dictated. I wanted the diagnosis immediately, but I wasn't going to get it until it was ready. My kid had cancer and I was on fire with urgency, but the diagnosis was going to come whenever the lab made the diagnosis. It was going to take the time it was going to take. One of the skills I had to embrace was slowing down and learning how to handle only the thing in front of me, because that was all we could do. At that point, the one thing I could do was celebrate her birthday because we knew we had this one.

We still had the BTS tickets, and we were just sitting in the hospital waiting so I begged the doctors to tell me if she could go to the concert. When they said yes, I went into a flurry of action—upgrading our flights to first class, trading the swanky downtown hotel for something near the stadium, trading our regular seats for front-row floor seats, and arranging for a wheelchair because she was too tired to stand for long, let alone walk around a stadium.

We boarded the flight, giddy, like prison escapees. And then, somewhere over Virginia, I realized I'd forgotten the concert tickets. I burst into tears.

Krissy comforted me. "It's fine, Mom. I'm still having fun." That's the kind of kid she is.

I sat with my disbelief. This was not the thing I would fail at. And praise God for the Internet—immediately I went online to some back-alley scalper site and paid an ungodly sum for new front-row seats.

At the concert, Krissy lit up so bright, I felt like I was seeing her for the first time.

Afterward she told me, "This is the best day of my life."

CHAPTER TWENTY-SEVEN

MUSTARD SEED OF HOPE

While we waited for the diagnosis, I still had to work—I had bookings I couldn't back out of and I knew that cancer would be expensive, especially since Krissy wasn't on our insurance yet. I was due in New York to do an ad campaign.

Right before I left, Gayle checked in and asked what room Krissy was in. Without my asking, without her even offering, I knew she'd be staying with my daughter while I was gone. There was a grain of peace in that.

When I got on set, I turned on my smile, and I worked. Everything would be fine and then I'd think, *My daughter has cancer.* The thought would crack me open, and I'd take a quick bathroom break as the tears pooled along my lash lines. I'd dab them with a tissue before they could ruin my makeup, pull myself together, and get back to work. No one there ever found out what was going on.

As soon as the shoot was over, I raced to JFK. The Delta terminal was abuzz. It was Delta's annual fundraiser for pediatric cancer research. Everywhere I looked there were people wearing bright T-shirts and pictures of kids with cancer. I tried not to fall apart. Someone asked me if I'd like to make a donation to help a child with pediatric cancer.

They were collecting change, but I wanted them to run my credit card. I made a four-figure donation.

"Are you sure?" Suddenly everyone was whispering, trying to figure out how to process that kind of donation unexpectedly, and searching my face for understanding. They didn't know I was donating money that might save my daughter's life. I believe that God delivers you from suffering so that people who are still in it can be saved as well. That is how suffering can be meaningful. I'm fortunate that I haven't lived a life of suffering—I don't have a terminal illness, I haven't suffered continual abuse, I haven't lived in constant poverty. But I do have a little bucket of suffering that I carry around every day, and I try to alleviate a little bit of it by giving. Money is a fluid, circular thing. The money I gave that day might make its way back to my kid. That money might have gone to the research that was going to save my kid from whatever her diagnosis would be.

As I passed the Delta person my credit card, I tried to keep my hand from shaking, trying to keep my whole self from breaking into a million little pieces.

I made it all the way back to Atlanta. As I was walking through Hartsfield-Jackson International Airport, past the chapel near the Martin Luther King Jr. exhibit, my phone rang. I was on speakerphone with Dr. Keller, the oncologist who would be overseeing Krissy's treatment, and a team of people. I stumbled and leaned against the wall.

"Hi, we have Krissy's results. It's stage four." I was ready for that. Then he said, "And it's Hodgkin's."

They were quiet for a moment because they were used to the chaos of responses people have; they do this all the time and know the routine range of emotions. Maybe they were waiting for the questions: How long do we have left? What does this mean? But they'd never dealt with

Nicole Walters before. I'd already read everything, and knew that Hodgkin's was a blessing. Instead of seeing the darkness, I saw the pinhole of light, the mustard seed of hope.

"I'm sorry, it's Hodgkin's?" I had to be sure I hadn't heard static around the prefix *non*. Dr. Keller confirmed that it was Hodgkin's lymphoma and I fell down sobbing on the cold floor saying "thank you" over and over.

Dr. Keller couldn't understand why I was thanking him. He was diagnosing cancer, but all I heard was that Krissy had a shot. I had prayed for God to just give me a window. Hodgkin's lymphoma was our window. I could hear the confusion on the line; it usually takes time for people to see the hope. But I let the doctors know I understood. "We have a chance to beat this thing and that's not lost on me."

"You're right. Her prognosis is very good," Dr. Keller told me.

The busy airport, the streams of people pouring in and out of Atlanta, the whole world disappeared. I was crying and thanking God right there in front of the chapel. Elated, I just kept saying thank you. *Thank you. Thank you so much, God. What you're telling me is that we're doing this. I know it's going to be hard. We can make it through; our life is a testament to that.*

I went straight from Hartsfield to the hospital, and when I floated into Krissy's room with the good news, there was Gayle, who hadn't left Krissy's side the whole time I was gone.

While Gayle was at the hospital, Josh was home. Whenever we would talk about our marriage, Josh would say he was good at the routine, the day-to-day stuff, and that I was good at the chaos, the crazy, the ad hoc. Josh considered himself the paperwork guy, so while Krissy was sick, he stayed home to do things like pick up her prescriptions, pay bills, and spend time with Ally. He said he thrived better if he didn't have to mess up his routine, and, considering his condition, I just accepted that he couldn't stay up all night with Krissy, that he couldn't handle the stress of it all, and that, for her health and well-being, I had to *always* be the person. Given how much I loved Krissy, this was a responsibility I was willing to rescue him from.

The problem with our division of labor is that life—particularly our life—is anything but routine. And frankly, whose is? It's never just taking the kids to school, it's arriving at school and being asked, "Where's my lunch?" It's putting dinner on the table for family members who have different food allergies. It's handling the problem whenever anything goes awry. I don't know about you, but I signed up to be a mom, not a firefighter. Life has a lot of fires, though. Being a firefighter is too much, so sometimes we just want to do the day-to-day. It's a lot to always be *the* person. It's a lot to always be rescuing.

Rescuing is inserting your energy where it isn't warranted, required, or necessary. Rescuing shows up in many ways: financially, with the emergency funds to fix a situation you did not create; physically, with the car ride or the cleanup of a mess you didn't make; and mentally, with the vent session, phone calls, and advice you know won't be applied. There is *always* a cost when you are excessively invested in the lives of others, and it's paid from the bank of your own wellness.

Friend, if there's only one thing you deserve most in the world, it's the love and energy of investing your time in yourself. Almost by force, I've had to learn to stop rescuing others so I could save myself.

Self-control is the highest form of maturity—and the most impressive sign of growth. There is a peace, freedom, and pride in being able to remain silent when our inclination is to speak or do. Frankly, minding matters that aren't yours is exhausting. And I don't mean not speaking up in spaces that don't serve you—I mean holding emotional space, dedicating mental figure-outing, and committing anxious energy to problems that are not yours to hold.

There are people out there that everyone needs to watch out for. They're the people who like to place a problem in the center of the room and stare at it. There are also people who set a problem in the middle of the room and then yell at it, but those people are more obvious. We know to get rid of those people. You really have to run when someone can sit in a room with a problem that they put there and try to tell you the problem isn't really a problem. How can you fix a problem if you're spending all your time arguing over whether this massive problem you're both staring at is even in the room?

This is what I've learned about rescuing. If you align with this at all, and I'm not playing here, if you feel even a twinge of truth to any aspect of what I am saying, you are rescuing somewhere, somehow, with someone, and it has to stop.

CHAPTER TWENTY-EIGHT

LET FAITH FILL THE GAPS

There's no right time to have kids. You'll never have enough money. You'll never know enough or have enough time. And there's no good time for your daughter to have cancer, because cancer is awful and no one deserves to have it, ever. It's always a bad time. However, some bad times are better resourced than others. When Krissy got sick, we lived fifteen minutes from one of the best treatment facilities in the region. My business was growing by leaps and bounds and I could write the checks and take the time to give Krissy the care she required. Gayle lived fifteen minutes from our house. God had been keeping us season after season. All we had to do was cancer. We didn't have to do: How are we going to pay for this? We didn't have to do: How am I going to take this much time off work? We didn't even have to think about who was going to make dinner. For the last three years, since we'd moved to

Atlanta and watched the business truly soar, God had been preparing us to fight cancer.

With the diagnosis, they moved Krissy to the pediatric oncology unit, a place they tried to infuse with hopefulness. The ward was painted in bright colors, and there were unlimited popsicles, fun volunteer-run activities, and a playroom with toys, which had to be sanitized every time they were used because the kids were all so vulnerable. There were lots of families around, but there were also kids who were by themselves because their parents had to work or because they lived far away and couldn't afford to stay in Atlanta. We forget how often nurses stand in the gap of the parents. Nurses pushed around five-year-olds with their IV stands, and everybody was bald. God talks about how your hair is your crown, but here everyone has shed everything that makes them look distinctive. Everyone there is a kid with cancer. Everyone's time there is fleeting. They are either going to live or die. We all knew we were there to get our kids better, but this floor shouldn't even exist. Cancer in kids shouldn't exist. Cancer shouldn't exist. But it does. And it was a brutal reminder that at any point you can be called for the fight of your life.

My faith was ready. From the moment I knew Krissy had cancer, I had faith that she would make it through. God had made me a promise. I stayed in constant communication with Him. I prayed without ceasing. I gave thanks when she ate, when she slept, when she breathed. I gave thanks for the nurse who was able to find a vein with ease. I gave thanks when I could pay a bill. After her diagnosis, people would come up to me all the time and tell me that they had had Hodgkin's, that they had survived, that they were forty and had three kids. They were proof of what was possible.

We were also blessed that my bank account was ready. We were paying for everything out of pocket. As part of chemo, you have to do a series of shots that cost between $3,000 and $7,000 each. Regularly, I'd get bills for tens of thousands and I could just pay them. Once, while I was standing at the vending machine getting a Pop-Tart for Krissy, I got a call from the hospital's billing office that something had cost $22,000, and I was able to just give them my bank account. The cost registered, of course, but I did not care. This is what the money was for. I didn't worry; I didn't even have to check my balance. That season reaffirmed the fluidity of money. Money is a tool of survival.

But even with all our many blessings, this season was still very hard. Krissy was really sick and she was in pain. She hated needles and was stuck all over with them all the time. On one really tough day, when I could see her suffering, all my guilt bubbled up. "I'm so sorry that I didn't catch it sooner. If I hadn't been working, maybe I'd have caught it sooner. I feel like I let you down."

"Mom, if you weren't my mom, and this happened to me, I'd be dead right now."

As serious as cancer is, we laughed a lot. That's how our family got through cancer. Cancer wasn't something that was going to take us; it was just visiting. We joked about it all the time. My daughter would walk down the hall with her elegantly shaved head and big eyes and call out, "Here comes Cancer Krissy." That was her new nickname. She made a video diary we called "Krissy's Cancer Diaries." And mostly we sat around and watched shows and cracked jokes.

"All I really want is some cereal."

"Oh, man, they're spoiling you here. I hope you really understand that post-cancer, this is not going to be your life. So live it up, push all those buttons. Call those nurses." Though if I'm being honest, I chased down anything she craved. She'd gone so long without eating because she wasn't feeling well that once she started getting her treatments and taking steroids, all she wanted to do was eat. One day, she cried out, "I'm just really going to miss eating this much."

There was a lot of joy in our room; we were buoyed by our optimism.

Dr. Keller was very candid and clear, very practical and matter-of-fact. He'd been practicing for forty years; he'd been to weddings of kids he'd treated years earlier.

I told him, "Cancer is a good thing for us, because we're going to make it through this, and when we come out on the other side, we'll have learned about ourselves."

He told us, "You guys are the most optimistic, positive people. A lot of people say that cancer is one of the best things that's ever happened to them, because it really has changed the course of their life for the better, but they don't realize that until after it's done. You're the first person who's ever said it during the journey."

Krissy did all the hard work. The journey was hers, but I got to accompany her, and I had never felt so much like a mother.

When your kids are babies and toddlers, they look at you to see if it's safe, they hide behind your legs, and after they fall they check your face to see how bad it is before crying. It's a quick look to ask, Am I okay to proceed? Is it okay to feel what I'm feeling? Is this a safe place? Because I'd gotten my children when they were girls and not babies, I'd never had those moments with them. But sitting in the hospital, I realized that whenever Krissy looked at me, I was her safe place.

As a mother, the biggest thing for me wasn't sleeping in the hospital with Krissy, and it wasn't the running around checking every single vending machine to find the one that had Cheetos. It was when the doctors would come in and they would talk about the next decision that needed to be made and I would watch Krissy while she listened intently, whether it was about her treatment or if she wanted to donate her cells for research. And then the doctors would say, So we could do this or this? And Krissy would look to me.

Every time her doctor arrived, flanked by the student doctors, and started talking about what the numbers meant, or which drugs were having which effects, she would have no reaction to what they were saying. Instead, she would look at me for my reaction or for what she should think. I've never felt more like a mom.

"You make whatever decision you want."

Then she would decide something and look back at me. "I think that's a good decision," I'd say, even if sometimes I didn't agree with it. Something can be a good decision for someone else even if we don't agree with it. The respect of boundaries and autonomy is so critically important to our interactions with each other. At the very least, that is something we want for ourselves. That was an important part of mothering. She wasn't a baby. She had a whole body and a whole life and she needed to know what was going on. I was teaching her that she had the right to make decisions about her body.

Despite my unwavering knowledge that Krissy would be okay, I lived on a knife's edge. I never let down my guard. For three months I barely slept. I watched her constantly. I bathed her and helped her with the things she didn't want the nurses to do, like going to the bathroom. If I wasn't by her side, I was sending her all my energy, the way Gayle's mom had sent her energy, the way I had done years before when they weren't with me all the time. There were times when I literally could do nothing for her but pray and I saw things happen that made no sense, things that even the doctors couldn't explain.

One night at 3:00 a.m., I saw Krissy in her bed at the station we'd set up for her in the family room with all her meds and webcams so I could monitor her. I saw her in distress, and when I got to her bedside, she told me she didn't feel good. I started taking her temperature at regular intervals, and when it crept to one hundred degrees, I called the hospital and told them we were on our way.

They pumped her with a broad range of antibiotics to treat whatever the infection was, but her fever was still spiking. Her blood pressure was dropping. Something else was happening, but no one knew what. Nothing was working. Her numbers were going haywire. She was drifting in and out of consciousness, and the doctors and nurses were crowded around her frail, little seventeen-year-old body.

Someone had rolled in a crash cart.

With Krissy crashing in front of me, all I could do was pray two-word prayers. *Come quick. Send help.*

I *knew* what she needed was blood. But there was a protocol they had to follow. They were pumping her full of fluids and trying to find a doctor to approve the transfusion. Only then would the blood be brought from the blood bank.

Krissy and I have the same blood type. I told the doctor to just take my blood and pump it into her. But the staff insisted they couldn't do that and then they stepped into the hall trying to get a supervising lead doctor on the phone. I was left standing over her body, watching her disappear.

I could hear the doctors in the hallway. I could hear someone on the phone. We all knew what she needed.

Finally, I said, "You need to get blood in her now. I don't care about these approvals. I don't care about anything. You need to get blood in her now." I could feel my voice rising.

I peered into the face of a short doctor and said, "Go get her blood." I don't know what he saw in my face—urgency, crazy mother, or just the truth. But he left the room with purpose.

I turned to Krissy and watched her numbers steadily ticking down. She started to fade.

"Krissy. No. Stay awake." She had so many wires and tubes wormed into her that I didn't know where to touch her, but I had to shake her. "Krissy. No. Stay awake," I repeated.

All the doctors were in the hallway.

I grabbed her foot and shook her. "Krissy, stay here." She roused a little then faded again. I shook her every time her eyes fluttered closed, and I kept talking to her, "Krissy, come back. Krissy, stay here with Mom."

"I'm so tired," she mumbled.

"You can't sleep right now. You can't sleep right now. Krissy, you can't sleep right now."

She looked at me. "I just want to sleep for a little bit."

Somehow I knew I could not let her sleep.

The doctors stayed in the hallway; they knew the only thing to do was get her blood.

I was calling out to my daughter, insisting she stay with me. I was also saying, "Come on, God." I don't know if I was saying it in my head, out loud, or yelling it into the room. "God, do whatever you have to do."

I told Krissy, "You will stay here right now, young lady. You cannot go. Absolutely not." And Krissy, being the sweet, obedient child she is, slowly nodded all right.

And then the blood showed up. The nurse hooked it onto the stand. I saw a few bubbles at the top of the bag and could see it steadily pulsing into Krissy. When the bag was half-full, the numbers started ticking up and up and up. I exhaled loudly. The color came back to Krissy's face, and I felt like I saw the color surge in the faces of all the people in the room.

We knew what happened.

Death goes left and death goes right. Death came into our room, but it left. It didn't touch my baby.

Then there were fewer doctors in the room. A nurse switched out the empty bag of blood with a fresh one. Krissy's numbers kept ticking up. I didn't know exactly what they meant, but I knew this was better. Then she went to sleep, and it was okay.

I heard the door click shut and I realized there was no one in the room anymore. It was just me and Krissy.

She was still here.

I crawled into the little bed they have for parents and slept a deep, deep sleep. Hours later I started awake and there was Krissy, sitting up eating Lucky Charms.

"I woke up and I just wanted some cereal," she said, as if nothing had happened.

That afternoon when they checked us out, I asked the doctor what had happened. I'm fiercely logical. There's a cause and there's an effect. I wanted to know what had happened and how to keep it from happening again. But they didn't know.

"What infection was it?"

"We don't know."

"What did you do to fix it?"

"We don't know."

"How do I prevent it from happening again?"

"We don't know."

"Does this happen often?"

"No."

"So then what the hell happened?"

The doctors couldn't explain it.

The only explanation was that in that moment, God had held us. But I still didn't trust that nothing was missing. I ran myself ragged, feeling like I needed to collect everything so I wouldn't miss anything. I needed to collect all the money, all the opportunities, all the doctors. I needed to know all the research. I even looked at alternative therapies in Australia, just in case one day Dr. Keller told us that the treatment wasn't working. I had a private jet membership at the ready in case we had to go.

It's amazing the power of just being present in the moment and engaged. All along, we had everything we needed. Nothing was ever missing. Again and again we had learned the hardships of life, but we were never lacking. This was a horrible season. Everything was wrong, everything was right, but nothing was missing.

Before Krissy got sick, some nights she would be up really late getting through her homework and I would stay up with her and when she got sick, sometimes all I could do was lend her my energy.

Even before Gayle's mom had passed the idea of lending energy on to me, I understood. In the early stages before my kids lived with me, I did everything I could to protect them. I'd send them back to their mother's house with food and clean clothes and made sure they knew how to call me if they needed me. Sometimes I would just drive by and send my energy out to them.

I still felt that protective bubble stretched over all of us. There was a boy across the hall, Jason, who was the same age as Krissy and whose parents are pastors. He didn't make it. I didn't know who he was before; we never even spoke, but I will never forget him. That little boy isn't here anymore, and his parents are coping with that every day, and I still have my kid. I know his parents prayed. They did all the things they were supposed to. They had a whole congregation standing around them, hoping this wouldn't happen, and it still didn't work out. I can't explain that. Jason's life provides a lesson for me every single day. I am very aware that in the blink of an eye, my circumstances can be different. Death is arbitrary. It could turn right or left. None of those other kids on the ward made it. I realized how lucky we were. More than lucky, we were blessed.

There was chemo at the hospital—infusion therapy—and then after about a month, there was chemo at home—the pills to keep the process going. But she still wasn't out of the woods.

One night we were home when Krissy spiked a fever. She was really tired and said, "I don't feel good, Mom," right before she fainted. My primal brain broke the laws of physics and I caught her up before she hit the ground. In an instant I had swooped her into my arms, opened the front door and the car door, and settled my baby in the back seat. Krissy roused enough to say, "I didn't even know you could pick me up like that." I hadn't known I could either. She passed in and out lying in the back seat as I kept my foot on the gas. I got all green lights on the way to the hospital. Eleven in a row.

The emergency room doctors were running tests looking for the infection, because they had to give her the right antibiotic to fix it. Her body couldn't do it by itself. While they worked, she said the pain felt like fire was coursing through her bones.

I frantically prayed over her body. I don't mean I was laying my hands on her and saying the Lord's Prayer. By that standard, I'm a terrible prayer. A lot of us feel like we can't speak to God because it needs to sound or look or be a certain way. But if He's the one who understands us in and out from the moment we are born to the moment we die, the last thing we need to worry about is coming to Him and saying it messy. Prayer, to me, sounds a lot like conversation. It's me talking to Him. Sometimes prayer for me is one sentence: *Please don't let me screw this up.* Sometimes that's all I can muster. He knows the real feelings of my heart. Sometimes my prayer is just two words: *I can't.* Or *I'm done.* Or *Please help.*

Whenever my kids seem like they're struggling with communicating their feelings, I tell them, "Say it messy, and we'll sort it out afterward." A lot of times what I find is, it's not that the words are messy, it's just that the feelings are confused, and I can understand them just fine. I never want the fear of sounding messy to keep them from saying what they need to. I apply that to my relationship with God. I don't want to let the fear of sounding messy keep me from saying what I need to say. Praying on the way to the hospital was a lot of *Please, God. Please, God. Please, God.* I knew He would fill in the blanks because He knew how I felt. Praying over Krissy's body was as simple as: *Not now. Not now.* I want to encourage you to know that that's enough. And also know that, believe it or not, you already pray more than you think you do. If you've ever looked at a car accident and said, "Send help." If you've ever had a moment and said "Thank you" to the greater world, you're praying, although maybe you didn't realize it.

People often say that the perfect prayer is the Lord's Prayer—it hits all the points, and it sounds poetic, especially during Mass when you say it with everyone else. But people can say those types of prayers and sound totally hollow. I'm pretty sure we serve a God who would rather have us say things with meaning than sit around and pretend. So you better believe that my *Please help* can hold a whole hell of a lot more weight than somebody else's Lord's Prayer said in an automatic way that lacks meaning.

I prayed over my daughter, and she revived. The fire in her bones had been a rare reaction to the meds she'd taken earlier. But, surprisingly, for a second time while we were at the hospital, they had also found an infection, which they were able to treat.

Every day, Krissy's survival was a miracle. All I could do was accept it. When I was in corporate I worked with a beloved older lady who complimented me on my dress one time, and I immediately said, self-deprecatingly, "Oh, thank you. I got this from Target on the sale rack." You know, it's that thing women do. Some of us are taught that we should always be submissive, or modest. This lady schooled me: "Just say thank you." That's enough.

That's how I feel about the fact that I got to keep Krissy. I can't explain it, except to say, "By the grace of God, thank you."

That's a lesson I apply everywhere, because a lot of stuff doesn't make sense. I'm just thankful I get to be in the room. I regularly say, "Thank you, God, for choosing me."

If God is the perfect parent, I don't believe He would test you with the intent to fail. I would never do that to my kids. You wouldn't either. But sometimes hardship happens and the best I can do is stand next to them while they go through it. In the midst of hard things, sometimes people turn from their faith and ask, "Where is God?" But, in that moment, I was able to dive deep and say, "He is everywhere." He was in everything. He was in the results. He was in the testing. He was in the nurses with the gentle hands with the needles when Krissy was nervous. He was in the green traffic lights.

I'm grateful because the journey I had been on let me see God in everything.

All our recent crises—from Daya's leaving home to Krissy's cancer—required me to let go of these big, positive, grandiose experiences as the markers of God's presence and start accepting His presence as being a whisper, not a yell. While I was with Krissy in the hospital, all those moments He was whispering in my ear, "Sleep, peace, ease." It was always okay. It always worked out.

Faith is finding things to keep you moving forward, despite the fact that the world is filled with things that will make you question. If you really learn how to do Christianity right, it's creating moments that help bolster other people's faith so that they don't question. You get to be His hands and feet.

Faith sustained me through Krissy's cancer, just as it had carried me through the uncertainty of my early twenties and the challenges of entrepreneurship, and the constant crisis of my marriage. Faith is essential.

I won't sugarcoat this: If you're going to succeed in life—whatever "success" means to you—you need to be more than driven. You need to be *about* success. And you need to have faith, unshakable faith that pushes through the fear. When you jump into the unknown, you have to have faith that the ground will rise to catch you.

Faith is not a strategy. Sitting around having faith that things will happen and work out isn't going to get you anywhere. You must get to work. But your faith is what fills in the gaps when times get tough, when you're not sure what to do. Anytime you're afraid, scared, or unsure, you must have faith to help push you through.

I recognize that this is all "easier" because I have a label for my belief: God. But even if you don't, you need belief, and you need to give it a name. Because if you do, then you can find your way. The one thing God gave me was a way. We were in a total pit of darkness and He offered us a speck of light. I'm an advocate for God. It's easy to call myself a Christian, but what I am is a believer. When things are bad, He makes sure I'm okay. When I'm dealing with hard lessons, He helps me learn. He never lets it get worse than I can handle. I tell you it doesn't even feel like Christianity because it just feels like truth. You are free not to believe me. In a way, I don't want to believe it myself. If I hadn't seen it with my own eyes, I wouldn't believe it. But I have experienced it, I've touched it, and it's as real as water, food, or air. It's not something intangible to me.

In the Bible, Jesus and His disciples were out at sea in a boat. One of Jesus's favorite miracles is to walk on water, so He does, and then He tells His disciples that He can make them walk on water too. Peter, who was known as a skeptic, is the only one who agrees to try. Now, the way the miracle works is that you must maintain eye contact with Jesus. That's the key. Don't look down. Jesus tells Peter, "Come." All Peter had to do was believe and keep his eyes on Jesus. Peter was serving two roles: One, he was building his own belief. Two, he was bolstering everybody else's. It was windy and there were waves, and then, sure enough, Peter looked down. Why? Because he didn't really believe— because he wanted more data.

Sometimes it's not about relying on your own data. You've got to just focus on the endgame. For me, with Krissy's cancer, I was keeping my eyes on the finish line because I had received my promise that she would be okay from the beginning. I had to get the hell out of the boat. I asked for a way, God told me there was a way, He showed me there was a way. He walked it first. I knew it was going to be frightening. I knew there would be waves. But He told me to keep my eyes on Him.

When we got her all clear, I wanted to say, "Of course." Not out of hubris but because it was what God told me would happen, which is why I never looked down. I kept my eyes on Him. I had to because if I didn't, the risk was too big. I stayed the course, and it worked.

The end of cancer is gradual. You have your last treatment, and after a month, you have a scan. If the scan is clear, you have monthly scans, and if you make it to a year cancer-free, then you have annual scans. You have to learn to have gratitude for having made it through each phase.

That summer, Krissy had her last treatment. I had known the treatment would work since the day her cancer had been diagnosed. God had assured me. So, on our way to pick up the first scans, Krissy and I talked about how excited we were to see that the cancer was gone. We talked about how excited we were to know that this was finished. We were going to pick up the package of faith God had left for us.

To celebrate, I found the perfect beach house in Tampa, Florida. It wasn't extravagant, but it was close enough for Krissy to walk to the beach and there was enough room for *all* of us. Daya was coming. We had so much to celebrate.

On our first family vacation to California, years before, we were on a tight budget. It was the first time the kids had been on a plane. We flew coach and had a tiny two-bedroom apartment where someone had to sleep on the couch, and we went grocery shopping so we could cook all our food and stay on budget.

On our flight to Tampa, we had the good seats, and everything was a little nicer; the bumps had been worked out before we left.

A few days earlier, the rental agency called to tell me that the house I'd rented wasn't available. The disappointment swept through me, and then I told them everything. At this point, I was beginning a new season of asking for what I needed. We hadn't told very many people about the cancer, but on the phone with this stranger I laid it all out—the chemo, the survival, Daya's return. I'd done everything I could as a mom; I needed the person on the other end of the line to, as a fellow human, figure it out.

The agency called me back to say they'd found another house and told me not to worry about a thing. The house I'd rented was nice. The house they put us in was God-sized. It was so big that we each had our own floor. It had a pool. Inside, there was a display of bright red balloons along the stairs and a spread of truffles, cookies, and wine. I dissolved into a hot mess of tears and relief and gratitude. The man who let us in said, "We just hope everything is perfect for you." And it was. We could walk to the beach. They'd coordinated bikes and a golf cart so that Krissy wouldn't have to walk, and I spent the whole week watching the girls be happy. I knew Krissy was healing, but I had been worried about the wellness of our whole family. Here was proof that we would be okay. My kids are walking reminders of what God can do.

There's a level of happy I can express only by stripping off all my clothes and running around naked. But I won't actually do that because the world isn't ready for that type of trauma. It's not like watching your team win the Super Bowl but instead like winning the Super Bowl yourself with a Hail Mary pass on the final play.

When we got back from Florida, Gayle called. She had helped so much while Krissy was sick—in my life and my business, and while she was helping, she'd noticed things she wanted to improve. She wanted to come on, briefly, as a consultant again. I said no. I didn't want to work with her again. It wasn't worth the risk. I loved her so much. "You're right here, you're family. I love that you filled in for me like this, but I can't risk losing you again." She told me she was coming over and twenty minutes later she was walking through my door.

"I know that this is something I need to do, and you need to come on as a client. If I'm going to help, I need to know now because there's going to be some changes for me." I was cancer-weary and something in her voice scared me.

"What do you mean?"

She shifted the loose top she was wearing and showed me her

stomach. She was five months pregnant. She'd found out she was expecting the day Krissy's pediatrician had told me she had cancer. She'd been planning to tell me that day, but in that moment, what mattered most to her was being there for me. I fell to the ground crying. In a season where it felt like there could have been so much loss, Krissy's life was preserved and there was new life. God kept us and He doubled down.

In that season, everywhere I turned, I saw Him.

CHAPTER TWENTY-NINE

TAKE UP SPACE

People often say that if you believe, you will receive. But it's not that—it's actually applying that belief: if you actually transform it, if you sync it up with some resources, then you'll receive. When you go through hard things, granting yourself grace is essential. Grace is not beating yourself up as you go through the process. But grace is not a free pass to not do anything. Let's stop feeding into our desire to magically have things now and start telling the truth about the fact that we already have everything we need to succeed inside of us because nothing is missing, and if we're willing to leverage those gifts, the pieces of us that we already have, we can have anything we want. Nothing is missing.

When you go out into the world, you are supposed to be as big as possible, to take up as much space as possible with your God-given gifts. The best way to honor Him is to use your gifts well to serve others.

Me not taking up space would be launching a business, getting a hand-ful of clients, and then saying, *Okay, I did it.* Take up space. Let me go out there and reach as many people as possible because my job is to do things as big as I can. We often worry about stepping on someone else's toes so we don't take up the space that we should.

Don't let someone dim your light because it's shining in their eyes. We're encouraged to be small in a lot of spaces. There's this mentality of scarcity, that if some of us don't focus on making ourselves small, there won't be enough room.

When in reality I believe that rooms expand to meet the amount of joy and talent that's in them. This concept, that in the boardroom, in your home, in the community you need to be less, is so damaging. We're told we have to be meek and humble with our gifts in all spaces—but the only place you're required to be humble is before God.

Part of taking up space is going out there and claiming things for yourself. It's the real estate of life. It's starting your website. It's reserv-ing your own name on the Internet. It's going into an office and person-alizing your desk and leaving your sweater on the back of your chair. It's the last-bite-of-food dance, where no one wants to take the food but we're all hungry. The person who's not afraid to take up space is the one who thrives.

One time, when I was in corporate, I went into a meeting I was leading and asked my colleague, who was more tenured than I was, "Where should I sit?" They looked at me quizzically. "At the head of the table." I was leading the meeting, after all. Why wouldn't I sit at the head of the table?

Women are always thinking about everyone else, and often the result of thinking about and for others is that we shrink ourselves. For me, that started with my dad. In his presence there was no room for anyone else with a big personality.

When I got my girls, one of the things I was incredibly aware of was making sure they always felt like they had space and that they were wanted in the space. It's why we moved out of the house we'd bought before we met them in Baltimore into a house that included them. I didn't want them to feel like they were just fitting into our space. That was something I'd always had to do as a kid—like sleeping on the blue pullout couch. I wanted them to know that space was being created with them in mind, space that was distinctly theirs. Because if my kids can't feel like they can take up space in their own home, how are they going to take it up in the world?

I didn't have enough space in my marriage. If you looked at it from the outside, it probably felt like I had everything because I have such a big personality. But I didn't have space in my own home, or my own life. I didn't have space to rest or space to grow. I didn't have space to *not* do. I didn't have space to steer toward my goals as I saw God calling me because that wasn't my husband's priority. And I didn't feel like I deserved to take up that space. Here I was, preaching to everyone else, including my girls, that they deserve to take up space, that they were worthy, that they were enough, but I wasn't living it.

I assumed that because I'd spent so much time dedicating myself to everyone else, that I would get space to work just on me. I thought my turn would come. It doesn't work that way. You have to claim that space.

After Krissy's recovery, after filming our TV show, after living through a year of the pandemic, after eight years of marriage, my body gave me an ultimatum. I started feeling my heart racing, my head pounding, my blood pressure out of sorts. I found myself sitting in parking lots, like a mom sitting in the garage for a few moments of stillness before going into the house to her family—only I was doing it to try to calm my body.

A couple of days before the premiere of our show, I was so panicked that I couldn't sleep. I was incredibly anxious—not first-day-of-school energy but flat-out fearful. My body felt terrible, so, since we were in the thick of the pandemic, I scheduled a virtual consultation. My blood pressure was 173 over 141. A normal, healthy blood pressure is less than 120 over 80. I was a hair's breadth away from stroke range. My blood pressure was so high that the doctor told me I had to get it under control or he'd have to put me on medication. I didn't want that if I could avoid it. But something had to change.

When I told Josh, he seemed unaffected. I was staring at the edge of an emergency, and I could see that he may not have understood how serious it was. Josh has never been my emergency contact. Even if there was an emergency, he wasn't the person I would call for either comfort or resolution. This was a glaring sign that I didn't feel safe. I live too hard and too big to be with someone who can't take over if I don't make it, and who can't say, *Hey, slow down, you're about to die.* I realized that not only was I with someone whom I didn't believe could do either, I was also with someone who when I said I needed to slow down would say go harder. The problem was that *I* thought I needed to figure out how to be smaller.

A lot of clients come to me because they're burned out. Often, they've found a consultant because they can't think for their businesses at that time. They're too tired, and they want to quit. If you're an entrepreneur and you've built something, odds are you still love what you're doing; it's not really that you want to quit, it's that something is out of sorts.

With these health scares, for the first time in my life, I wanted to completely shut down my company. I was not going to die behind this business. I was not going to die behind this stress. I wasn't okay and I couldn't pay someone else to be Nicole Walters—without me, there was no business. Something was going to give—either the business or me.

For years I'd been telling Josh that my energy level wasn't going to last forever. It was entrepreneurship, and you have to adjust. That is a well-known entrepreneurial lesson. You're not always going to be that young person who is going to keep up the fire. The most important thing is to make your money, invest it well, and be prepared for the transitions that will happen, because you can be sure that how you built it today is not how it's going to operate tomorrow.

When I told Josh that I thought I needed to start closing the business, he looked me in the face and said, "You can't. It would put us in financial ruin."

"I don't think I'm gonna live. I don't know how I can keep going like this. I'm scared that I won't be alive."

"It's not just about you."

And, friend, I hate to admit this, but at that point, I believed him. I was angry, I was disappointed, and I made it known that I didn't appreciate the lack of consideration of my health. I didn't want to be selfish, but my body was matching my thoughts. I wasn't just feeling that I couldn't keep going; my body couldn't go anymore.

Two months later, I wanted to watch the season finale of my show. It was COVID, so there was no season-finale party; the kids had gone to bed, and Josh was upstairs, but I wanted to celebrate in some way. I had made it to the finish line of a major milestone: I had a television show that aired on the number-one cable network in America. I got a hot pizza and chilled a bottle of wine. I was going to clap for my own damn self.

A few minutes before the show started, I sat down with my modest feast and turned the TV on, and Josh came down the stairs. He stood in front of me and said, "I'm not happy. What are you going to do about it?"

In the past when he said something like that, I wanted to fight to be understood, argue my stance on how I was trying, spend hours recounting everything I'd done to illustrate how I prioritized his needs—I just had to prove my point. Or I'd feel guilty, as if I had done something wrong. Or I would start coming up with solutions. But on this night I had reached my point of surrender. I couldn't even fight anymore because my body and spirit were so weak.

I turned the TV off just as the announcer said, "*She's the Boss* season finale starts now." I knew my wine was gonna get warm, and my pizza was gonna get cold. "What is it that you want me to do, Josh?"

During our relationship, I always used to ask him that question. I would ask him and get some new answer, and every time I would intend to do it—lose the weight, make the money, buy a new house. I asked that question to genuinely explore it. But this time I was asking with a totally different tone. I was asking, "What else do you want from me?"

Before therapy, I used to heavily engage, asking questions as I would with a client and treating him as a concerned wife would, but I was no longer concerned. As I was listening—I'm not going to lie—I was realizing that what it seemed he really meant was that I wasn't enough for him. I wasn't what he wanted.

All my life I've been told I wasn't enough. All my life I have felt like something was missing. But in that moment, I thought, *Sir, with me, today, I can't say it all the time, but in this moment, nothing is missing.* He was in our million-dollar house, watching our TV show on a major TV network, with our beautiful family asleep upstairs. I could feel my blood pressure rising. I said, "Josh, I don't know if I'm enough for you."

"I don't know if you are either. Probably not."

I told him I was going to book a session with my therapist to see if I could work through that. "That makes me very happy," he said, because it appeared that what he heard was that I was going to go fix myself for him. And in the past, that's exactly what I had tried to do. I'd gone to other therapy sessions with a list of issues Josh had given me to work on. I wasn't friendly enough. I didn't work hard enough in the house. I didn't give him enough grace around stuff he didn't want to do. There was always something I needed to work on, and I did, and would come back "better," meaning I'd learned to have less anxiety around my annoyance in a particular situation.

Only this time, when I booked the session, I was going because I needed to figure out if I was safe to stay where I was because my blood pressure was still spiking and nothing was changing. I also knew that I wanted to work on whether I had the ability to be what he wanted. Had I done everything to be what he wanted? Which, now, I realize, is a crazy question. I had spent fourteen years trying to figure out how to make my marriage work. And then I realized, *Oh, it doesn't work.* I wondered what it would look like for me to just accept that it did not work. I told you before that there's nothing scarier to me than not being able to figure out who I am independent of everything else—whether that's what my hair looked like naturally, or what making money looked like without a corporate job, or what my happiness looked like without a partner.

I went to California to do a series of intensive therapy sessions. But after I started therapy, I couldn't go back to Atlanta. I kept calling Josh and telling him I needed another week to sort out what I was doing. I needed more rest. I was in therapy for about three weeks. I went there trying to work on my marriage and instead I worked on myself, which was the actual work.

When I finally went home, I'd assumed that the time apart was well spent for both of us. I'd learned a lot about myself, and still held a sliver of hope that in the past three weeks, we'd both done solid work on the next chapter. I wanted to save my marriage. I booked a trip to Jamaica for the whole family. I rented the fabulous hexagonal villa with white stone walls I'd seen as I walked the beach on that trip years earlier. This trip was confirmation of everything I'd realized while I was away.

And after almost five years in Atlanta, the same issues were coming up on a different day, in a different location, with a different bank account. Materially, we had more of everything, but nothing had changed. I was still holding up the sky, and I was tired.

After that trip, I went where people go whenever they need their dreams to be bigger: California.

The one thing that's worked for me is being brave and having hope that there could be something better on the other side, but also knowing that if there isn't, I'm enough.

Everything is right, everything is wrong. Nothing is missing.

EPILOGUE

SEASONS

All we need to do is be honest, willing to show up for the hard work, and learn as we live. And hopefully, each time we start over, things will be better than they were before. Starting over happens often. I started over with my hair. I started over with my business. I started over as a mom. I started over when Krissy got sick and again when she got well. And I'm starting over now, after divorce. This is a new season.

We all go through seasons. Seasons of chaos and creativity, seasons of stability and stillness, seasons of change and growth, and seasons of need and plenty. We know how to do seasons. What we don't know how to do are things that feel endless, unwavering, and constantly painful. During long stretches of uncertainty, we can get confused and unsettled.

We often forget that seasonality doesn't just exist in nature but is also *our* nature. We don't recognize that things happen in seasons all around us—in the weather, our aging, even in our meals: appetizer, entrée, dessert. The idea that every single thing we do must tie into the next rather than drawing to a close that is appropriate, necessary, and warranted is really damaging to our sense of self and can be an impediment to our progress.

Many of us make the mistake of thinking we're living a life that is a continuum, a single journey with an ultimate goal. Many of us think the end goal is happiness. I used to think I had to put my happiness on hold if I was in a hard season, but you don't have to wait for it to not be hard to be happy. That messaging that happiness comes at the end is harmful. If you buy into that, even if happiness shows up, you might reject it. You might push it away because you feel like it's not appropriate or allowed, or you might create circumstances that won't permit happiness to come in because you think it doesn't have a home with you. So many of us pray for happiness and ease in hard moments, but then we don't accept them when they show up. Sometimes that ease might be a funny movie, a manicure, a walk with a friend, but we don't accept it because we don't think we deserve it. You don't have to put your happiness on hold. Our happiness helped carry us through Krissy's cancer.

If you can't find happiness—if it's too hard or too heavy or too difficult—lean into gratitude. Gratitude begets happiness.

By finding gratitude in the hard seasons, you're honoring yourself better than ever before, and that is a natural affirmation that helps you grow. If you can say, "I don't care what anyone else says—this is what feels right to me and is in alignment with my values; I'm going to do it," things are more likely to work out.

You can't take directions from people who don't know your destination. You can coach yourself, do affirmations, read self-help books all the time, but your body knows if you mean it. If you take actions that counter what you're affirming with your mind, your body is going to know that too.

While I was married, I was constantly telling myself, *I love you, Nicole. You're worthy, Nicole.* But I kept going home to Josh. My body didn't believe my affirmations. Every time my blood pressure spiked, my internal belief—my spirit and soul—was saying: *If you love us, why are you keeping us here? You don't treat us well.*

I want to be where I feel loved, safe, and wanted. At some point I'm going to work a fifteen-hour day, and at the end of it, all I'm going to be able to do is crawl into bed. I want to crawl into bed next to somebody who's going to hold me. I deserve that. And if that is my little bit of happy in a season of overwhelming work, if that gives me the energy to get up the next day and log back on and deal with all the hard stuff, I deserve that. And you deserve that too, friend.

You deserve.

There are so many things I am keenly aware that I don't know. But there's some stuff I do know, which is that everything has context, that it's grayer than I thought, that grace is required, that things are blurry, that people are individuals, that life is difficult, and that you want to chase an "all life," settle for a "both life," and avoid an "or life." A life that has the most choices, and not one that's limited by money, partners, circumstances, or self.

When I got to California, everything was still wrong; in fact, it was more wrong than usual, but everything was so right. There's *so* much I haven't even talked about yet. I've only been here for a year and there has been everything from sex, drugs, and rock and roll to rehab, sickness, death, dating, and divorce. It's a lot of life. I promise to tell you about it one day.

We're all people. We're all moms and aunts and sisters and we worry about people, so I want you to know that I'm all right, just like you're gonna be all right. As of the publication of this book, I am divorced. I am seeing someone new. I still believe in love. And the kids are all right. Ally should be a sixth grader, Krissy should be a year away from finishing college, and Daya should be about two years sober and out of treatment. This is where everyone *should* be. But, if you've been keeping up with us, you'll know as well as I do how life really turns out.

But what I can tell you, no matter what, is that I have learned that nothing is missing. I have what I need to heal, to grow, to change, and to thrive. I have learned to look for the mustard seed of hope in every difficult circumstance; indeed, I have learned that survival depends on it. As I wrote this book and relived the seasons, what I could see most clearly was that in every season, something was wrong. Maybe you are reading this book saying to yourself, *Well, my partner is wrong, or my work is wrong, or my purpose is wrong, or I'm wrong.* I want to let you know that everything is wrong and right at the same time. Find the happy in each season and keep moving forward knowing that what you have within you is always enough.

ACKNOWLEDGMENTS

Writing a book is an incredibly rewarding endeavor. Rarely do we take the time to go back through our lives, review the most important moments, and extract the lessons that created impactful change—it's a gift and privilege to do this and share it with the world. That said, there's no way to share this gift without the help of those closest to us. I couldn't have created the time and content, and weathered the emotional journey, without the support of friends, family, mentors, and my publishing team.

My mom: Parenting is complex. I have a new appreciation for how you've shown up, the gift that life is, and the nurturing required to raise a child. I see what you've done. It's not easy, and you truly did your best. Thank you for loving me with what you had. Thank you for the sacrifices. Thank you for giving me a sister. Thank you, Mom.

My daughters, Daya, Krissy, and Ally: You three cutie-pies are the light of my life and my reason for being. I love you more than air. My sweet tinies, I am so grateful for the privilege of being your mother. I couldn't imagine a greater joy than witnessing you grow into the dynamic, hardworking, and brilliant women you are today, and I thank you for choosing me. I will work every day to continue to honor this choice—and Mom is never ever leaving.

My sister, Maame (and the best brother in love, Jeremy!): I am so grateful for the mirror you serve as in my life to remind me of who I am and who I belong to. Through the highs and lows, you understand me on levels no one else ever could. I appreciate you just as you are. Thank you for being there in ways I cannot measure.

My Other Sister, Gayle: Through tsunamis, from living coast to coast, with lifesaving missions on sandy beaches in Negril and many, many adventures. You can't get rid of me, and I will forever be in your corner. Ghana Girls for life.

My fiancé, Alex: Never in a million years would I have expected to know and experience love and life the way I have with you. Your love deepens my desire to serve God well, and lean into the best version of myself to help this world we are all in. Every day I work to heal from where and who I was, and I get the gift of doing it in the safest arms (for me) outside of Christ Himself. It's a simple love. Thank you for choosing us every day. You are the key. I love you.

The Squad—Jadah, Jen, Nikki: You've been my friends, my sisters, and mothered me. You've held me up, fed me, chastised me, and lent me so much belief, my cup runneth over. God knew when He sent you three that you were exactly what I needed, and I will honor this friendship for a lifetime. #sQuad.

To the mother of my children: Thank you so much for the greatest gift in my world. We've done a good job together working hard with what we can, and I'm so proud of you for showing up every day and doing your best. I promise you I will always love and protect our girls my entire life, and I will always honor the sacrifice of presence to give them a future.

To my wasband, Joshua: I'm grateful for who you've been to me, and the season we had. I learned so much. While we grew up together and grew apart, ultimately we grew—and that's what matters most. I hope you get every single thing God has for you.

Dr. Mcayla: You've saved me, my family, and my purpose many times over. I'm eternally grateful for the peace and the tools to understand every moment that's in this book and apply them to help me grow. Thank you for answering your calling, and helping me stay and serve in mine.

Seth: From an elevator to a street-side coffee shop, to the banks of the Hudson, never would I want to share a dosa with anyone else. You've lifted me, pushed me, and nurtured me. I'm deeply thankful for our friendship and will work every day to be a precious part of your legacy.

Mary: In one of the most complex seasons of my life, you kept me (and my calendar) together. Thank you for showing up for my business, and my heart.

My managers, Meg and Liz: Your ability to think bigger than me and lend your knowledge and labor to every opportunity is the greatest gift. I am so appreciative for what you've done for me—and, by extension, my sweet girls. Thank you, and let's keep going!

My agent, Anthony: Thank you for always showing up honestly and with so much heart. There isn't a better one out there, and I'm so grateful you're on my team!

My incredible PR team at Luna: Lauren, you make dreams come true!

Alexis Gargaliano: Thank you. Long hours, late nights. Endless grace. Thank you.

My publishing and marketing team at Simon Element: Easily the biggest privilege to work with such a dynamic, dedicated, and brilliant team. Richard, Leah—thank you.

And my countless friends from these chapters of life and the chapters to come . . .

Danny: *Estoy muy agradecido por ti. Durante un momento difícil me recordaste quién era y lo que podría ser. Gracias querido amigo.* 0.27%.

Mr. and Mrs. Ervin, Kia, Justin and Ashley, Mr. and Mrs. Montang,

Hilarie, Sophia, Danielle, the DB crew, Jimmy, Sharon, Jen Hatmaker, Olando, the Csillag family, Paolo, Sarah, Viraj, Rhea, Elaine, Demetria, Candace, Keith, Erica, Luvvie, Michela, Deesha, Rachel C., Ree, Glennon, Nedra, Pastor Albert, Morgan, Jamie, Lauryn, Amy, Chalene and Bret, Melissa, Nischelle, Octavia, Oprah, Yasmine, Tabitha, Gabrielle, Boz, Sarah, Maria and Keven, Scott, Avi, Sam, Joe, and I know there are SO many more people that have impacted me along the way—I could fill another book. THANK YOU for being a part of the story, complete with your gifts, your words, your support, and your love.

Lastly, but above all else, I thank God. I'm so grateful to have given my life in service to Jesus Christ. I never would've made it to where I am without the love, direction, protection, and consistency of my faith in the Lord. And while I recognize that this is a complex relationship for many, for me it is clear, and I wouldn't want it any other way. This book is a testament to what is possible, and how others use it is proof that if He can do it for me, He can do it for you. I pray that when others see me that they see Him in everything I do. Thank you, God, for always being true to your word. I surrender all. 1 Peter 4:10.

ABOUT THE AUTHOR

Nicole Walters is a former top-selling corporate executive who quit her six-figure sales job in front of ten thousand people, took what she knew, and built a million-dollar business in one short year. Now the host of a popular podcast, *The Nicole Walters Podcast*, a TV personality, and an in-demand motivational speaker, Nicole is passionate about teaching everyday people how to own their power and trust they already have everything they need to succeed. She currently resides in Los Angeles, California, with her three beautiful daughters and her trombone-playing fiancé, Alex.